CAR-FREE®
in BOSTON

A Guide for Locals and Visitors

TENTH EDITION

Editor
Jeff Perk

Contributing Editors
Madeleine Noland
Andrew Rubel

Cartography
Madeleine Noland

Cover Design
Steve Novick

**Published by
Rubel BikeMaps
Cambridge, Massachusetts**

**for the
Association for Public Transportation, Inc.**

Dedication and Thanks

This tenth edition of *Car-Free in Boston* is dedicated to the memory of Guy Rosmarin. As Governor Sargent's transportation advisor in the late 1960s, Guy proposed a diversified transportation system instead of building Boston's Inner Belt and Southwest Expressway, projects whose wisdom were being questioned. His plan, further developed by the Boston Transportation Planning Review, was hugely successful and received widespread acclaim. Twenty years later, the plan's principles formed our new national transportation policy, enacted by Congress in 1991 as the Intermodal Surface Transportation Efficiency Act (ISTEA).

Special thanks to Suzanne Heywood, John Hostage, and Rosemary Jason for getting the ball rolling so we could publish this new edition of *Car-Free*, and also to James "Kibo" Parry for helping find those elusive computer files. Rubel BikeMaps also thanks the entire APT board, particularly Fred Moore, President, for his unflagging confidence in our work. Many thanks also to the MBTA, Jonathan Belcher of CTPS, and all the other reviewers not named but not forgotten.

Copyright and Publishing Information:

Copyright © 2003, Association for Public Transportation, Inc. Car-Free® is a registered trademark of the Association for Public Transportation, Inc. (APT); Registered U.S. Patent & Trademark Office. All rights reserved. Cover photo credits: Jeff Perk (State House); Massachusetts Bay Transportation Authority (transit photos). For APT contact and membership information, see page vi.

Published by Rubel BikeMaps, Cambridge, Massachusetts. No part of this book may be reproduced or transmitted in any form by any means, electronic or mechanical, including information storage and retrieval systems, except brief extracts for purpose of review, without written permission from Rubel BikeMaps (contact information below).

ISBN 1-881559-76-9   Printed in the United States of America   3   2   1

Every effort has been made to obtain accurate information prior to publication. However, transit services and schedules do change. We urge you to confirm schedules with the carrier before making your trip. Note that MBTA fares may go up in 2004. Please send updates and suggestions for this book to Rubel BikeMaps (contact information below).

Text pages printed on chlorine-free paper, ♻ 30% post-consumer waste.

Purchasing Information:

For additional copies, send $9.95 each copy plus $2.50 (media mail) or $4.50 (first class to New England locations) postage and handling for up to three copies to Rubel BikeMaps, or for additional information, contact:

Rubel BikeMaps

PO Box 401035   info@rubel.com
Cambridge, MA 02140   www.rubel.com

Contents

Introduction

While Boston is notoriously difficult for driving, its extensive public transit system and small walkable neighborhoods make traveling car-free easy and fun. This comprehensive guide to transit and places to go presents the basics of Boston public transit, specific directions to hundreds of destinations in Eastern Massachusetts, plus maps and detailed route information for virtually every train, bus, and ferry. Since 1977 this book has been helping locals and visitors alike enjoy the best of Boston *Car-Free*.

Boston has crooked, narrow, one-way streets; bad drivers; scarce on-street parking; expensive garage parking; and ever increasing traffic volumes. These conspire to make driving in Boston more challenging every year. The massive road construction project known as the "Big Dig" has only made matters worse. Owning and operating a car in Boston is expensive, too. Even with occasional use of taxis and rental cars, it is much less expensive to use transit than to own a car. Many families find that by using transit they can save thousands of dollars per year by owning one car instead of two. If you add up the time waiting in traffic, hunting for parking, getting lost, shoveling snow, and dealing with repairs and insurance, you may find transit significantly less time-consuming in the long run. And transit riders can use their time to read, work, or just relax.

While traffic gets worse, transit gets better. Boston's primary transit operator, the Massachusetts Bay Transportation Authority (a.k.a. the MBTA or "the T") has made a number of recent improvements. Old Colony Commuter Rail service to the South Shore has been revived and will soon be expanded to include the Greenbush Line to Scituate. Night Owl bus service has been added to extend rapid transit hours on Friday and Saturday nights. And the partially completed Silver Line Bus Rapid Transit (BRT), albeit controversial, will provide the South Boston Waterfront with rapid transit service for the first time, as well as link Roxbury with South Station and Logan Airport. Private transit companies have also seen many changes; Zipcar, a new Boston-based car-sharing company, offers "wheels when you want them," making owning one less car (or no car) even more convenient.

Our goal is to encourage people to use public transit. To this end, *Car-Free* has also seen some improvements. The overall organization and format have been improved to make it easier to use. Section 1, "Using

Transit" is now even more useful for newcomers. The "Destinations" section has been brought up-to-date with a few deletions and many additions. And, of course, all the route details have been updated, and many new services added. An expanded, carefully-constructed index makes it simple to find any topic, destination, station, map, or service.

While the transit in Boston continues to improve, there is still much to be done. The Association for Public Transportation (APT) is a non-profit organization that advocates for better public transportation and promotes increased ridership. Improvements get funded when lots of people want them. Joining APT adds your voice to APT's advocacy. If you want to do more, let your elected officials know how important a good public transit system is to you. But first, join APT to help us shape the future of public transit in Boston.

The Association for Public Transportation

I'd like to join APT; enclosed is my tax-deductible donation:

$15 Students/Seniors $50 Dispatcher
$25 Regular $100 Friend of Charlie on the MTA
$35 Conductor   _____ Other

Members receive APT's newsletter, *Mass. Transit News*, and a copy of the next edition of *Car-Free* when it is published.

NAME

ADDRESS

CITY   STATE   ZIP

Optional PHONE (H)   PHONE (W)

Optional EMAIL (for APT updates, will not be given to third parties)

Association for Public Transportation, Inc.
PO Box 51029
Boston, MA 02205-1029
(617) 482-0282
email: apt@car-free.com   web: www.car-free.com

Using Transit

APT FILE PHOTO

Green D Line train at Park Street Station

1 The T (MBTA Transit)

2 Not the T (Non-MBTA Transit)

3 More Local Transportation

4 Services for Seniors and Persons
   with Disabilities

T ransit information in this book is divided into two categories: that provided by the Massachusetts Bay Transportation Authority (MBTA), known as "the T," and everything else, or "Not-the-T." The T includes rapid transit, Commuter Rail, MBTA buses, and MBTA ferries. Not-the-T includes other public or private buses and ferries plus Amtrak.

Note that in print—within both this guide and most other media you encounter in Greater Boston—"the T" is shorthand for the entire MBTA system. However, when asking for or giving spoken directions, "the T" customarily refers only to the rapid transit and Commuter Rail portions of the MBTA.

MBTA Fast Facts for Beginners

$ The standard fare for rapid transit Red, Green, Orange, and Blue Lines is $1; the Silver Line BRT and most buses cost 75¢; Inner Harbor Ferries are $1.25. Commuter Rail and Commuter Boat fares vary by distance. Subway-to-subway and bus-to-bus transfers are generally free (request transfer slip bus-to-bus); most other transfers require a new fare. Fares may go up in 2004.

Anyone—tourist or resident—intending to make extensive use of the T should consider purchasing either a Visitor Pass or a Weekly or Monthly Pass (see page 10 for details).

◷ The T is not a 24-hour system—from Sun.-Thur., rapid transit and buses wrap up their last runs between midnight and 12:30am. On Friday and Saturday nights "Night Owl" bus service extends rapid transit routes and some bus routes until 2:30am. Although some commuter trains, buses, and ferries do not operate on weekends or holidays, the bulk of the MBTA system—including all rapid transit lines—runs 365 days.

☺ MBTA personnel and your fellow T riders are generally very friendly and will happily answer questions or give directions. Your courtesy is also appreciated—always allow passengers off before boarding, stand clear of the doors to make room for others, and obey the state law prohibiting smoking on all MBTA property and vehicles. Regarding safety, Boston is a big city, but if you are aware of your surroundings and use common sense, you will find the T, like Boston itself, to be generally safe.

ⓘ Point your browser to **www.mbta.com** for the latest schedules and special service updates anytime day or night. Or call 800/392-6100 or 617/222-3200 to speak to live MBTA customer service, Mon.-Fri. 6:30am-8pm, and Sat.-Sun. 7:30am-6pm.

Chapter 1:
The T (MBTA Transit)

The MBTA operates rapid transit, Commuter Rail, bus, and commuter ferry service throughout Boston and over 170 surrounding communities in Eastern Massachusetts, plus Providence, RI. An introduction to each type of service—including fares—follows, but for detailed route and schedule information refer to chapters 8 through 11.

Ⓣ Rapid Transit (route details in Chapter 8)

Rapid transit, the heart of the T system, includes the subway, streetcars, and the newer Bus Rapid Transit (BRT). Service runs often enough that you do not need a schedule, and it runs 365 days per year through any and all weather, even the Great Blizzard of '78. If it's a day—the trains are running.

There are four main lines—Red, Green, Orange, and Blue—plus the new Silver Line BRT, which radiate like spokes from downtown Boston out to surrounding neighborhoods and towns. The lines intersect at four major downtown stations: Park Street, Downtown Crossing, Government Center, and State. If travelling *toward* one of these four hubs, use the **"inbound"** platform; if heading *away* from the hubs, you want **"outbound."** (Within these four stations, pick your platform by the name of the last station in the direction you're headed, or, on the Green Line, by "eastbound" or "westbound.") This *hub & spoke* design facilitates travel into and out of the metropolitan core. For travel between the outer ends of the spokes, you must go all the way into and out from downtown, or take a bus across town.

Rapid Transit Lines

- **Red Line** – runs south to Quincy, Braintree, Dorchester (Ashmont), and Mattapan; and northwest to Cambridge and Somerville. The southern end divides at JFK/UMass into two branches, Braintree and Ashmont; at Ashmont you can continue to Mattapan on the above-ground Mattapan trolley, a.k.a. the Mattapan High Speed Line. JFK/UMass is the last station for south-bound riders to change between Braintree and Ashmont trains.

- **Green Line** – runs west to Allston, Brighton, Brookline, Newton, and Jamaica Plain; and east (actually north) to East Cambridge. The western end separates into four branches: B (Boston College), C (Cleveland Circle), D (Riverside), and E (Heath St./Arborway)—the "A" line was discontinued long ago. Western stops are above-ground. See "Special Notes about the Green Line" on page 4 for more information.

- **Orange Line** – runs southwest to Roxbury and Jamaica Plain; and north to Charlestown, Wellington (in Medford), and Malden.

- **Blue Line** – runs northeast along the coast to Logan Airport and Revere.

- **Silver Line BRT** – a work in progress until 2010, this new Bus Rapid Transit line currently runs from Dudley Square to Downtown Crossing.

Major Transfer Stations

- **Park Street** – Red and Green Lines (with underground walkway to the Orange Line at Downtown Crossing)
- **Downtown Crossing** – Red and Orange Lines and Silver Line BRT (with underground walkway to the Green Line at Park Street)
- **Government Center** – Green and Blue Lines
- **State** – Blue and Orange Lines

Other Transfer Stations

- **Haymarket** and **North Station** – Green and Orange Lines
- **Boylston** – Green Line and Silver Line BRT
- **New England Medical Center** – Orange Line and Silver Line BRT
- **Chinatown** – Orange Line and Silver Line BRT (not a free transfer)

Underground stations are identified by large round Ⓣ logos; surface streetcar stops typically have signs bearing the name of the stop, and the western-most portion of the Green E Line branch has signs posted at the street curb. A schematic map of the subway line is posted at every train station, most streetcar stops, and in the trains themselves. A subway map is also inside the back cover of this book, and detailed station-by-station maps, including addresses and bus connections, can be found in Chapter 8, "MBTA Rapid Transit."

Special Notes about the Green Line

Not all eastbound Green Line trains run to the last stop (Lechmere); many of them, usually with a red slash through their label, turn around at Park Street or Government Center (red slashes on other trains are obsolete and can be ignored). Passengers bound for Haymarket, North Station, Science Park, or Lechmere should not be surprised if the conductor calls out "Last stop!" before reaching your intended station. Simply catch the next train running in the same direction.

Westbound Green Line riders wanting to stop at Kenmore or Hynes Convention Center/ICA can board any Green Line branch except the E Line, which splits from the other three branches after Copley (see map inside back cover). Riders headed for Prudential or Symphony must take an E train.

Above-ground western B, C, and E trains behave a little like buses: if a fare is due you pay it to the driver (see "Rapid Transit – Fares" below); the routes follow major streets with stops every few blocks; and you must push the "stop request" button when you want to get off.

Rapid Transit – Fares

The basic fare for the Red, Green, Orange, and Blue Lines is **$1,** and the Silver Line BRT is **75¢.** Subway station turnstiles accept only tokens and magnetic-stripe passes. Where there are no turnstiles (at streetcar stops, BRT stops, and some Green Line stations, for example) use your token, pass, or exact change—no pennies or dollar bills—to pay as you board, unless no fare is due (see below). See page 10 for information on money-saving Monthly, Weekly, and Visitor Passes, and page 13 for information on special reduced fares.

There are staffed booths at most underground stations where a collector can sell you tokens, make change, and help with directions or other questions. Many stations also have token vending machines which dispense 1, 5, or 10 tokens—no change is given. Note: the current fare collection system will be replaced by an automated system, with pre-paid fare cards replenished at station kiosks. This new system is scheduled to be operational by 2005 and will replace the token system. Fares may increase in 2004.

Transfers from one line to another are free, and except for the two southernmost Red Line stations, Quincy Adams and Braintree, you can ride as far as you want without paying anything extra. Transfers to and from the Silver Line BRT require a paper transfer slip available from Silver Line drivers or in-station automated dispensers. Note that if you must reverse direction, free transfer between inbound and outbound platforms is possible at most but not every station. In particular, inbound riders on the Green E Line wishing to transfer to outbound Green B, C, and D trains should do so at Arlington.

Special Notes about Rapid Transit Fares
Outbound travel on any Green Line train is **free** if you board at a surface stop west of Kenmore Square. The Mattapan trolley (Ashmont to Mattapan) is also free for all outbound travel, and free for inbound travel, too, if you transfer at Ashmont (where full fare is charged to transfer to the regular Red Line trains). Inbound trolley riders who step off before Ashmont pay **75¢** upon exiting.

Higher fares are charged upon entering Quincy Center, Quincy Adams, and Braintree on the Red Line ($2), and when boarding at all above-ground inbound stops on the Green D Line ($1.25 at Fenway through Reservoir, $2.50 at Chestnut Hill through Riverside). An additional fare ($1) is also charged upon exiting at Quincy Adams and Braintree. Short trips between these higher-priced suburban stations are discounted as follows:

• When boarding at Braintree through Quincy Center on the Red Line, pay the $2 full fare by purchasing a $1 token and a $1 local travel warrant; redeem the warrant for $1 in cash upon exiting any station from Braintree through North Quincy.

• Pay full $2.50 fare from Riverside to Newton Centre on the inbound Green D Line and request a $1.25 "Newton local" coupon from the driver when exiting between Woodland and Chestnut Hill. The coupon is good toward your next trip.

A **10-ride ticket** for inbound rides on the Green D Line is sold at all staffed Green Line collector's booths for $22.50—a 10 percent discount for riders who board between Chestnut Hill and Riverside.

Holiday Service

MBTA service operates every day of the year, but service is sometimes reduced or increased for holidays or special events. The schedule adjusts year to year for holidays that fall on varying days of the week.

Bus and subway lines operate on special schedules as follows:

- Sunday schedule: New Year's Day, Memorial Day, Fourth of July (buses only), Labor Day, Thanksgiving, Christmas.

- Saturday schedule: Martin Luther King Day, President's Day, Patriot's Day (buses only), Columbus Day, Friday after Thanksgiving (Red, Green, and Orange Lines only), and Christmas Eve (Red, Green, and Orange Lines only).

- Special Events with increased rapid transit (not bus) service: Patriot's Day (Boston Marathon), Fourth of July, New Year's Eve.

Commuter Rail lines follow slightly different holiday schedules:

- Sunday Schedule: New Years Day, Memorial Day, Labor Day, Thanksgiving, Christmas.

- Saturday Schedule: President's Day.

- All other holidays have service consistent with the particular day of the week on which the holiday falls.

Rapid Transit – Hours of Operation

MBTA rapid transit operates 20 hours, roughly 5am to 12:30am, 365 days per year. On Friday and Saturday nights, extended rapid transit service is provided by Night Owl buses which run until 2:30am. Sunday service begins about 40 minutes later than other days. Bowdoin station on the Blue Line is closed weekends, holidays, and Mon.-Fri. after 6:30pm. See sidebar on page 118 for information about first and last trains.

🚆 Commuter Rail (route details in Chapter 9)

The Commuter Rail is the MBTA's regional train service with 11 lines serving one-fifth of Massachusetts' cities and towns, plus Providence, RI. Three more lines are under construction and scheduled to be completed by 2007. Lines serving points north and northwest depart from North Station and those serving points south and southwest depart from South Station.

- North Station lines: **Newburyport/Rockport, Haverhill/Reading, Lowell,** and **Fitchburg/South Acton.** Transfer to the subway is possible at North Station (Green and Orange Lines across the street), and for select lines at Porter (Red Line), and Malden Center (Orange Line).

- South Station lines: **Framingham/Worcester, Needham, Franklin, Attleboro/Stoughton, Fairmount, Middleborough/Lakeville,** and

Plymouth/Kingston. At South Station it is possible to transfer to the Red Line, Amtrak, and interstate and commuter buses. Subway transfers for select lines are also possible at Back Bay Station, Ruggles, and Forest Hills on the Orange Line, and at JFK/UMass, Quincy Center, and Braintree on the Red Line.

Commuter Rail is quite different from rapid transit in that it runs further afield, service is heavily skewed to favor commuter rushes, and trains come less frequently. You will want to know the schedule to avoid long waits. See "Where to Find MBTA Maps and Schedules" at the end of this chapter. Easy transfer from a Commuter Rail train to a subway train is possible at certain shared stations (see above), but bear in mind that the systems are completely separate using different tracks, trains, tickets, and fares—and there are no free transfers between the two systems.

Commuter Rail stations are identified by a purple sign with a T logo. Many have large parking lots and many are not staffed. For a complete list of stations and addresses see Chapter 9, "MBTA Commuter Rail." A map of the Commuter Rail system appears inside the back cover foldout of this book.

Note that there is no Commuter Rail connection between North and South Stations. To travel between them you must take the subway, transferring between Red and Green Lines at Park Street, or a 25 minute bus trip, so travel between points north and points south by Commuter Rail is cumbersome. (For southern Commuter Rail trains that serve Back Bay Station, the Orange Line provides an easier connection to North Station.) The Association for Public Transportation (APT) continues to advocate for a North-South Rail Link along with the Sierra Club (www.sierraclub.org) and other organizations. Visit www.car-free.com or see page vi for information about APT.

Commuter Rail – Fares
Adult Commuter Rail fares range from **$1** to **$5.75**, based on distance. A **12-ride ticket,** valid for 180 days, may be purchased for the cost of 11 one-way fares. Prices for the 11 incremental fare zones plus information about money-saving passes are found on pages 10-13; information about special reduced fares appears on page 13. Fares may increase in 2004.

Commuter Rail tickets are sold aboard all trains, but if your station's ticket office was open when you boarded, a fee is added to tickets purchased on the train ($2 rush hours, $1 off-peak). Tickets are also available at North Station, South Station, Back Bay Station, and at or near some suburban stations.

Commuter Rail – Hours of Operation
More than just commuter service, most Commuter Rail trains operate nights, weekends, and holidays (the Needham Line runs only Mon.-Sat., and the Fairmount and Stoughton Lines run only Mon.-Fri.). Weekday inbound service begins 5-6am and ends 9-11pm; outbound service generally starts and ends 1-2 hours later. Weekend and holiday service starts an hour or so later than on weekdays.

USING TRANSIT
DESTINATIONS
ROUTE DETAILS
INDEX

🚌 MBTA Buses (route details in Chapter 10)

Most of the MBTA's 170-some bus routes operate feeder service, linking subway stations to neighborhoods not directly served by rapid transit. Some routes provide connections between different subway lines without going into downtown. The few bus routes that actually enter downtown Boston are mostly *express* buses from the suburbs. *Night Owl* buses extend the hours of all rapid transit lines (except the Mattapan trolley) plus select bus routes until 2:30am on Friday and Saturday nights. For most bus routes you will need to know the bus schedule to avoid long waits; the exceptions are the *frequent* buses which generally run every 6-15 minutes much like rapid transit. For detailed information see Chapter 10, "MBTA Buses."

Buses stop only at designated stops, and the driver will not automatically make every stop on every route. You may need to wave as the bus approaches to let the driver know you want to get on, and if you're getting off, ring the bell to signal the driver to stop for you. Curbside stops are typically marked at each end with narrow vertical signs displaying the T logo and route numbers of all buses which frequent the stop. Some stops also feature three-sided bus shelters with the name of the stop across the top. A few communities persist in marking bus stops with signs that too-closely resemble the ubiquitous local parking signs, but even these have a small T logo.

All MBTA buses display their route number and final destination in digital panels above the front windshield. On certain routes, the addition of the word "limited" means the bus doesn't make all stops; if in doubt, ask the driver before boarding.

An increasing number of buses have digital displays inside, too, that identify each upcoming stop. Otherwise stops are supposed to be announced by the driver, but don't count on it. Your best bet is to ask the driver or a fellow passenger for guidance—as a rule T personnel and riders are happy to help strangers.

MBTA Buses – Fares

The basic adult bus fare is **75¢**. On a few long local routes, a fare of $1.25-1.75 is charged and express bus fares range from $1.75-2.75. Exact change, tokens, or passes are required on buses; no pennies are accepted. No change is returned for tokens or dollar bills. Change for buses can be obtained from any rapid transit collector's booth. See page 10 for information on money-saving passes, and page 13 for special reduced fares.

Special Notes about MBTA Bus Fares

For connections between buses, ask the driver for a **free transfer.** These slips of paper are good only for onward travel on a different local bus route than the one on which they're given, and must be used within two hours. Upon payment of an additional 25¢ above the regular bus fare (i.e., $1 total), you may also request a transfer between the following selected buses and subway stations:

- Between bus 39 (Forest Hills-Back Bay) and the Green Line at Copley or the Orange Line at Back Bay Station.
- Between bus 1 (Harvard-Dudley) and the Orange Line at Massachusetts Ave. station when boarding at any stop between Dudley and Massachusetts Ave. station.

Free transfer coupons to the above two buses are also issued by subway station fare collectors at Copley, Back Bay Station, and Massachusetts Ave. station.

Finally, no fare is charged:

- Inbound from Dudley Station to Ruggles (Orange Line) on buses 15, 19, 23, 28, 42, 44 and 45.
- Inbound from Egleston Square to Jackson Square (Orange Line) on buses 22, 29 and 44.

Three types of discounted **10-ride tickets** ($16, $22.50, and $25) are available for all express buses with fares of $1.75, $2.50, and $2.75, respectively. Money-saving Monthly, Weekly and Visitor Passes described later in this chapter are also available. Fares may increase in 2004.

MBTA Buses – Hours of Operation

Bus schedules vary greatly. Some routes match the subway's 20-hour, 7-day service. Others operate weekday only, daytime only, or even rush hour only. On Friday and Saturday night (or, for the literal-minded, early Saturday and Sunday morning) there is Night Owl bus service between 1-2:30am along the routes of all rapid transit lines (with the exception of the Mattapan trolley) and five additional local bus routes. See buses marked "N-OWL" in Chapter 10, "MBTA Buses."

⚓ MBTA Ferries (route details in Chapter 11)

Year-round, in all but the stormiest gales, a fleet of MBTA vessels ply the waters of Boston Harbor and the South Shore. The boats are comfortable, most sporting both indoor and outdoor seating, restrooms, and concessions. There are two groups of ferries—Inner Harbor Ferries with short runs in Boston Harbor, and Commuter Boats with longer runs to points south.

Inner Harbor Ferries link various points in Boston Harbor: **North Station** (Lovejoy Wharf); **Charlestown Navy Yard** (in Boston National Historical Park); downtown's **Long Wharf;** the **World Trade Center** in South Boston's Seaport District; and the **US Courthouse** on Fan Pier, at the edge of the Fort Point Artist District. Long Wharf is at Aquarium station on the Blue Line, and Lovejoy Wharf is less than 10 minutes' walk from North Station. The ferry schedule at Lovejoy is designed to meet many Commuter Rail trains.

The longer-distance Commuter Boats serve three shorefront communities— **Quincy, Hull, and Hingham**—on the rim of Cape Cod Bay south of Boston. Only Quincy earns full daily service; Hingham and Hull (Pemberton Point) get weekday and weekday-rush hour service respectively. The Quincy and

Hull vessels stop at Logan Airport's water transportation dock en route to their Boston berth on the north side of Long Wharf. (For additional boat service to Logan Airport see Chapter 14, "Regional Airports.") Hingham boats arrive and depart from **Rowes Wharf,** midway between Aquarium station (Blue Line) and South Station (Red Line).

MBTA Ferries – Fares

The basic adult one-way fare for Inner Harbor Ferries is **$1.25** with a 60-trip ticket available for $57. The basic adult one-way fare for the Commuter Boats is **$4** (Hull) and **$5** (Quincy and Hingham) with 10-trip tickets available for $36 and $45 respectively. South Shore passengers disembarking at Logan pay **$12.** See below for information about passes, and page 13 for information about special reduced fares. Fares may increase in 2004.

MBTA Ferries – Hours of Operation

Inner Harbor ferries between Long Wharf and Charlestown operate daily, Mon.-Fri. 6:30am-8pm and Sat.-Sun. 10am-6pm; the rest run only Mon.-Fri. (excluding major holidays) from 6:30-7am until about 7pm.

The Quincy Commuter Boats operate daily: weekdays 6-7am to around 11pm, and weekends from 8-9am to around 11pm. Service to and from Hull is limited to Mon.-Fri. early morning and evening rush hours only, plus one midday trip. Hingham Commuter Boats operate Mon.-Fri. only, 6-7am to 7-8:30pm. Neither the Hull nor Hingham boats operate on major holidays.

Monthly, Weekly, and Visitor Passes

Money-saving T passes are available by the month or the week. Monthly subway, bus, and combo passes cost no more than 17 or 18 round trips; monthly Commuter Rail passes are generally equivalent to 15 or 16 round trips. A pass gives you unlimited rides—at night, on weekends, anytime. On Sunday monthly passholders may bring along a companion at no extra charge. Weekly combo passes, like their monthly counterparts, are valid on both buses and rapid transit, and cost less than a daily round trip via subway. There's also a special pass for tourists, designed for maximum flexibility, but, depending on the timing of your visit and the likelihood of your using the Inner Harbor ferries, the weekly pass may be a superior value. Monthly passes have magnetic stripes that can be swiped at turnstiles. Weekly and Visitor passes are shown to the collector or driver who will let you through.

Monthly Passes

Monthly passes can be purchased on-line at the T's website, **www.mbta.com,** through the 22nd day of the preceding month. They're mailed for free, too. You can also buy passes in person on the last four and first four business days of each month from the Amtrak ticket windows at North Station, South Station, and Back Bay Station (all three of which take credit cards), or from pass booths at the Government Center, Downtown Crossing, Harvard, and Alewife rapid transit stations (cash or check only). A wide variety of neighborhood stores also sell monthly passes—call 617/222-3200 for locations and hours, or find the full list of sales locations on the T's website. Note that pass prices may increase in 2004.

The **Annual Pass Program** offers 12 passes for the price of 11 when fully prepaid by check or money order. Call 617/222-5218 to have an application mailed to you, or print it out from the T's website.

Over 800 companies make monthly passes available directly to their employees via the **Corporate Pass Program,** and many even pay part of the cost as an employee benefit. Refer to the sidebar "Tax Breaks for Employers and Commuters" later in this chapter for details.

Car owners can save up to $75 per year on auto insurance by purchasing monthly passes for at least 11 of the 12 months preceding your insurance policy's anniversary date. Ask your insurance agent for details.

Monthly Bus (75¢) Pass – $25

Valid on all MBTA buses with 75¢ fare (for higher fares, you can pay the difference in cash). Valid on the Mattapan High-Speed Line; on the Silver Line BRT; on all street-level stops on the Green Line's B, C, and E branches west of downtown; and on the Green D Line from Reservoir to Fenway. Also valid on the Green D Line from Riverside to Chestnut Hill (i.e., all Newton stops) with cash payment of $1.25 or a Newton local coupon.

Monthly Subway ($1) Pass – $35

Valid at all rapid transit stations where the fare is $1 or less (you cannot show this pass and pay the fare difference at higher-priced stations, you must pay full fare). Valid on the Silver Line BRT and the Green D Line from Reservoir to Fenway (i.e., all above-grounds stops in Brookline). Also valid for Commuter Rail zones 1A and 1B; buses 39, CT1, CT2, and CT3; and bus 1 between the Orange Line station at Massachusetts Ave. and Dudley Station. *Not* valid on other buses (see Combo pass below).

Monthly Combo ($1.75) Pass – $57

Valid on all rapid transit lines and bus routes, except at the Red Line's southernmost stations, Quincy Adams and Braintree. You cannot show this pass and pay the extra $1 at these stations; you must pay the full $2 fare. For bus fares over $1.75 you *can* pay the difference in cash. Also valid for Commuter Rail zones 1A and 1B.

Monthly Combo Plus ($2) Pass – $63

Valid on all rapid transit lines, all Inner Harbor Ferries, and all buses on which the fare is $2 or less (for higher fares, you can pay the difference in cash). Also valid for Commuter Rail zones 1A and 1B.

Monthly Commuter Rail Pass – $85-169

Valid on all Commuter Rail services through the zone specified on the pass. Valid on all rapid transit lines, all Inner Harbor ferries, and on all bus routes up to the indicated zone fare (difference payable in cash). Refer to Chapter 9, "MBTA Commuter Rail," to find out what zone your station is in.

- Zone 1A ($1.00) – see Subway Pass
- Zone 1B ($1.50) – see Subway Pass
- Zone 1 ($2.50) Pass – $85
- Zone 2 ($2.75) Pass – $94
- Zone 3 ($3.00) Pass – $102
- Zone 4 ($3.50) Pass – $119

- Zone 5 ($4.00) Pass – $136
- Zone 6 ($4.25) Pass – $145
- Zone 7 ($4.50) Pass – $153
- Zone 8 ($5.00) Pass – $159
- Zone 9 ($5.75) Pass – $169

Monthly Interzone Pass – $56-135

Valid only on Commuter Rail for travel between zones. Not valid for boarding at any Boston, Cambridge, Chelsea, or Medford station. See any Commuter Rail Schedule card for details.

Monthly Commuter Boat Pass – $169

Valid on all MBTA services: rapid transit lines, buses, all Commuter Rail zones, Inner Harbor ferries, and Commuter Boat service to Hingham, Hull, and Quincy. Sold only at each ferry terminal, and on-line.

Weekly Passes

Valid from Sunday through end of Saturday service. Though not sold on-line, weekly passes are available from 15 rapid transit stations (cash only). Passes for the week ahead are sold Thurs.-Fri.; current week passes are sold Sun.-Wed. No passes are sold on Saturday. Sale hours vary, but most locations are open during standard business hours, and the six italicized stations are open through midnight. **Red Line:** Alewife, Harvard, *Fields Corner*, Ashmont, and Quincy Center; **Green Line:** *Kenmore*, Park Street (westbound side), Government Center, *Haymarket*, and Lechmere (closed Sunday); **Blue Line:** Maverick; **Orange Line:** *Sullivan*, *Ruggles*, and Forest Hills; **Silver Line BRT:** Dudley Station (closed Sunday). Note that pass prices may increase in 2004.

Weekly Combo ($1.75) Pass – $12.50

Valid for the same services as the Monthly Combo Pass.

Weekly Combo Plus ($2) Pass – $14

Valid for the same services as the Monthly Combo Plus Pass. In addition to the sales locations cited above, this pass is sold at Quincy Adams and Braintree on the Red Line.

Boston Visitor Pass

Available for one (**$6**), three (**$11**), or seven consecutive days (**$22**). Valid for unlimited travel on all rapid transit lines, any bus route on which the fare is 75¢, plus all Inner Harbor ferries. Pass prices may increase in 2004.

Boston Visitor Passes can be purchased on the T's website, www.mbta.com, or at these stations: **Red Line:** Alewife, Harvard, South Station, Quincy Adams; **Green Line:** Government Center, Copley, Hynes Convention Center/ICA; **Blue Line:** Airport; **Orange Line:** North Station, Back Bay Station. **Additional sales locations:** Copley Square Hotel, Cambridge Marriott Hotel, the Visitors Booth just outside Park Street station, and BosTix outlets at Faneuil Hall and Copley Square.

Senior, Student, and Other Special Fares

Senior citizens (65 and over) with MBTA ID cards pay only 25¢ for Red, Green, Orange, and Blue Lines and 15¢ for Silver Line BRT and local buses. On zoned and express buses, and on Commuter Rail, senior citizens pay half the regular fare. Monthly passes are reduced to $13. Note that fares may increase in 2004. A driver's license and other ID forms showing proof of age are accepted on Commuter Rail, but on buses and the subway you must have an MBTA senior citizen card. The cost of a card is 50¢, and it's valid for life (see below for how to get one).

Persons with disabilities who have an MBTA Transportation Access Pass (TAP) pay the same amount as seniors. TAPs from other regional transit authorities in Massachusetts are also accepted on the T. TAPs cost $3.00 and are valid for five years if permanently disabled, or one year if temporarily disabled. Medicare recipients under age 65 automatically qualify for a one-year TAP. Blind persons with a travel card from the Massachusetts Commission for the Blind ride free.

Senior citizen cards and TAPs can be obtained at Back Bay Station on weekdays, 8:30am-5:00pm. Call 617/222-5976 (TTY 617/222-5854) for further information, or to request a mail-in application.

Up to two **Children** under five ride the MBTA system free when accompanied by an adult. Children age 5-11 pay half fare.

Students through high school with an MBTA student badge pay half fare for travel to and from classes. A monthly high school pass is available through your school for $7.00. Students' fares and passes are only valid until 8pm on days when school is in session. They are not valid on Commuter Boats or on Commuter Rail trains beyond Zone 1.

College students whose school belongs to the **Semester Pass Program** can buy a semester's worth of discounted monthly passes. Contact your school directly or the MBTA at 617/222-5218 to find out more, or view a directory of participating institutions on-line at www.mbta.com.

Commuter Rail **Family Fares** for a group of up to five people—one adult and four children under 18, or two adults and three children—are available for the price of two adult roundtrips and are good for a roundtrip on the day of purchase on any trains except morning rush trains.

Where to Find MBTA Maps and Schedules

The free, full-color **Official Public Transit System Map** showing all MBTA-operated services is sometimes available at the Park Street information booth (in the center of the westbound Green Line platforms), at the Transportation Library in the State Transportation Building, 10 Park Plaza (see Downtown Map, page 30), or at the MBTA Operations Center at 45 High Street in downtown Boston. All MBTA maps can also be downloaded from www.mbta.com.

Printed **pocket-sized schedules for all MBTA rapid transit and bus routes** are available at kiosks in Park Street, Government Center, Back Bay, and Harvard Square subway stations. Bus drivers usually can provide schedules for their own

Tax Breaks for Employers and Commuters

Federal Tax Code section 132(f) lets employers offer pre-tax **Commuter Choice** benefits covering up to $100 of an employee's monthly transit, ridesharing, or parking expenses. This national program gives employers complete flexibility to mix benefits with employee contributions.

One of the two principal Commuter Choice options lets employees **purchase public transit passes through deductions** from pre-tax income, saving both employer and employee from the payroll taxes on the amount set aside for each pass. Passes that cost more than the $100 monthly benefit ceiling must have the difference paid for with taxable dollars. Alternatively, employers may offer their workers a subsidy of up to that same $100 per month to commute via transit, which can then be taken as a business expense on the employer's taxes. The T's Corporate Pass Program qualifies as this type of benefit: employers order transit passes from the T (minimum of five per month), and then distribute them to their staff. Call 617/222-5218 or visit www.mbta.com to obtain an application for your company.

The second option lets employees **receive up to $100/month in vouchers** to pay for public or private transit passes or tokens, commuter or interstate bus or rail tickets, or vanpool services. In Massachusetts the vouchers, provided by Commuter Check Services Corp. (CCSC), come in six denominations from $20-45. Participating employers may either distribute Commuter Checks free to their employees and write off the resulting business expense; let employees pay for them through pre-tax payroll deductions; or split the expense with each employee in whatever proportion is desired. For more information call New Jersey-based CCSC at 201/833-9700, or go to **www.commutercheck.com**.

Visit **www.commuterchoice.com** to obtain a directory of non-profit and for-profit service providers able to help your company administer these benefit programs. For the official word on what's allowable by law, check out the Federal Transit Administration's website, www.fta.dot.gov, and follow the link to Commuter Choice.

route. **Commuter Rail schedules** are available at South Station's Customer Information desk (next to the Amtrak ticket office), in North Station's lobby, at Back Bay Station's rail ticket office, and from Commuter Rail ticket agents. Schedules for all routes—rapid transit, bus, Commuter Rail, Commuter Boat, and privately operated MBTA "commuter coach" services—are available at the MBTA Operations Center at 45 High Street in downtown Boston, and at the Transportation Library at the top of the escalators in the State Transportation Building. Schedules are also distributed to over 400 community locations, including public libraries, city and town halls, stores, banks, and colleges.

For schedule information you can also call the MBTA's **Travel Information Line** at 800/392-6100 or 617/222-3200. Phones are staffed Mon.-Fri. 6:30am-8pm, and Sat.-Sun. 7:30am-6pm. The MBTA's Web site, which features fares, schedules, service advisories, and on-line forms for purchasing passes, is at **www.mbta.com.** You can even download T schedules to your Palm Pilot.

Commendations, Complaints, and Suggestions

The MBTA's "Write to the Top" program promises prompt responses to your input. Call MBTA Customer Relations at 617/222-5215, write MBTA Customer Relations, 10 Park Plaza, Rm. 6720, Boston, MA 02116, email feedback@mbta.com, or look for the red "suggestion" boxes in many stations which are (usually) stocked with blank comment cards.

The MBTA also guarantees timely service, offering a free fare for anyone whose trip is delayed more than one-half hour. Mail an On-Time Service Guarantee card (available from MBTA collectors and drivers) or complete an on-line form within 30 days of the delayed trip to receive your free fare.

All MBTA services rely on financial assistance from federal, state, and local governments. Let your elected officials know that the T is important to you. These officials may also be able to help get better service in your community. If you have a question or comment about the level or quality of service, or a suggestion for improving service, you can contact your state senator or representative, or your city or town's representative on the MBTA Advisory Board. Call 617/426-6054 for the name of your Advisory Board representative.

The **Association for Public Transportation,** the private, non-profit group that produced this book, is also interested in your comments on transit service. Send them to APT, PO Box 51029, Boston, MA 02205-1029. For more information about APT visit www.car-free.com or see page vi.

Chapter 2:
Not the T (Non-MBTA Transit)

A number of other carriers besides the MBTA operate transit services in and near Boston. Most services favor weekday commuters, particularly to and from MBTA stations, but exceptions abound for mall shoppers, sightseers, and day-trippers.

Amtrak (route details in Chapters 12 and 13)

Acela Express, the high-speed, European-inspired, electrified rail service from Amtrak, provides 10 daily roundtrips between Boston and New York City via Providence, RI, continuing onward to Philadelphia, Baltimore, and Washington, DC. There are also daily **Amtrak** trains to New York City via Springfield, MA and central Connecticut; to Chicago, IL, via Springfield and Albany, NY; and to Portland, ME aboard the new "Downeaster" service.

Service to Portland departs from North Station (Green and Orange Lines). All other Amtrak trains depart from South Station (Red Line) and stop at Back Bay Station (Orange Line). Trains via Providence stop at Route 128 Station (Rte. 128/I-95 Exit 13), and trains via Springfield stop in Framingham and Worcester.

Non-MBTA Buses (route details in Chapters 12 and 13)

There are several different types of bus services available including longer-distance commuting routes into Boston, connections to MBTA services, inter-state routes, and local or regional around-town routes. For transit service to a particular city or town, see Chapter 7, "Cities and Towns."

Commuter Buses and TMAs

A number of companies offer commuter service into Boston to augment MBTA service. Most of these heavily favor rush hour, with as few as one morning trip inbound and one evening trip outbound, but some offer Saturday and midday service as well. Trips are usually 40-90 minutes long and fares are generally $4-5 for the longer trips. Many buses make just a few stops in outlying towns or offer "flag stops" (wave the bus down at any safe place along its route), and then run express into Boston to stop at one or more of: Copley Square, Park Square, Park Street, Government Center, Haymarket, the Financial District, South Station, or Logan Airport. These locations, except Logan, are shown in the maps in Chapter 5, "Popular Sights and Excursions."

Transportation Management Associations (TMAs) are non-profit organizations, often state-subsidized, that serve large employers by helping commuters find alternatives to solo driving. TMA services are sometimes restricted to employees of member companies. Many TMAs offer scheduled bus service, as well as park-and-ride, van- and car-pooling, bicycle route recommendations, and more. Bus routes are usually shuttles from MBTA transit stations or large parking facilities to the workplace. They are free to member employees and are sometimes open to the public for a small fee. The particularly useful Longwood Medical Area shuttle, open to the public for $2, connects that area with Harvard Square. To see if there are TMA services that you can take advantage of, ask your employer or visit www.masscommute.com.

Local Buses – RTAs and Neighborhood Shuttles

Local bus transit in Massachusetts is provided by public **Regional Transit Authorities** (RTAs) and public or private neighborhood shuttles. These connect residential areas with shopping areas, large employers, schools, post offices, libraries, and other transit hubs like Commuter Rail stations. Many offer door-to-door service by pre-arrangement for the elderly and disabled.

The MBTA is the largest of the RTAs, serving scores of towns around metropolitan Boston, but there are 17 other RTAs serving 90 cities and towns from Western Massachusetts to Cape Cod. Neighborhood shuttles are rarer, offered by just a few towns in Eastern Massachusetts. Some RTAs and neighborhood shuttles primarily serve one town, while others cover a multi-town region. To see if a specific town is served by an RTA or neighborhood shuttle, see Chapter 7, "Cities and Towns."

Some local services operate on Saturdays, but very few operate on Sundays. Fares are usually $1 or less for short routes and up to $3 for longer routes. Discounted monthly passes or multi-ride tickets are almost always available along with special reduced-rate services for the elderly and handicapped.

Interstate Buses

Many private interstate bus companies concentrate on various parts of New England. The two largest serve destinations beyond New England: **Peter Pan Bus Lines** (a Trailways affiliate) serving the northeast from New Hampshire to Washington D.C.; and **Greyhound Lines,** serving the entire United States and parts of Canada. Both coordinate their long-distance schedules wherever connections between them exist. Their routes, including frequent daily express service between Boston and New York City, are listed together in Chapter 12, "More Rail, Bus, and Ferry (Not the T)."

All major interstate buses use the **South Station Transportation Center,** which is connected by walkway to the train station's cavernous main waiting room. Peter Pan and Greyhound also share a ticket counter inside South

South Station, Boston's Intermodal Hub

Boston's largest (no contest) intermodal hub serves MBTA rapid transit and Commuter Rail, Amtrak, and is adjacent to a large interstate bus terminal serving all major carriers. The rail station also has an attractive waiting area with food services, shops, and a regularly-staffed information booth. The only landbound transit you can't easily access via South Station is northbound rail (Amtrak and MBTA Commuter Rail), which can be found at North Station.

Station, next to the Red Line subway station escalators, as well as at Riverside in Newton, the western terminus of the Green D Line.

Non-MBTA Ferries (route details in Chapters 12 and 13)

Most non-MBTA ferry services are seasonal, connecting points around Boston Harbor to the Boston Harbor Islands National Park Area, Gloucester, Salem, and Provincetown. There are also year-round ferries from Cape Cod to the islands of Martha's Vineyard and Nantucket. Some ferry companies also offer seasonal harbor cruises, fishing charters, and whale-watching excursions.

Of special note is the year-round **Airport Water Shuttle**, the fastest public transit connection between downtown Boston and Logan International Airport. The Water Shuttle departs from Rowes Wharf, behind the Boston Harbor Hotel, midway between Aquarium station on the Blue Line and South Station on the Red Line.

Tours and Charters

A wide variety of sightseeing tours is available in the Boston area, from one-hour "trolley" tours of downtown to weekend- or week-long tours of New England. Look in the Boston Area Yellow Pages under "Sightseeing Tours" for some options. If your group is planning an outing, you can obtain group rates on many carriers, including the MBTA Commuter Rail. If you have enough people, you can charter a bus, a boat, or even a whole train.

ANDREW RUBEL

The New England Aquarium gives harbor tours featuring "Science at Sea" on the Doc Edgerton, named in memory of the MIT scientist who pioneered strobe and underwater photography and explored the oceans with Jacques-Yves Cousteau. The Aquarium also offers whale watches aboard the larger Voyager III, built specifically for whale watching. For harbor tour and whale watch information or reservations, call 617/973-5281.

Chapter 3:
More Local Transportation

Carpools, Vanpools, Park-and-Ride, Special Buses

CARAVAN for Commuters, Inc., www.commute.com, is a private, non-profit, state-supported organization that helps commuters in Massachusetts find alternatives to driving alone. Their **Commuter Information Line,** 888/4-COMMUTE, provides free information on train, bus, and ferry routes, carpools, vanpools, and park-and-ride lots.

Your employer or college may be a member of a Transportation Management Association (TMA). Call your human resources or commuter services office, CARAVAN (see above), or visit www.masscommute.com to find out if there are TMA services you can take advantage of. See also "Commuter Buses and TMAs" on page 16 for more details, or for transit service to a particular city or town, see Chapter 7, "Cities and Towns."

Many employers and some apartment and condominium developments hire private transit companies to run special bus or van services for their employees or residents. If your employer or management office does not already offer this service, call CARAVAN for a free consultation.

Taxicabs, Rental Cars, and Zipcar

Even if you don't use a car regularly, you may occasionally need one. So rent one, by the mile (taxi), by the day (rental car), or via the potentially more cost-effective Zipcar. Any of these is cheaper and easier than car ownership.

For the most up-to-date list of taxis and car rental companies, look in your telephone directory's Yellow Pages under "Taxicabs" or "Automobile Rental & Leasing." Some rental companies, such as Enterprise Rent-A-Car, will pick you up and bring you to the rental agency.

Zipcar is a membership organization offering "wheels when you want them." It has a fleet of well-maintained cars conveniently parked throughout the Boston area. A Zipcar is parked within a five minute walk of 600,000 people, with new locations added frequently (Chapter 5 maps show select locations). Members may reserve a vehicle from a specific location and period of time. Zipcar cleans and maintains the cars, so upkeep is not a concern for Zipcar members. Depending on your usage, Zipcar may be more economical than taxis or rental cars, and if Zipcar allows you to sell a car, the savings can be significant. Zipcar can be reached at 866/4-ZIPCAR or visit www.zipcar.com

Bicycles

Transit and bicycling are powerfully synergistic. Each increases the range of the other. If you are primarily using transit, a bicycle can greatly extend your useful range from the nearest MBTA station. By biking 10 minutes to rapid transit instead of walking, you cover about two miles instead of only one-half mile. If you're willing to travel 20 minutes to reach the T, you can be located about four miles away—not so convenient for walking, but a cinch on a bike.

Many Bostonians use bicycles as transportation to work or school or to run errands, and more employers are providing facilities for cyclists. Secure bicycle racks are now installed at many MBTA stations and, within certain time and route restrictions, you can also take your bike on the T (see sidebar).

Transit can also be used to extend bicycling range. For example, by first taking your bike to the end of a Commuter Rail line, it becomes easy to bicycle long distances, such as round trip from Boston to many points in New Hampshire in one day, while logging very few cycling miles in urban traffic.

Most **ferries** let you roll your bike aboard for a small fee, sometimes for free. Check with the carrier in advance before traveling.

Amtrak has roll-on service for bicycles on the Downeaster from Boston to Portland, Maine and on the late-night Twilight Shoreliner to New York City. Reservations are required, a fee applies, and stops for disembarking with bicycles are limited, so call in advance. Other Amtrak trains only accept boxed bicycles if they carry checked baggage, and only through stations that accept checked baggage. A large bicycle box can be purchased from Amtrak at South Station. Boxes from bicycle shops usually require much more bike disassembly.

Some **commuter buses and interstate buses** accept bicycles (often on a space-available basis). Policies and fees vary widely, sometimes leaving it up to the driver, so less busy times are best. Call the specific bus company for details.

Safe on-road bicycling is very feasible if you know what you're doing. Resources for urban cycling include "Bicycle Driver Training" courses, the compact booklet "Bicycling Street Smarts," and "Boston's Bikemap," which includes a brief but effective article about bicycling in Boston traffic (see resources below).

The Boston area also offers several bikepaths that take you downtown or to a rapid transit station where you can board the train. "Boston's Bikemap" shows these paths as well as recommended on-road bicycle routes:

- **Dr. Paul Dudley White Bikepath** runs along both sides of the Charles River from west of Watertown Sq. to the Museum of Science (19+mi).
- **Minuteman Commuter Bikeway**, from Alewife station (Red Line) to Bedford via Arlington and Lexington (11mi). Paths also lead from Alewife to Belmont and to Davis Square (Red Line) in Somerville.
- **Southwest Corridor linear park** includes a bikepath from Forest Hills to Copley Place (3.5mi).
- **Jamaicaway Bikepath** from Jamaica Pond to Brookline Village (2mi).
- **Muddy River Bikepath** runs along the Muddy River bordering the Longwood Medical Area and on to Fenway station (1.5mi).
- **Neponset River Trail** runs along the north side of the river from the coast to Central Ave. station on the Red Line (Mattapan) (2.5mi).

Bikes on the Ⓣ

Selected portions of the MBTA welcome cyclists and their two-wheeled companions at no extra charge as follows:

- Red, Blue, Orange lines: allowed Mon.-Fri. 10am-2pm and after 7:30pm; also Sat.-Sun. all day. Only two cyclists may ride at any given time, at either end of the last car of the train. If those spots are already taken—or the car is too crowded—wait for another train.

- Green Line and Silver Line BRT: not allowed.

- Commuter Rail: allowed at all times except weekday rush hours in the direction of the rush (shaded portions of timetables). Follow the conductor's instructions for boarding and exiting.

- Buses: not allowed, except on the exterior front-mounted racks of buses on the CT1, CT2, and CT3 routes.

- Ferries: allowed at all times.

Temporary bans on bikes are enacted from 8:30-11pm during major sporting events or performances at Fenway Park or FleetCenter. Other bans may also be in place during special events near a given station.

Holiday bans are in effect systemwide for the St. Patrick's Day parade (Sunday closest to March 17); Patriots Day (third Monday in April); and Independence Day (July 4).

For safety reasons, cyclists may not enter or exit at the following stations: Downtown Crossing, Government Center, Park Street. Transfers *between* the Red and Orange Lines at Downtown Crossing are permissible. For more information about Bikes-on-the-T, call the MBTA at 617/222-3200 or the Massachusetts Bicycle Coalition (MassBike) at 617/542-BIKE.

Bike paths are also listed by town in Chapter 7, "Cities and Towns." The following resources may also be of help:

- Massachusetts Bicycle Coalition (MassBike), 59 Temple Place #669, Boston, MA 02111; 617/542-BIKE; www.massbike.org; an information resource that promotes improved cycling conditions.

- Charles River Wheelmen, 19 Chase Ave., W. Newton, MA 02465; 617/325-BIKE; www.crw.org; sponsors recreational group rides year-round.

- Rubel BikeMaps, Box 401035, Cambridge, MA 02140; www.bikemaps.com; publishes Boston's Bikemap; general-purpose road and bicycle maps for Eastern, Central, and Western Massachusetts, plus Cape Cod; *Pocket Rides* recreational rides; and *Bicycling Street Smarts*, a bite-sized guide to riding confidently, legally, and safely on the road. All are available at bookstores, bike shops, mail-order, and on-line.

Chapter 4: Services for Seniors and Persons with Disabilities

Regional Transit Authorities (RTAs), including the MBTA, offer services for seniors and persons with disabilities as required by the Americans with Disabilities Act. Accommodations can include accessible vehicles and reduced fares. Normally, you must apply for these services, but once you have the appropriate pass, you are eligible for services from RTAs across the state. Carriers often need advance notice, so call at least 24 hours before traveling.

Information about accessible MBTA stations and buses appears in Chapters 8-10, however, accessibility is continually being improved. For updated information, visit www.mbta.com or contact the MBTA Office for Transportation Access (OTA). OTA oversees all MBTA services for seniors and persons with disabilities, addresses questions about MBTA accessibility, and operates the programs outlined below, as well as providing travel information for customers who require an accessible route to their destination. For OTA fixed-route services call 617/222-5976 or -5854 (TTY); for paratransit services call 617/222-5123 or -5415 (TTY); or visit www.mbta.com/traveling_t/disability_ota.asp.

- Senior and Access Pass Program – Reduced-fare passes. Back Bay Station office (Mon.-Fri. 8:30am-5pm); 617/222-5438 or -5854 (TTY). See also "Senior, Student, and Other Special Fares" on p. 13.

- Call-A-Lift Bus Program – Many MBTA bus routes are regularly run with lift-equipped vehicles (denoted "LIFT" in Chapter 10). For those that are not, you can order a lift-equipped bus for the route by calling in the morning the day before you travel. (If you cannot use a regularly-scheduled route, see THE RIDE below.) Back Bay Station office (Mon.-Fri. 8:30am-5pm); 800/LIFT-BUS or 617/222-5854 (TTY).

- THE RIDE – Also known as "paratransit" service, THE RIDE provides transportation for people who cannot use general public transit because of a physical, cognitive, or mental disability. THE RIDE is also available to ADA-certified out-of-state visitors (please make advance arrangements). For questions or to apply for eligibility: 10 Park Plaza office (Mon.-Fri. 8am-5pm); 617/222-5123, 800/533-6282 (in-state), or 617/222-5415 (TTY). For tickets: Back Bay Station office (Mon.-Fri. 8:30am-5pm).

- Travel Training Program – Teaches interested users of THE RIDE to travel on MBTA rapid transit, Commuter Rail, and buses. Back Bay Station office (Mon.-Fri. 8:30am-5pm); 617/222-5970 or -5854 (TTY).

Amtrak stations in most large cities are wheelchair-accessible, including South Station and Back Bay Station in Boston. Advance reservation is required for wheelchair accommodation. Call 617/482-3660 or 800/523-6590 (TTY).

Most Massport shuttle buses at Logan Airport are accessible, and the Accessible Van also serves all terminals and the closest accessible subway station, Wood Island (Blue Line). Call 617/561-1769 or 617/561-1770. See Chapter 14 for more information about Logan Airport and Massport shuttles.

Destinations

JOHN HOSTAGE

The Public Garden lagoon, home of the Swan Boats

A nyone who shares the *joie de vivre* of a three-year-old knows that transit is, by itself, as good as an amusement park ride. Even as adults we like to say that getting there is half the fun. But to experience all the fun, most of us require a destination.

This section's three chapters are designed to satisfy that need to have goals in life. Full of suggestions, Chapter 5, "Popular Sights and Excursions," offers descriptions for the most popular spots in Boston and Eastern Massachusetts. If you already know where you want to go, consult Chapter 6, "Place Listings – How to Get There" or Chapter 7, "Cities and Towns" for complete transit directions.

Visitor Information

- **Massachusetts Office of Travel and Tourism** 617/973-8500, www.massvacation.com. Call for their annual *Getaway Guide,* a statewide summary of attractions, lodgings, and tour operators.

- **Boston Visitor Information Line** 888/SEE-BOSTON or 617/536-4100, www.bostonusa.com. A service of the Greater Boston Convention & Visitors Bureau, which also operates the **Boston Common Information Booth** on the Tremont Street side of the **Boston Common.** *Red Line or Green Line to Park Street.*

- **Cambridge Office of Tourism Information Booth** 800/862-5678 or 617/497-1630, www.cambridge-usa.org, in Harvard Square. Cambridge information and tours. *Red Line to Harvard.*

- **Boston National Historical Park Visitor Center** 617/242-5642, 15 State St. at Devonshire St., opposite the Old State House Museum. Freedom Trail information and tours; public restrooms; wheelchair accessible. *Orange or Blue Line to State.* The National Park Service also staffs the **Information Center** in Faneuil Hall off New Congress St. (*Orange or Blue Line to State; Green Line to Government Center*), and the **Bunker Hill Pavilion** visitor center at Charlestown Navy Yard (*Inner Harbor Ferry F3 or F4 to Charlestown Navy Yard*).

- **BosTix** 617/482-BTIX; www.artsboston.org; adjacent to Faneuil Hall, off New Congress St. (Tues-Sat 10am-6pm, Sun 11am-4pm), and at Copley Square (Mon-Sat 10am-6pm, Sun 11am-4pm). Exclusive vendor of half-priced, day-of-show tickets to local performing arts; full-priced advanced tickets to arts and professional sports; TicketMaster outlet. *Orange Line or Blue Line to State; Green Line to Government Center; Green Line to Copley.*

- **The Travelers Aid Society** 617/542-7286, offices at 711 Atlantic Ave. (*Red line to South Station*); booths at South Station and Logan Airport Terminals A and E (*Blue Line to Airport*).

Chapter 5:
Popular Sights and Excursions

This chapter has two sections: **Boston Area** alphabetically lists and describes Boston neighborhoods and the adjacent communities of Brookline, Cambridge, and Somerville—all accessible via the easy-to-follow rapid transit lines and Inner Harbor Ferries. **Outside Boston** describes popular destination communities elsewhere in Eastern Massachusetts within an easy day trip from Boston via public transit.

Neither list is intended to be encyclopedic—instead, they provide some basic orientation and highlight the region's most popular destinations. Maps, when present, are noted with the ⊕ symbol. Rapid transit stations are listed in outbound order from downtown Boston. **Bold face** indicates an attraction whose contact information (including directions by T) can be found in Chapter 6, "Place Listings – How to Get There." Additionally, a comprehensive list of transit service to the communities can be found in Chapter 7, "Cities and Towns." The following symbols are used in the maps in this chapter:

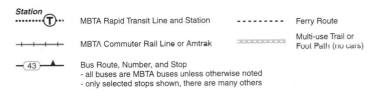

Station ········(T)···	MBTA Rapid Transit Line and Station
┼─┼─┼─┼─┼	MBTA Commuter Rail Line or Amtrak
─(43)──▲	Bus Route, Number, and Stop - all buses are MBTA buses unless otherwise noted - only selected stops shown, there are many others
- - - - - - - -	Ferry Route
▭▭▭▭▭▭	Multi-use Trail or Foot Path (no cars)

BOSTON AREA

BOSTON – Back Bay   ⊕ page 27

GREEN LINE (all branches): Arlington, Copley
GREEN B, C, AND D LINE: Hynes Convention Center/ICA
GREEN E LINE: Prudential, Symphony
ORANGE LINE: Back Bay Station, Massachusetts Ave.

From its inception as a state-sponsored urban development built entirely atop landfill, this neighborhood of elegant 19th-century townhouses, churches, and shopping areas between Arlington Street and Massachusetts Avenue has been one of Boston's most desirable addresses. It is also home to such attractions as the **Gibson House Museum, Trinity Church,** the **Boston Public Library,** the **Institute of Contemporary Art** (ICA), and the **Christian Science Center,** with its walk-through **Mapparium.** Chic boutiques, galleries, and restaurants line elegant **Newbury Street.** The 50-story Prudential Center tower, known to locals as "The Pru," welcomes visitors to its top-floor observation deck. The tower's namesake, a vast office, residential, and retail center, connects via covered footbridge to **Copley Place,** Back Bay's other large indoor retail-cinema-office mall, and to the **Hynes Convention Center.** A number of upscale hotels—Fairmont, Hilton, Marriott, Sheraton, Saunders, and Westin, among others—are clustered in the vicinity.

The Public Garden marks the Back Bay's east edge. Here you'll find the pedal-powered **Swan Boats** (Apr.-Sept.) and Boston's most popular public artwork, the Mallard family sculptures based on Robert McCloskey's children's classic, *Make Way for Ducklings.* After the **Boston Common**, the **Public Garden** is considered the second jewel in Boston's **Emerald Necklace** (see page 33).

To the north is the bank of the **Charles River Basin and Esplanade,** a popular spot for jogging, in-line skating, and bicycling on the Dr. Paul Dudley White Bikepath, which extends upriver 9.5 miles to a mile beyond Watertown Square. You'll find people sunning on the **Esplanade** beside the landscaped lagoons and arched footbridges. Sailing lessons and inexpensive sailboat rentals are available from April to early November at Community Boating, Inc. (617/523-7406), the nation's first public boating program. The **Esplanade** is also home to the **Hatch Memorial Shell,** where the Boston Pops Orchestra and other performers have given free public concerts each summer since 1940.

Recommended Excursions

1) The Pru: start with a lofty view of Boston from the **Prudential Skywalk,** and then browse the acres of shops in the "city under glass" at the tower's base. [Green E Line to Prudential]

2) **Newbury Street**: the eight blocks between Massachusetts Avenue and the **Public Garden** are a people-watching window-shopping delight in any weather. [Green Line to Arlington, then north one block]

3) The **Esplanade**: from Arlington station walk north along the edge of the **Public Garden** to the end of Arlington Street (four blocks), then cross Beacon St. to the pink-hued Fiedler Footbridge to the river. [Green Line to Arlington] See map at right for other access points to the **Esplanade,** plus handicap ramp at the Harvard (Mass. Ave.) bridge east side.

BOSTON – Beacon Hill   ⊕ page 30 (Downtown Boston)

RED LINE: Park Street, Charles/MGH
GREEN LINE: Government Center, Park Street
BLUE LINE: Bowdoin

Beacon Hill is a quiet enclave in the middle of the busy city. Since its one-way streets have been purposely designed to frustrate drivers, it is an excellent place for walking. Atop the hill is the Massachusetts **State House,** flanked by some of the city's finest mansions and by **Suffolk University.** Louisburg Square, with its patrician townhouses, is the centerpiece of Beacon Hill. At the foot of Beacon Hill is quiet Charles Street, a popular area with many restaurants and antique shops. Around the corner on Beacon Street across from the **Public Garden,** the Bull & Finch pub is still a magnet for fans of television's **"Cheers"** **bar.** Facing the base of the hill's north side along busy Cambridge Street are the **Suffolk County Courthouse** and **Massachusetts General Hospital.**

The Black Heritage Trail winds its way across Beacon Hill; begin at the **Boston African-American National Historic Site** next-door to the African Meeting House, a.k.a. the **Museum for Afro American History.** For information call 617/742-5415; or pick up a free brochure at any of the city's visitor centers.

Back Bay, Boston

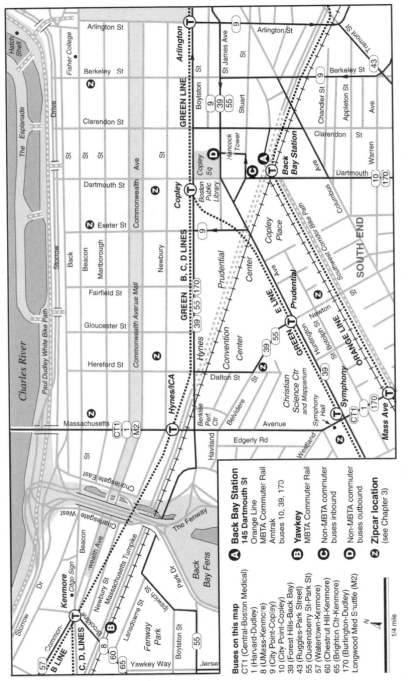

Buses on this map
CT1 (Central-Boston Medical)
1 (Harvard-Dudley)
8 (UMass-Kenmore)
9 (City Point-Copley)
10 (City Point-Copley)
39 (Forest Hills-Back Bay)
43 (Ruggles-Park Street)
55 (Queensberry St-Park St)
57 (Watertown-Kenmore)
60 (Chestnut Hill-Kenmore)
65 (Brighton Ctr-Kenmore)
170 (Burlington-Dudley)
Longwood Med Shuttle (M2)

A Back Bay Station
145 Dartmouth St
Orange Line
MBTA Commuter Rail
Amtrak
buses 10, 39, 170

B Yawkey
MBTA Commuter Rail

C Non-MBTA commuter buses inbound

D Non-MBTA commuter buses outbound

N Zipcar location
(see Chapter 3)

1/4 mile

USING TRANSIT

DESTINATIONS

ROUTE DETAILS

INDEX

Recommended Excursion

Beacon Hill: Walk along the edge of **Boston Common** to the **State House,** turn left on Beacon Street, and right on Joy Street, entering the sedate brick cloister of Beacon Hill. Meander westward onto Charles Street. [Red or Green Line to Park Street]

BOSTON – Charlestown   ⊕ next page

ORANGE LINE: Community College
INNER HARBOR FERRIES: Lovejoy Wharf (F3) or Long Wharf (F4) to Charlestown Navy Yard

Divided from the rest of Boston by the Charles River, this predominantly residential neighborhood was originally a separate town founded in 1629, a year before Boston itself. The **Bunker Hill Monument,** commemorating the Revolutionary War battle that put Charlestown in the history books, towers over intimate blocks of 18th- and 19th-century townhouses. The waterfront is dominated by the **Charlestown Navy Yard,** part of **Boston National Historical Park** and home of "Old Ironsides," the 18th-century **U.S.S. Constitution.**

Recommended Excursion

Charlestown Navy Yard: Visit the **U.S.S. Constitution Museum, Old Ironsides,** and **Bunker Hill Monument** (three blocks northwest). [Ferry F3 or F4 to Charlestown Navy Yard or 15-minute walk from North Station]

The Freedom Trail

The Freedom Trail is a self-guided walking tour of 16 historic sites associated with the founding of the United States. Marked by a stripe of red brick or paint, it wends for 2.5 miles from **Boston Common,** past **Faneuil Hall** and through the North End to Charlestown. Among the stops along the way are the **Old South Meeting House, Old State House, Paul Revere House,** the **Old North Church,** "Old Ironsides" (**U.S.S. Constitution**), and the **Bunker Hill Monument.** Several of the trail's sites are also part of the **Boston National Historical Park.**

The trail begins at the Boston Common Visitor Information Booth. Maps of the trail can be obtained there or at the National Park Visitor Center, 15 State St. (617/242-5642) across from the **Old State House.** The Park Service also offers free ranger-guided tours of portions of the trail daily from Patriots Day (third Monday in April) to Thanksgiving weekend (end of November). For a schedule of the various special events held along the trail throughout the summer, request a guide from the Freedom Trail Foundation by calling 617/227-8800, or visit www.thefreedomtrail.org.

The Freedom Trail has provided inspiration for two other trails: The Black Heritage Trail (described under "Boston: Beacon Hill" elsewhere in this section) and the Women's Heritage Trail. Featuring walks in downtown, the North End, Chinatown, and Beacon Hill, the Women's Heritage Trail includes sites associated with Amelia Earhart, Rose Kennedy, Phillis Wheatley, Mary Baker Eddy, Louisa May Alcott, and Julia Ward Howe.

Charlestown and the North End, Boston

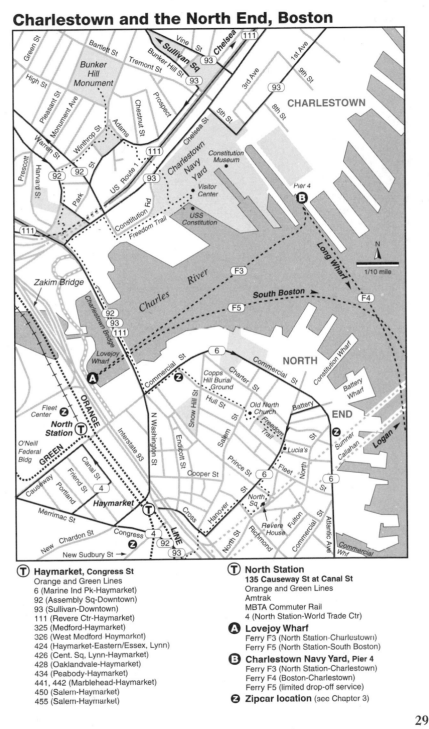

USING TRANSIT

DESTINATIONS

ROUTE DETAILS

INDEX

Ⓣ **Haymarket, Congress St**
Orange and Green Lines
6 (Marine Ind Pk-Haymarket)
92 (Assembly Sq-Downtown)
93 (Sullivan-Downtown)
111 (Revere Ctr-Haymarket)
325 (Medford-Haymarket)
326 (West Medford Haymarket)
424 (Haymarket-Eastern/Essex, Lynn)
426 (Cent. Sq, Lynn-Haymarket)
428 (Oaklandvale-Haymarket)
434 (Peabody-Haymarket)
441, 442 (Marblehead-Haymarket)
450 (Salem-Haymarket)
455 (Salem-Haymarket)

Ⓣ **North Station**
135 Causeway St at Canal St
Orange and Green Lines
Amtrak
MBTA Commuter Rail
4 (North Station-World Trade Ctr)

Ⓐ **Lovejoy Wharf**
Ferry F3 (North Station-Charlestown)
Ferry F5 (North Station-South Boston)

Ⓑ **Charlestown Navy Yard, Pier 4**
Ferry F3 (North Station-Charlestown)
Ferry F4 (Boston-Charlestown)
Ferry F5 (limited drop-off service)

Ⓩ **Zipcar location** (see Chapter 3)

29

Downtown Boston

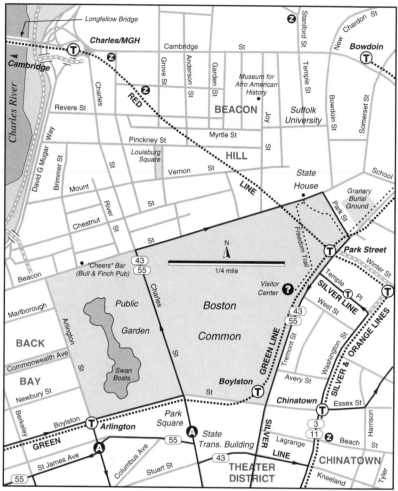

Ⓐ Commuter Buses
Park Square and Arlington
Brush Hill - St James Ave
Cavalier Coach - Trans. Bldg
The Coach Co - St James Ave &
  Berkeley St
Gulbankian - Trans. Bldg
Interstate Coach - Trans Bldg
MVRTA - Transportation Bldg
Peter Pan Greyhound -
  St James & Arlington Sts
Plymouth & Brockton -
  Stuart & Charles Sts
Trombly - Transportation Bldg

Ⓑ Chinatown Buses
(see map at right)
500 (Riverside-Downtown)
501 (Brighton Ctr-Downtown)
504 (Watertown-Downtown)
505 (Waltham-Downtown)
553 (Roberts/Brandeis-Downtown)
554 (Waverley-Downtown)
556 (Waltham Highland-Downtown)
558 (Auburndale-Downtown)
Cavalier Coach - Essex St
Fung Wah - 68 Beach St
Gulbankian - Essex & Lincoln Sts
Interstate Coach - Beach & Lincoln
MVRTA - Essex & Lincoln Sts
Travel Pack - Harrison & Beach
Trombly - Essex & Lincoln Sts

Ⓒ Downtown Crossing Buses
(see map at right)
Federal & Franklin Sts and
  Otis & Summer Sts
7 (City Pt-Downtown)
448 (Marblehead-Downtown)
449 (Marblehead-Downtown)
459 (Salem-Downtown)
500 (Riverside-Downtown)
501 (Brighton Ctr-Downtown)
504 (Watertown-Downtown)
505 (Waltham-Downtown)
553 (Roberts/Brandeis-Downtown)
554 (Waverley-Downtown)
556 (Waltham Highlnd-Downtown)
558 (Auburndale-Downtown)
Gulbankian - Franklin & Hawley Sts

Downtown Boston

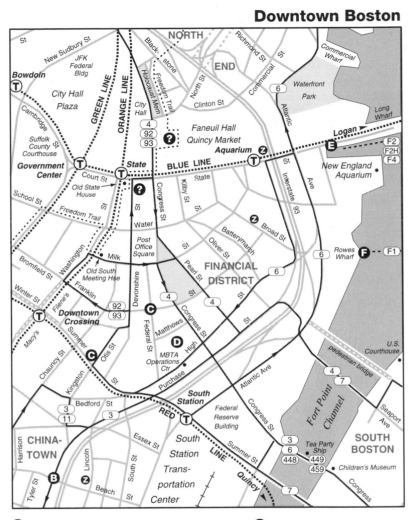

(T) South Station Trans. Ctr.
Summer St and Atlantic Ave

Red Line
MBTA Commuter Rail
Amtrak
MBTA buses at Summer St:
  3 (City Pt-Chinatown)
  6 (Marine Ind Pk-Haymarket)
  7 (City Pt-Downtown)
  448 (Marblehead-Downtown)
  449 (Marblehead-Downtown)
  459 (Salem-Downtown)
American Eagle
Bloom Bus Lines
Bonanza
Brush Hill - Beach & Lincoln
C&J Trailways
Coach New England

Concord Trailways
Dartmouth Coach
Greyhound
Interstate Coach -
  Beach & Lincoln Sts
JBL Bus Lines - South St
Peter Pan Trailways
Plymouth & Brockton
Vermont Transit
Yankee Bus Co. (am drop-
  off only)

D Commuter Buses
Financial District
Gulbankian - Federal & Matthews Sts
JBL Bus Lines - Congress & High Sts

E Long Wharf
F2 (Quincy, Boston, Logan)
F2H (Quincy & Hull, Boston, Logan)
F4 (Charlestown)
Boston Harbor Cruises
  (Harbor Islands and Provincetown)

F Rowes Wharf
F1 (Hingham)
Airport Water Shuttle

Z Zipcar location (see Chapter 3)

BOSTON – Dorchester

RED LINE: Andrew, JFK/UMass
RED LINE (ASHMONT): Savin Hill, Fields Corner, Shawmut, Ashmont
Annexed by the city of Boston some 240 years after being founded as a separate town, Dorchester is the city's largest neighborhood, occupying the large swath of coastline between South Boston and the Neponset River. Public access to the water is facilitated along the **Dorchester Shores Reservation,** which includes **Malibu** and **Savin Hill** beaches. The **John F. Kennedy Library and Museum** also sits on the waterfront of Dorchester Bay, next to the very modern commuter campus of the **University of Massachusetts,** better known as **UMASS Boston.** The Neponset River Trail marks the southern edge, running west 3.5 miles from the mouth of the Neponset to Dorchester Lower Mills.

Recommended Excursion
John F. Kennedy Library and Museum: Exhibits, including recreated White House "rooms," chronicle Kennedy's presidency and early life, and special exhibits feature Jackie and Robert Kennedy. [Red Line to JFK/UMass, connect to free shuttle bus (usually less than 15-minute wait)]

BOSTON – Downtown   ⊕ page 30,31

RED LINE: Park Street, Downtown Crossing, South Station
GREEN LINE: Haymarket, Government Center, Park Street, Boylston
ORANGE LINE: Haymarket, State, Downtown Crossing, Chinatown, New England Medical Center
BLUE LINE: Aquarium, State, Government Center, Bowdoin
SILVER LINE: Downtown Crossing, Chinatown, New England Medical Center
INNER HARBOR FERRIES: Charlestown Navy Yard to Long Wharf (F4)

Downtown Boston is a blanket term for the irregular, often labyrinthine blocks gently sloping from Beacon Hill to the Inner Harbor's edge—the "Central Business District," in the parlance of the city's planning authority. It's primarily the territory of office workers, shoppers, and tourists wandering the **Freedom Trail** (see sidebar page 28), but there are residential pockets, too—in luxury condos on the waterfront and in the upper floors of many commercial blocks.

At the heart of downtown lies the Financial District, centered around Congress Street's diminutive Post Office Square. Along the western edge lies **Downtown Crossing,** a pedestrian-only series of shop-lined blocks anchored by the city's flagship department stores (Filene's and Macy's), and the park-like **Boston Common,** home to the Frog Pond (ice skate rentals available in winter) and public art such as August Saint-Gaudens' memorial to Col. Robert Gould Shaw and the Massachusetts 54th Regiment. On the north side of downtown are Government Center, comprising **Boston City Hall** and numerous state and federal offices, and **Faneuil Hall** and **Quincy Market,** 19th-century buildings reincarnated as the nation's original pushcart- and food-court-filled festival marketplace. The city's waterfront firmly defines downtown's eastern boundary, its historic old wharves now covered in hotels, luxury condominiums, prime office space—and the **New England Aquarium.**

Boston's Emerald Necklace

Many of the nine parks in this seven-mile chain were designed by Frederick Law Olmsted in the latter 1800s. With a few short interruptions, you can walk along greenways and through parks from **Boston Common** and the **Public Garden** all the way to **Franklin Park**—Boston's largest—straddling Roxbury, Jamaica Plain, Forest Hills, and Dorchester.

Between the Common's pedestrian-filled walkways and Franklin Park's golf course and zoo are the **Commonwealth Avenue Mall, Back Bay Fens, the Riverway, Olmsted Park, Jamaica Pond,** and **Arnold Arboretum.** Most are mentioned with their Boston neighborhoods in this chapter. For park directions, see "Beaches and Parks" in Chapter 6.

Contact the Boston Parks and Recreation Department for more information (617/635-4505, www.cityofboston.gov/parks), or, for a recorded schedule of ranger-led tours and events, call 617/635-7383. For special events, to lend support, or to join in advocacy, contact the Emerald Necklace Conservancy, 617/232-5374, www.emeraldnecklace.org..

Downtown's southern side is segmented into several distinct mini-neighborhoods. The historic 19th-century Leather District, on Lincoln and South Sts., includes blocks of residential and commercial loft buildings bordering the bustling rail and intercity bus terminals at South Station. A large ceremonial Chinese gate marks the formal entrance to next-door Chinatown, known for being one of Boston's only neighborhoods where restaurants stay open well past midnight. Chinatown is hemmed in on its western and southern edges by **Emerson College,** the **New England Medical Center,** and isolated remnants of the so-called Combat Zone, Boston's all-but-vanquished adult-entertainment area. A small Theater District, centered on Tremont Street, abuts the southern edge of **Boston Common** and segues westward into residential Bay Village and hotel-filled Park Square, which together mark downtown's boundary with neighboring Back Bay.

Recommended Excursions

1) **Faneuil Hall** and **Quincy Market:** the scores of shops and eateries in and around these historic buildings play year-round host to a lively parade of tourists and office workers. In warmer weather, buskers, jugglers, and other street performers entertain the passing crowds. [Blue Line to Aquarium; Green Line to Government Center; Orange Line to State]

2) **Downtown Crossing:** shop till you drop. [Orange, Red, or Silver Line to Downtown Crossing]

3) **Boston Harbor Islands National Park Area:** from Long Wharf, ride Boston Harbor Cruises to George's Island. From there four other islands are accessible by free water taxi. Camping is even permitted on some; call 617/223-8666 for information, and 617/727-7676 and 877/I-CAMP-MA for permits. [Blue Line to Aquarium; Inner Harbor Ferry F4 to Long Wharf]

BOSTON – Fenway/Kenmore

⊕ this page (partial coverage)

GREEN B LINE: Kenmore, Blandford St., B.U. East, B.U. Central
GREEN C LINE: Kenmore, Saint Mary's St.
GREEN D LINE: Kenmore, Fenway
GREEN E LINE: Symphony, Northeastern University, Museum of Fine Arts

This multifaceted district encompasses commercial, institutional, and residential areas on either side of the **Back Bay Fens,** a piece of the **Emerald Necklace** (see sidebar page 33) which follows a sweeping tree-lined curve of the shallow

Longwood Medical Area, Boston

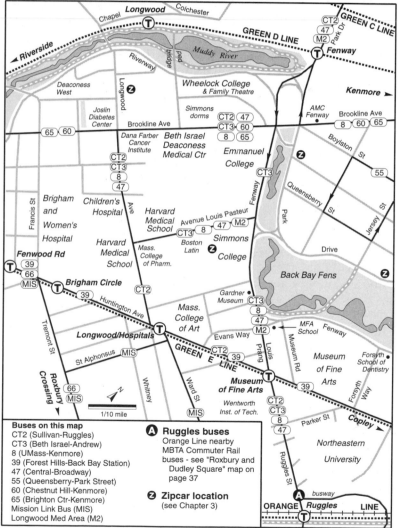

Buses on this map
CT2 (Sullivan-Ruggles)
CT3 (Beth Israel-Andrew)
8 (UMass-Kenmore)
39 (Forest Hills-Back Bay Station)
47 (Central-Broadway)
55 (Queensberry-Park Street)
60 (Chestnut Hill-Kenmore)
65 (Brighton Ctr-Kenmore)
Mission Link Bus (MIS)
Longwood Med Area (M2)

Ⓐ **Ruggles buses**
Orange Line nearby
MBTA Commuter Rail
buses - see "Roxbury and
Dudley Square" map on
page 37

Ⓩ **Zipcar location**
(see Chapter 3)

Muddy River. Be sure to visit the Rose Garden near the end of Jersey Street. North of the Fens lies Kenmore Square, which seems to come alive at night: its giant neon Citgo sign is visible from all along the Charles River basin, and its sidewalks are usually filled with young clubgoers headed for Avalon, Embassy, Atlas, and other hot nightspots clustered along Lansdowne Street in the shadow of **Fenway Park** where the Red Sox have played since 1912. West of Kenmore the Green Line becomes a streetcar, rising from underground in distinct branches that make frequent local surface stops.

Some dozen colleges and conservatories enliven Fenway/Kenmore with their students; the largest, **Boston University** and **Northeastern University,** bracket the neighborhood on two sides. **Symphony Hall,** the **Museum of Fine Arts** (MFA), and the **Isabella Stewart Gardner Museum** are found on or near Huntington Avenue, along the southern edge.

Recommended Excursion
Museum of Fine Arts: Plan to spend several hours with this large and interesting collection. [Green E Line to Museum of Fine Arts]

BOSTON – Jamaica Plain
GREEN E LINE: Back of the Hill, Heath St.
ORANGE LINE: Jackson Square, Stony Brook, Green St., Forest Hills

Historically a district of the once-independent town of Roxbury (see below), "JP" is a residential neighborhood known on the one hand for its parks and on the other for its social and racial diversity. The greenspace includes **Olmsted Park,** among the quieter parks in the **Emerald Necklace** (see sidebar page 33); **Jamaica Pond,** where one can rent a rowboat or sailboat or fish the stocked waters; **Arnold Arboretum,** a 265-acre living museum of 15,000 trees and shrubs, curated by **Harvard University;** and Southwest Corridor Park, a narrow linear park and bike path built along the route of the Orange Line from Forest Hills to Back Bay's **Copley Place.**

Recommended Excursion
Arnold Arboretum: The trip is well worth making any time of year, but a spring visit is richly rewarded with spectacular lilacs. [Orange Line to Forest Hills, follow the signs to the Arboretum]

BOSTON – The North End ⊕ page 29 (with Charlestown)
GREEN and ORANGE LINES: Haymarket, North Station
INNER HARBOR FERRIES: F3, F5, or F5X to Lovejoy Wharf

The North End is considered the cornerstone of the city's Italian-American community, although demographically it is becoming less so every year. Colorful Catholic festivals fill the narrow streets on summer weekends, while a high concentration of intimate restaurants and bakeries keep the sidewalks filled with steady year-round throngs of hungry tourists and residents from elsewhere in the city. Several prominent historical sites—including the **Paul Revere House** and the **Old North Church**—dot the **Freedom Trail** (see page 28) as it meanders through the neighborhood.

Recommended Excursion
In early evening, pick up the **Freedom Trail** (see page 28) on Hanover Street and walk to the **Old North Church,** checking menus as you go. Then turn left on Salem Street to check more menus before finally returning to the most appealing restaurant for dinner. Looking for a recommendation? Try Lucia's (415 Hanover St.), an editor's personal favorite and voted among the top ten family-run restaurants nationwide by *Bon Appetite* magazine (September 2002). [Green or Orange Line to Haymarket, follow the signs to the North End]

BOSTON – Roxbury ⊕ next page

ORANGE LINE: Ruggles, Roxbury Crossing
SILVER LINE: Lenox St., Melnea Cass Blvd., Dudley Station

Before being absorbed into Boston in the 19th century, Roxbury had been a country town known for its farms and orchards. Now it's the geographic center of Boston. Although two centuries of urbanization have all but obliterated any rural aspects of the community, vestiges remain, including some of Boston's last surviving 18th-century homes. One, the 1750 Dillway-Thomas House, is the centerpiece of the **Roxbury Heritage State Park.** A touch of Roxbury's undeveloped landscape has also been preserved in **Franklin Park,** Boston's largest park and one of landscape architect Frederick Law Olmsted's masterpieces. Nearby stands Abbotsford, one of the earliest grand suburban mansions to be built after Boston annexed the community, and now home to the **National Center for Afro-American Artists.**

Recommended Excursion
Franklin Park Zoo: Of the many exhibits to see, be sure to visit Butterfly Landing (seasonal) and the 3-acre indoor Tropical Forest featuring tropical birds, monkeys, capybaras, gorillas, a black panther, and more. [Orange Line to Ruggles, connect to T-bus 45 (usually less than 15-minute wait)]

BOSTON – South Boston

RED LINE: South Station (15 min. walk or free Boston Coach shuttle to Seaport District), Broadway, Andrew
INNER HARBOR FERRIES: F5 and F5X to Fan Pier and World Trade Center

South Boston, commonly called "Southie" (not to be confused with the South End), occupies Boston's southeastern waterfront. On one side are the lettered and numbered residential streets running from the brackish Fort Point Channel to the shores of Dorchester Bay. The neighborhood's other side is former industrial waterfront now occupied by the **U.S. Courthouse,** the **World Trade Center,** and a host of other projects around the construction site of the mammoth new Boston Convention Center. As part of the redevelopment of this area, newly christened the Seaport District, Silver Line BRT stops, scheduled to open in 2004, are being constructed for Court House, World Trade Center, and Convention Center.

In between are the 19th-century brick warehouses colonized decades ago by hundreds of loft-dwelling artists who collectively give the area its identity as the Fort Point Arts Community. Boston's **Children's Museum** also sits amid these warehouses a scant few blocks from downtown.

At Southie's far eastern tip is **Castle Island,** now linked to the mainland by landfill topped by pedestrian promenades. This popular fishing spot and its small, seawall-sheltered beach are crowned by historic Fort Independence, whose current incarnation dates from the 19th century. Just south of **Castle Island** are the more open-water swimming areas of **Carson Beach** and **L and M Street Beaches.**

Recommended Excursions

1) **Children's Museum:** Hands-on, fun exhibits for kids up to age 10. [Red Line to South Station, walk one block northeast on Atlantic Ave., turn

Roxbury and Dudley Square, Boston

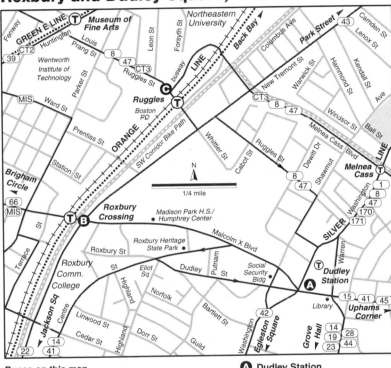

Buses on this map

CT2 (Sullivan-Ruggles)
CT3 (Beth Israel-Andrew)
1 (Harvard-Dudley)
8 (UMass-Kenmore)
14 (Roslindale-Heath St)
15 (Kane Sq-Ruggles)
19 (Fields Corner-Ruggles)
22 (Ashmont-Ruggles)
23 (Ashmont-Ruggles)
28 (Mattapan-Ruggles)
41 (Centre & Eliot-JFK/UMass)
42 (Forest Hills-Ruggles)
43 (Ruggles-Park & Tremont Sts)

44 (Jackson Sq-Ruggles)
45 (Franklin Park Zoo-Ruggles)
47 (Central-Broadway)
66 (Harvard-Dudley)
170 (Burlington-Dudley)
171 (Dudley-Logan Airport)
Mission Link Bus

Ⓐ Dudley Station
Silver Line BRT
buses 1, 8, 14, 15, 19, 23, 28,
41, 42, 44, 45, 47, 66, 170, 171

Ⓑ Roxbury Crossing
Orange Line
buses 15, 19, 22, 23, 28, 42, 44, 45, 66
Mission Link Bus

Ⓒ Ruggles buses
Orange Line nearby
MBTA Commuter Rail
buses CT2, CT3, 8, 15, 19, 22, 23,
28, 42, 43, 44, 45, 47

Boston's other Neighborhoods

Boston has other, less-visited neighborhoods beyond those detailed in this chapter. Some are mentioned below and some, like Mission Hill and Hyde Park, are listed with the rest in Chapter 7. Each has a flavor all its own.

- **Allston:** With proximity to both **Boston University** and **Harvard University,** Allston is a teeming hub of off-campus student life with relatively inexpensive housing generously interspersed with cheap eats, nightclubs, and liquor stores. [GREEN B LINE: B.U. West through Warren St.]

- **Brighton:** A separate town until the mid-19th century, this affordable residential neighborhood enjoys a small "town center" at Market and Washington Streets. [GREEN B LINE: Summit Ave. through Boston College; T-bus 57]

- **East Boston:** Surrounded on all sides by water, "Eastie" is home to a small, dense residential core, but is dominated by Logan International Airport. [BLUE LINE: Maverick through Suffolk Downs]

- **Longwood Medical Area:** (⊕ page 34) Although historically part of the Fenway/Kenmore area, these tightly packed blocks have carved out their own identity courtesy of a half-dozen of the city's largest hospitals and medical schools. [GREEN D LINE: Longwood; GREEN E LINE: Longwood/Hospitals, Brigham Circle]

- **The South End:** Not to be confused with South Boston or "Southie," the South End epitomizes urban gentrification, with many young, often childless professionals occupying the Victorian-era townhouses, enjoying eclectic shops and cosmopolitan restaurants along Tremont St. [ORANGE LINE: Back Bay Station, Massachusetts Ave.; SILVER LINE: Herald St. through Lenox St.]

Brookline Village, Brookline

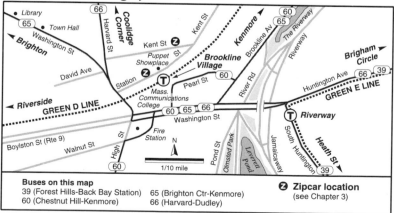

Buses on this map
39 (Forest Hills-Back Bay Station)   65 (Brighton Ctr-Kenmore)
60 (Chestnut Hill-Kenmore)   66 (Harvard-Dudley)

❷ **Zipcar location**
(see Chapter 3)

Cleveland Circle, Boston

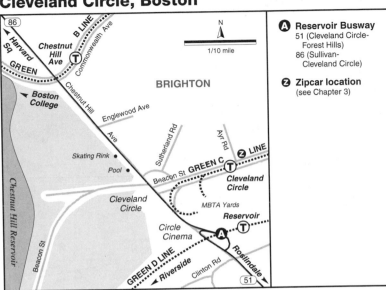

A Reservoir Busway
51 (Cleveland Circle-
Forest Hills)
86 (Sullivan-
Cleveland Circle)

Z Zipcar location
(see Chapter 3)

right on Congress St., cross the Fort Point Channel]

2) **Castle Island:** As part of your visit to this 22-acre urban park, take a tour of Fort Independence conducted by the Castle Island Association (seasonal) or use the interpretive signage for a self-guided tour. [Red Line to Broadway, connect to T-bus 9 or 11 (both offer frequent service) to City Point, walk two blocks east]

BROOKLINE   ⊕ previous page (partial coverage)

GREEN C LINE: Saint Mary's St., Hawes St., Kent St., Saint Paul St., Coolidge Corner, Winchester/Summit, Brandon Hall, Fairbanks St., Washington Sq., Tappan St., Dean Rd., Englewood Ave., Cleveland Circle
GREEN D LINE: Longwood, Brookline Village, Brookline Hills, Beaconsfield, Reservoir

A wholly separate town surrounded on three sides by Boston, Brookline is known for its affluence, its highly-regarded public school system, and its precedent-setting smoking ban throughout all restaurants and bars. Wide, townhouse- and tree-lined Beacon Street, on which the Green C Line makes all its surface stops, epitomizes the town's northern half with its Parisian-boulevard design. The southern half, by contrast, is characterized by spacious residential neighborhoods, rolling country club golf courses, and virtually no public transit. Brookline's eastern edge is bordered by **the Riverway** and **Olmsted Park,** two pleasant urban oases belonging to Boston's **Emerald Necklace** (see sidebar page 33).

A number of synagogues and kosher restaurants and bakeries, evidence of Brookline's large Jewish community, are found along Harvard Street between

Harvard Square, Cambridge

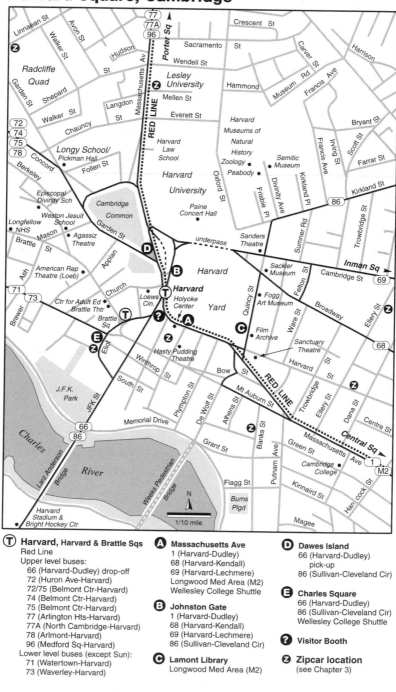

T **Harvard**, Harvard & Brattle Sqs
Red Line
Upper level buses:
66 (Harvard-Dudley) drop-off
72 (Huron Ave-Harvard)
72/75 (Belmont Ctr-Harvard)
74 (Belmont Ctr-Harvard)
75 (Belmont Ctr-Harvard)
77 (Arlington Hts-Harvard)
77A (North Cambridge-Harvard)
78 (Arlmont-Harvard)
96 (Medford Sq-Harvard)
Lower level buses (except Sun):
71 (Watertown-Harvard)
73 (Waverley-Harvard)

A **Massachusetts Ave**
1 (Harvard-Dudley)
68 (Harvard-Kendall)
69 (Harvard-Lechmere)
Longwood Med Area (M2)
Wellesley College Shuttle

B **Johnston Gate**
1 (Harvard-Dudley)
68 (Harvard-Kendall)
69 (Harvard-Lechmere)
86 (Sullivan-Cleveland Cir)

C **Lamont Library**
Longwood Med Area (M2)

D **Dawes Island**
66 (Harvard-Dudley)
pick-up
86 (Sullivan-Cleveland Cir)

E **Charles Square**
66 (Harvard-Dudley)
86 (Sullivan-Cleveland Cir)
Wellesley College Shuttle

? **Visitor Booth**

Z **Zipcar location**
(see Chapter 3)

the intersection of Beacon Street, a crossroads better known as Coolidge Corner, and JFK Crossing, a commercial stretch a few blocks north named after the nearby **John F. Kennedy Birthplace National Historic Site.** Smaller neighborhood-oriented shopping and dining districts are found at Audubon Circle near Boston University in the east and Cleveland Circle (⊕ page 39) near Boston College in the west, at either end of Beacon Street, and around Brookline Village and Chestnut Hill.

Recommended Excursion

Coolidge Corner: Wander the area, take in the scene, and grab a bite to eat. The area's great many kosher choices range from Chinese restaurants to donut shops. For bagels and other baked goods, Kupel's Bake and Bagel (421 Harvard St.) is a well-established landmark, and is open "wicked" early (closed Saturday). [Green C Line to Coolidge Corner]

CAMBRIDGE – Harvard Square   ⊕ previous page

RED LINE: Harvard

Harvard Square in Cambridge is known for its many bookstores, restaurants, street performers, and shops, as well as the nation's oldest college. **Harvard University** has several museums, including the **Busch-Reisinger, Fogg,** and **Sackler** art museums, the **Semitic Museum,** and the **Harvard University Museums of Natural History** complex. This last is famous for its unique collection of botanical models known as the "Glass Flowers." Campus tours are offered by the Harvard Information Center in Holyoke Center, a modern building behind the outdoor café a short block east of the subway station.

On Brattle Street is the **Longfellow National Historic Site,** George Washington's headquarters during the American Revolution. The square's south side is bordered by the Charles River and Memorial Drive, a major automobile arterial that's blocked off on Sundays from April to November to become "Riverbend Park," with cars banned between Western Avenue and the Eliot Bridge. Tours of historic Cambridge and Brattle Street are available seasonally from the Cambridge Office of Tourism booth in the center of Harvard Square.

Recommended Excursion

Harvard Square is a must-visit for anyone spending more than a day or two in Boston. Follow your interests – there is something for everyone here. For the outdoor inclined, visit Mount Auburn Cemetery which doubles as a botanical garden and birdwatcher's paradise (from the square, walk one mile west via Mt Auburn St. or take T-bus 71 or 73). [Red Line to Harvard]

Central Square, Cambridge

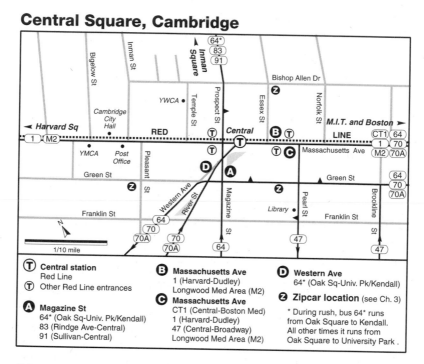

CAMBRIDGE – Central Square
🌐 this page

RED LINE: Central

Central Square, the seat of Cambridge city government, straddles Massachusetts Avenue midway between Harvard Square to the west and the **Massachusetts Institute of Technology** (MIT) to the east. Many shops and restaurants along Mass. Ave. cater to students, offering good ethnic cuisine, secondhand books and clothing, and unfinished furniture at bargain prices.

SOMERVILLE – Davis Square
🌐 next page

RED LINE: Davis

As Harvard Square has become more upscale over the past few years, Davis Square has become more like Harvard Square used to be. Numerous restaurants and cafés, eclectic shopping, a handful of highly-regarded nightclubs, and the **Somerville Theater** make Davis Square worth a visit. **Tufts University** is a 3/4-mile walk or shuttle-bus ride from the subway station.

Davis Square, Somerville

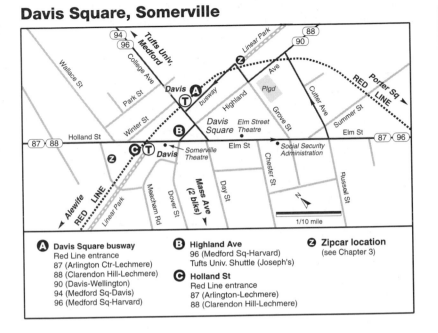

A **Davis Square busway**
Red Line entrance
87 (Arlington Ctr-Lechmere)
88 (Clarendon Hill-Lechmere)
90 (Davis-Wellington)
94 (Medford Sq-Davis)
96 (Medford Sq-Harvard)

B **Highland Ave**
96 (Medford Sq-Harvard)
Tufts Univ. Shuttle (Joseph's)

C **Holland St**
Red Line entrance
87 (Arlington-Lechmere)
88 (Clarendon Hill-Lechmere)

Z **Zipcar location**
(see Chapter 3)

OUTSIDE BOSTON

Lengths of time in parentheses indicate approximate travel time by the most direct transit option from downtown Boston. Estimates include expected waiting times for well-planned transfers when required. Additional time will be required to get to specific destinations from the nearest station.

CONCORD (45 minutes)

Concord is the site of the American Revolution's first battle (the "shot heard 'round the world") and also birthplace to the country's first native literary movement, Transcendentalism. Be prepared for some walking or bring a bike (see "Bikes on the T", page 21)—sights are often one-half to nearly two miles apart. The North Bridge, part of Minute Man National Historical Park, and the Concord Museum are worth the walk, and the homes of Ralph Waldo Emerson, Nathaniel Hawthorne, and Louisa May Alcott can also be visited. **Walden Pond,** where Henry David Thoreau marched to the beat of a different drummer, is very beautiful. Hike around the pond on a well-used trail (about two miles) or swim at the small, pleasant beach. For information call the Chamber of Commerce (978/369-3120), the National Park Service (978/369-6993), or Walden Pond State Reservation (978/369-3254).

Recommended Excursions

Take the Commuter Rail Fitchburg/South Acton Line to Concord. From the station turn right on Thoreau Street, then left on Sudbury Road and straight on Main Street to the town center (0.6 mile). The North Bridge and National Park Visitor Center is another 0.6 mile north (left at the elongated town green, right on Monument St.) **Walden Pond** is 1.8 miles south on Walden Street, or 1.7 miles from the station (right on Thoreau Street, right on Walden Street, straight across Rte. 2).

Gloucester

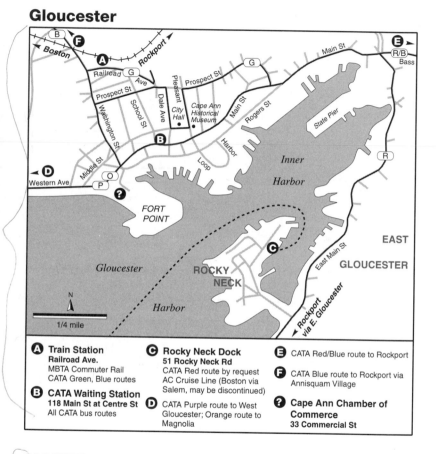

A **Train Station**
Railroad Ave.
MBTA Commuter Rail
CATA Green, Blue routes

B **CATA Waiting Station**
118 Main St at Centre St
All CATA bus routes

C **Rocky Neck Dock**
51 Rocky Neck Rd
CATA Red route by request
AC Cruise Line (Boston via Salem, may be discontinued)

D CATA Purple route to West Gloucester; Orange route to Magnolia

E CATA Red/Blue route to Rockport

F CATA Blue route to Rockport via Annisquam Village

? **Cape Ann Chamber of Commerce**
33 Commercial St

GLOUCESTER (1 hour)   ⊕ this page

The ancient fishing village of Gloucester has grown into a city, but it still retains touches of its 19th-century ambience. The Gloucester Maritime Trail comprises four self-guided walking tours of Gloucester aided by signs, painted lines, and a free map guide. Pavilion Beach, Half Moon Beach, and Stage Fort Park, all somewhat rocky harbor beaches, are within a mile of downtown and the Chamber of Commerce Visitor Center. For information, call the Cape Ann Chamber of Commerce at 978/283-1601.

Recommended Excursion

Take the Commuter Rail Rockport Line to Gloucester; walk 1/2 mile south on Washington Street or take a CATA bus to downtown, the industrial waterfront, and the Visitor Center on Commercial Street. The summer ferry across the harbor to Rocky Neck is well worth the trip.

IPSWICH (1 hour)

Although the historic center of this small, pretty North Shore town is filled with 17th- and 18th-century homes, the main attractions are Castle Hill and Crane Beach, a gorgeous tract of preserved coastline about four miles from town. Most of Ipswich's fine restaurants and interesting shops, on the other hand, are within a few blocks' walk of the train station.

Recommended Excursion

Crane Beach and Castle Hill: bring a bicycle on the Commuter Rail Newburyport Line to Ipswich (see "Bikes on the T," page 21); turn right on Topsfield/Market Street, right on South Main, right on County, and left on Argilla Road about four miles to the entrance. Taxis are also available.

LEXINGTON (1 hour)

Lexington's Battle Green is where the first shots of the American Revolution were fired. The Battle Green, **Munroe Tavern, Hancock-Clarke House,** Old Belfry, and **Buckman Tavern** are all within a short walk of the town center. The **Museum of Our National Heritage** is about a mile. The town center itself offers a few restaurants and shops to browse. For information call the Chamber of Commerce at 781/862-1450.

Recommended Excursion

Lexington by Bike: Find the Minuteman Bikeway at the northwest corner of Alewife station (Red Line, see "Bikes on the T," page 21) and follow it about seven miles to centrally located Lexington Visitor Center, right on the bikepath. For buses to Lexington, see Chapter 7, "Cities and Towns."

Lowell

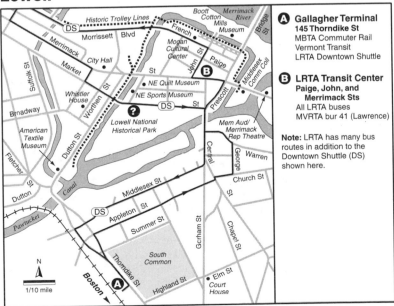

A Gallagher Terminal
145 Thorndike St
MBTA Commuter Rail
Vermont Transit
LRTA Downtown Shuttle

B LRTA Transit Center
Paige, John, and Merrimack Sts
All LRTA buses
MVRTA bur 41 (Lawrence)

Note: LRTA has many bus routes in addition to the Downtown Shuttle (DS) shown here.

LOWELL (45 minutes)   ⊕ previous page

Lowell was the first planned city of the American industrial revolution. Today many of its early 19th-century mills have been saved from dereliction and the wrecking ball of urban renewal, some as part of the **Lowell National Historical Park.** A restored, old-fashioned electric trolley links many of the park's historic sites. Of particular interest is the **Boott Cotton Mills Museum,** whose industrial history exhibits include a 1920s-era weave room with 88 operating power looms. Visitors experience the clatter, heat, and smell of the factories. Beat writer Jack Kerouac was born in Lowell, and each October a three-day celebration is held in his honor, with poetry readings and other events.

Recommended Excursion

Mill and Canal Tour: take the Commuter Rail Lowell Line to Lowell and catch the frequent shuttle bus (Mon.-Sat.) to downtown. Go to the Market St. Visitor Center and buy tickets to this justifiably popular tour (reservations strongly recommended, 978/970-5000).

LYNN (30 minutes)

Originally an upscale bedroom community of Boston, Lynn's mid-20th-century economic slump turned many of its grand ocean-front houses into two- and three-family rental units. However, as housing prices around Boston skyrocket, many people have rediscovered Lynn as an affordable suburb with good access to the city and gorgeous property well worth restoring.

The city's oceanfront features wide and sandy Lynn Beach with a well manicured sidewalk promenade and park. Northwest of downtown is Lynn Woods, a 2,200-acre park with nearly 30 miles of trails. Park maps are available and, weather permitting, skis can be rented (781/598-4212) at the headquarters on Great Woods Road.

Recommended Excursion

Surf and Turf: take the Commuter Rail Newburyport/Rockport Line to Lynn and visit the delightful historical museum at the **Lynn Heritage State Park** right near the station. Then walk 1/2 mile east on Carroll Parkway to the rotary and cross over to Lynn Shore Reservation. Lynn Beach is on your left and gorgeous **Nahant Beach** is on your right.

MANCHESTER-BY-THE-SEA (50 minutes)

This small coastal community is home to arguably the most beautiful transit-accessible beach in Massachusetts: **Singing Beach.**

Recommended Excursion

Singing Beach: take the Commuter Rail Rockport Line to Manchester; turn left on Beach Street and walk 1/2 mile to the beach. You cannot get closer to the beach by driving; people with cars must park at the train station. If you wish to bike the 1/2 mile, you can bring a bicycle on the train anytime except during rush hour (see page 21, "Bikes on the T"), or you may be able to rent one from Seaside Cycle, which is a short walk from the station (call ahead: 978/526-1200, www.seasidecycle.com).

New Bedford

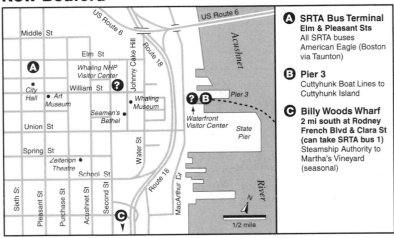

A SRTA Bus Terminal
Elm & Pleasant Sts
All SRTA buses
American Eagle (Boston
via Taunton)

B Pier 3
Cuttyhunk Boat Lines to
Cuttyhunk Island

C Billy Woods Wharf
2 mi south at Rodney
French Blvd & Clara St
(can take SRTA bus 1)
Steamship Authority to
Martha's Vineyard
(seasonal)

NEW BEDFORD (90 minutes)   ⊕ this page

New Bedford's storied past as a prosperous whaling port is celebrated by the **New Bedford Whaling National Historical Park,** which encompasses much of the historic downtown. Herman Melville's experiences aboard a New Bedford whaler are, of course, a cornerstone of American literature; the Seamen's Bethel described in his novel *Moby Dick* still stands, just across the street from the incomparable **New Bedford Whaling Museum.** Visitor information is available from either the National Park Service Visitor Center or the city-run Waterfront Visitor Center on the State Pier (508/991-6200).

Recommended Excursion

The Waterfront: take an American Eagle bus from South Station (4-13 trips daily), walk east on Elm Street a few blocks to the picturesque working waterfront, Visitor Center, Whaling Museum, and other attractions.

PLYMOUTH (90 minutes)

Here the Pilgrims established the first permanent English colony in New England. On the town's waterfront you can dine on seafood, sample cranberry products from Ocean Spray, marvel at the tiny size of **Plymouth Rock,** and board a full-scale replica of the *Mayflower.* **Plimoth Plantation,** a stockaded living-history re-creation of Plymouth circa 1627, is three miles south of downtown. Most sites are open from April to November. For information call the Chamber of Commerce at 508/830-1620.

Recommended Excursion

Plimoth Plantation: take the Commuter Rail Plymouth/Kingston Line to either Plymouth or Kingston and catch the local PAL bus (Liberty Link from Plymouth depot, Puritan Link from Kingston, return via Freedom Link) to the CVS Pharmacy on Main Street, then transfer to PAL Mayflower Link bus to **Plimoth Plantation.** These shuttle buses are not frequent: it is highly recommended to leave Boston by 10am in order to enjoy a full day at the Plantation. Information about private carriers offering service to Plymouth attractions are usually found posted on the station platforms.

Providence, RI

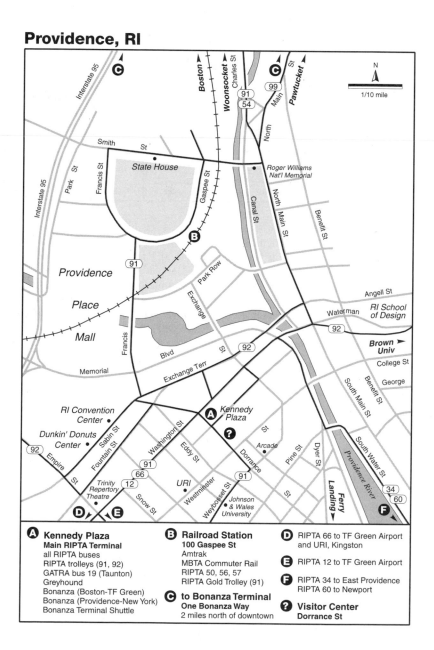

ⓐ Kennedy Plaza
Main RIPTA Terminal
all RIPTA buses
RIPTA trolleys (91, 92)
GATRA bus 19 (Taunton)
Greyhound
Bonanza (Boston-TF Green)
Bonanza (Providence-New York)
Bonanza Terminal Shuttle

ⓑ Railroad Station
100 Gaspee St
Amtrak
MBTA Commuter Rail
RIPTA 50, 56, 57
RIPTA Gold Trolley (91)

ⓒ to Bonanza Terminal
One Bonanza Way
2 miles north of downtown

ⓓ RIPTA 66 to TF Green Airport
and URI, Kingston

ⓔ RIPTA 12 to TF Green Airport

ⓕ RIPTA 34 to East Providence
RIPTA 60 to Newport

❓ Visitor Center
Dorrance St

PROVIDENCE, RI (90 minutes)   ⊕ previous page

Frequent transit service from Boston makes visiting Providence relatively easy, and given the city's renaissance in recent years, worthwhile, too. At the city's heart is the Providence River, lined with lovely promenades, public art, and attractive plazas that blossom with outdoor café seating in warmer weather. There are even Venetian-style gondola rides for the romantically inclined. The river's unique "WaterFire" performances, beginning at dusk on summer Saturdays, offer a mesmerizing procession of bonfires on the river itself accompanied by exotic, ethereal, or operatic music. Just east of the river, **Brown University** and **Rhode Island School of Design** occupy College Hill, adding elements of student life and culture to the lively riverfront mix. Downtown shoppers should visit the Arcade, a Parisian-style indoor shopping concourse just west of the river, and the upscale shops of Providence Place located north of downtown and a short walk west of the train station.

All Providence-bound Peter Pan interstate bus routes, all RIPTA local buses, and GATRA local service from next-door Attleboro, MA (see Chapter 12, "More Rail, Bus, and Ferry (Not the T)") stop at Kennedy Plaza, downtown's main bus terminal. The train station, serving both MBTA Commuter Rail and Amtrak, is a short walk north. The most frequent service from Boston is provided by Bonanza Bus Lines, many of whose routes stop at both their main terminal two miles north of downtown and at Kennedy Plaza (there's hourly shuttle service between the two, as well).

Recommended Excursion:

Take an early Bonanza or Greyhound bus to Kennedy Plaza. Spend the day wandering College Hill and the evening along the river (check the WaterFire schedule at www.waterfire.com). Buses run frequently from South Station; be sure to book one that stops at Kennedy Plaza.

PROVINCETOWN (90 minutes)

"P-town" is located at the very tip of Cape Cod. Beaches, whale-watching excursions, cycling through the windswept dunes of the Cape Cod National Seashore, dining on seafood, and simply strolling amid the carnivalesque atmosphere of this unabashedly gay resort are among the most notable diversions for visitors, but there are museums, galleries, and unique shops, too. For visitor information contact the Provincetown Chamber of Commerce (508/487-3424), www.ptownchamber.com.

Recommended Excursion

High-speed catamarans to Provincetown depart daily throughout summer both from Long Wharf (Blue Line to Aquarium) and from beside South Boston's World Trade Center (T-bus 7 from South Station or Inner Harbor Ferry F5/F5X to Commonwealth Pier). Generally the first boats arrive in P-town around 9:30am and the last boats depart at 7:30pm daily late May through early October. There are also ferries from Plymouth to P-town. For schedule and ticket info, refer to Chapter 12, "More Rail, Bus, and Ferry (Not the T)."

QUINCY (20 minutes)

Quincy, the "City of Presidents," was the hometown of Presidents John Adams and John Quincy Adams. Their mansion and humble birthplaces, now part of the **Adams National Historical Park,** are open April to November. Much of Quincy's long coastline is dominated by **Wollaston Beach**, a good place for sunning, walking, and enjoying scrumptious fried clams. **Blue Hills Reservation** (617/698-1802), a 5,800-acre parcel shared between Quincy, Milton, Canton, and Randolph, offers opportunities for hiking, mountain biking (with restrictions), downhill skiing (617/828-5070), swimming, fishing, and picnicking. Blue Hill's **Trailside Museum** in Milton offers trail maps and other park information. Note: **Quincy Market** is in downtown Boston, *not* in Quincy.

Recommended Excursion

Presidential Birthplaces: take the Red Line to Quincy Center, cross busy Hancock Street to the **Adams National Historical Park** Visitors Center where guided trolley tours depart frequently. Don't miss the life-size statues of John looking across the street at Abigail with young John Quincy.

Rockport

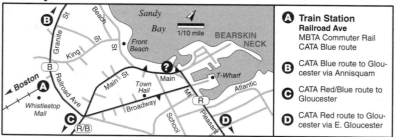

ROCKPORT (70 minutes)   ⊕ this page

Virtually everything in Rockport, including the Bearskin Neck artist colony, is a short walk from the train. The town is full of crafts shops, galleries, restaurants, and inns. Small and stony, nearby Rockport Beach is worth a visit, as is more distant Halibut Point Reservation, with its huge slabs of granite leading down to the surf.

Recommended Excursion

Take the Commuter Rail Rockport Line to Rockport and enjoy the picturesque town. If you like, make the two-mile walk to Halibut Point by heading north from town on Granite Street to the property's entrance on Gott Avenue.

Salem

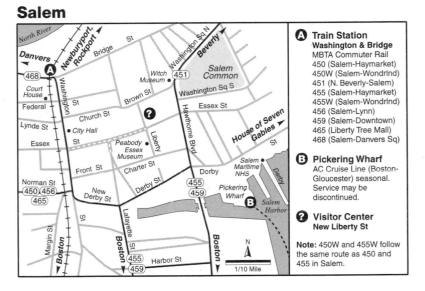

A Train Station
Washington & Bridge
MBTA Commuter Rail
450 (Salem-Haymarket)
450W (Salem-Wondrlnd)
451 (N. Beverly-Salem)
455 (Salem-Haymarket)
455W (Salem-Wondrlnd)
456 (Salem-Lynn)
459 (Salem-Downtown)
465 (Liberty Tree Mall)
468 (Salem-Danvers Sq)

B Pickering Wharf
AC Cruise Line (Boston-Gloucester) seasonal. Service may be discontinued.

? Visitor Center
New Liberty St

Note: 450W and 455W follow the same route as 450 and 455 in Salem.

SALEM (35 minutes) ⊕ this page

Salem, site of the infamous witch trials of the 1690s and later a prosperous port in the early 1800s, has many attractions, including the **Peabody Essex Museum,** the **House of Seven Gables,** the **Salem Maritime National Historic Site,** and various exhibits loosely purporting to relate to the 17th-century witchcraft hysteria. For more information call the Chamber of Commerce (978/744-0004).

Recommended Excursion

Take the Commuter Rail Newburyport/Rockport Line to Salem. Of all the attractions within a 15-minute walk of the train station, don't miss the three mentioned above. From spring through fall, the Salem Trolley (978/744-5469) links these sites and others, such as Salem Willows, an aging amusement arcade and tour-boat landing.

WORCESTER (70 minutes) ⊕ next page

New England's third-largest city, the birthplace of diner manufacturing, is the seat of the state university system's medical school. The excellent **Worcester Art Museum,** the scholarly collections of the **American Antiquarian Society,** and the local historical society's Salisbury Mansion (restored to its 1830s splendor) are near Lincoln Square, one-half mile north of downtown. The city's historical museum is at 30 Elm St., one block from City Hall. More out of the ordinary is the **Higgins Armory Museum,** showcasing medieval weapons and suits of armor. The downtown **Centrum Centre** is a major convention, concert, and sports venue. Just south are the Worcester Common Outlets for discount shopping. For more information call the Visitors Bureau at 508/753-2920.

Recommended Excursion

Worcester Art Museum: take the Commuter Rail Framingham/Worcester Line to Worcester and either walk 1/2-mile west to access local WRTA buses at City Hall Plaza or take a short taxi ride to the museum.

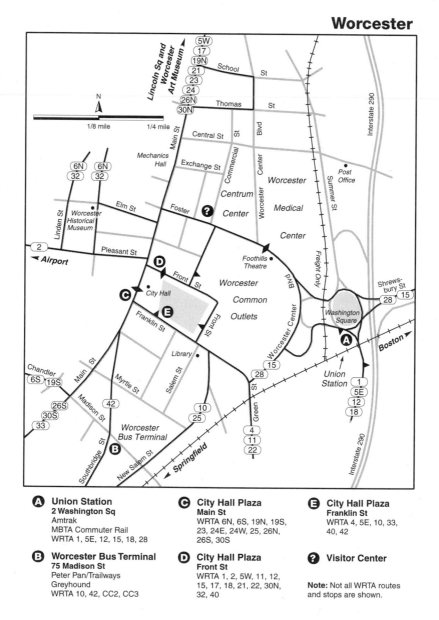

Worcester

Ⓐ **Union Station**
2 Washington Sq
Amtrak
MBTA Commuter Rail
WRTA 1, 5E, 12, 15, 18, 28

Ⓑ **Worcester Bus Terminal**
75 Madison St
Peter Pan/Trailways
Greyhound
WRTA 10, 42, CC2, CC3

Ⓒ **City Hall Plaza**
Main St
WRTA 6N, 6S, 19N, 19S,
23, 24E, 24W, 25, 26N,
26S, 30S

Ⓓ **City Hall Plaza**
Front St
WRTA 1, 2, 5W, 11, 12,
15, 17, 18, 21, 22, 30N,
32, 40

Ⓔ **City Hall Plaza**
Franklin St
WRTA 4, 5E, 10, 33,
40, 42

❓ **Visitor Center**

Note: Not all WRTA routes
and stops are shown.

Chapter 6:
Place Listings – How to Get There

Use this chapter to find transit directions to hundreds of specific locations throughout Eastern Massachusetts, plus some in Central Massachusetts and Providence, RI. For travel further afield, see Chapter 13, "New England and Beyond," and for directions to a city or town, see Chapter 7, "Cities and Towns." Destinations shown on a map are indicated by ⊕, and "CR" denotes Commuter Rail. For details about any rail, bus, or ferry route mentioned, see Chapters 8-11 (MBTA routes) or Chapter 12 (non-MBTA routes). Destinations are alphabetical within each category below. If you have trouble finding your listing, check the index on page 175.

Attractions, Museums, and Points of Interest

Adams National Historical Park
1250 Hancock St., Quincy
(617/773-1175), www.nps.gov/adam
• QUINCY CTR (Red Line-Braintree)

Addison Gallery of American Art
Chapel Ave., Andover (978/749-4015),
www.andover.edu/addison
• CR Haverhill Line to ANDOVER; take
  local MVRTA bus 22 (Ballardvale) to
  Phillips Academy

African Meeting House
See "Museum for Afro American History"

The American Textile History Museum
⊕ p. 45; 491 Dutton St., Lowell
(978/441-0400)
• CR Lowell Line to LOWELL; walk 15min
  N on Thorndike St

Black Heritage Trail
See "Museum for Afro American History"

Boott Cotton Mills Museum and New England Folklife Center
⊕ p. 45; 400 Foot of John St., Lowell
(978/970-5000)
• CR Lowell Line to LOWELL; take local

LRTA Downtown Shuttle to Boarding
House Park

Boston African-American National Historic Site
46 Joy St., Boston (617/742-5415),
www.nps.gov/boaf
• BOWDOIN (Blue Line)
• CHARLES/MGH (Red Line)
• GOVERNMENT CTR (Green or Blue Line)

Boston Historical Society
See "Old State House Museum," below,
and "The Bostonian Society," p. 88

Boston National Historical Park
Visitor Center, 15 State St., Boston
(617/242-5642), www.nps.gov/bost
• STATE (Orange or Blue Line)
• GOVERNMENT CTR (Green or Blue Line)

Boston Tea Party Ship and Museum
⊕ p. 31; Congress St. Bridge, Boston
(617/338-1773),
www.bostonteapartyship.com
• from SOUTH STA (Red Line or CR)
  walk NE on Atlantic Ave. one block,
  then right on Congress St. one block
  to bridge

The Botanical Museum
See "Harvard Museum of Natural History"

Buckman Tavern
See "Lexington Historical Society"

Bunker Hill Monument
⊕ p. 29; Monument Sq., Charlestown (617/242-5641)
- from COMMUNITY COLLEGE (Orange Line) 10min walk
- bus 92 (Assembly Sq.-Downtown) to Main and Winthrop Sts.
- bus **93** (Sullivan-Downtown) to Bunker Hill and Lexington Sts.
- Inner Harbor Ferry from Long Wharf to Charlestown Navy Yard; 10min walk
- Inner Harbor Ferry from Lovejoy Wharf to Charlestown Navy Yard; 10min walk

Bunker Hill Pavilion, National Park Service Visitor Center
55 Constitution Rd., Charlestown (617/241-7575)
See "Charlestown Navy Yard"

Busch-Reisinger Museum
⊕ p. 40, 32 Quincy St. (Fogg Art Museum), Cambridge (617/495-9400), www.artmuseums.harvard.edu
See "Harvard University," p. 74

Cambridge Historical Society
See "Hooper-Lee-Nichols House"

Cape Ann Historical Museum
⊕ p. 44; 27 Pleasant St., Gloucester (978/283-0455), www.cape-ann.com/historical-museum
- CR Rockport Line to GLOUCESTER; walk E on Railroad Ave. one block to Prospect St., continue E one block to Pleasant, turn right, one block

Center for Lowell History
See "Mogan Cultural Center"

Charles River Museum of Industry
154 Moody St., Waltham (781/893-5410), www.crmi.org
- from RIVERSIDE (Green Line-D) take local Waltham CitiBus 16 (Waltham Center-Riverside MBTA) to entrance
- CR Fitchburg/South Acton Line (or bus 70, 70A, 505, 553, 554, 556, or 558) to

WALTHAM Central Sq.; exit Moody St., walk one block S to just before the river

Charlestown Navy Yard
⊕ p. 29; Charlestown (617/242-5601)
- from NORTH STA (Green or Orange Line or CR) 15min walk across Charlestown Bridge
- bus 92 (Assembly Sq.-Downtown) to City Sq.; walk 5min E across Chelsea St.
- bus **93** (Sullivan-Downtown) to the Navy Yard
- Inner Harbor ferries from Long Wharf and Lovejoy Wharf

"Cheers" bar
⊕ p. 30; 84 Beacon St., Boston (617/227-9605)
- from ARLINGTON (Green Line) walk N on Arlington St. four blocks to Beacon St., turn right one block
- from PARK STREET (Red or Green Line) walk diagonally across Boston Common to Charles and Beacon Sts., then W two blocks

Children's Museum
⊕ p. 31; 300 Congress St., Boston (617/426-8855), www.bostonkids.org
- from SOUTH STA (Red Line or CR) walk NE on Atlantic Ave. one block to Congress St., turn right, cross the Fort Point Channel
- bus 6, 448, 449, or 459 to Sleeper St. at museum entrance

Christian Science Center
⊕ p. 27; Massachusetts Ave. at Huntington Ave., Boston (617/450-2000)
- from HYNES/ICA (Green Line-B, C, or D) walk S on Mass. Ave. two blocks
- SYMPHONY (Green Line-E)
- from MASSACHUSETTS AVE (Orange Line) walk N on Mass. Ave. two blocks
- bus **1** (Harvard-Dudley)

The Commonwealth Museum
200 Morrissey Blvd., Dorchester (617/727-2816), www.mass.gov/sec/mus
See "University of Massachusetts, Boston," p. 79

The Cyrus E. Dallin Art Museum
1 Whittemore Park, Arlington (781/641-0747), www.dallin.org
- bus 67, **77,** 79, 80, 87, or 350 to Arlington Center (Mystic St.)

Danforth Museum of Art
123 Union Ave., Framingham (508/620-0050), www.danforthmuseum.org
- CR Framingham/Worcester Line to FRAMINGHAM; two-block walk N on Concord St., bear left at Union Ave. two blocks, or walk E to Concord St. to take local LIFT bus 2, 3, or 5

Davis Museum and Cultural Ctr.
106 Central St. (Rte. 135), Wellesley College, Wellesley (781/283-2051), www.wellesley.edu/DavisMuseum
See "Wellesley College," p. 79

The Discovery Museum
177 Main St., Acton (978/264-4200)
- CR Fitchburg/South Acton Line to S. ACTON; walk 10min N on Main St.

Dreams of Freedom Immigration Museum
1 Milk St., Boston (617/695-9990), www.dreamsoffreedom.com
- from STATE (Orange or Blue Line) walk S on Washington St. to Milk St.
- from DOWNTOWN CROSSING (Red, Orange, or Silver Line) walk N on Washington St. two blocks

Faneuil Hall
⊕ p. 31; New Congress St. at North St., Boston (617/635-3105)
- from STATE (Orange or Blue Line) walk N
- from GOVERNMENT CTR (Green or Blue Line) walk E past City Hall
- from HAYMARKET (Green or Orange Line) walk S

Fogg Art Museum
⊕ p. 40; 32 Quincy St., Cambridge (617/495-9400),
www.artmuseums.harvard.edu
See "Harvard University," p. 74

Franklin Park Zoo
1 Franklin Park Rd. at Blue Hill Ave., Roxbury (617/541-LION), www.zoonewengland.com
- from ANDREW (Red Line) or FOREST HILLS (Orange Line) take bus 16 (Forest Hills-Andrew) to Peabody Cir.
- from RUGGLES (Orange Line) or DUDLEY STA (Silver Line) take bus 45 (Franklin Park Zoo-Ruggles) to Peabody Circle
- bus 14 (Roslindale Sq.-Heath St.) or

28 (Mattapan-Ruggles) to Franklin Park Dr.
- bus 22 (Ashmont-Ruggles) or 29 (Mattapan-Jackson Sq.) to Humboldt Ave. or Franklin Park Dr.

Frederick Law Olmsted National Historic Site
99 Warren St., Brookline (617/566-1689), www.nps.gov/frla
- from BROOKLINE HILLS (Green Line-D) walk two blocks S on Cypress St., right four blocks on Walnut St., bear left on Warren St. (after the church) one block
- bus 60 (Chestnut Hill-Kenmore) to Warren St.; cross Rte. 9 and walk two blocks S on Warren St.

Freedom Trail
⊕ p. 29, 30-31; Boston-Charlestown (617/227-8800), www.thefreedomtrail.org
See "Boston Common" p. 61 for start or "Charlestown Navy Yard" above for end

Fuller Museum of Art
455 Oak St., Brockton (508/588-6000), www.fullermuseumofart.org
- from ASHMONT (Red Line-Ashmont) take BAT bus 12 (Ashmont-Brockton), transfer to BAT bus 4A (Westgate Mall via N. Warren)
- CR Middleborough/Lakeville Line to BROCKTON; take BAT bus 4A

Gibson House Museum
137 Beacon St., Boston (617/267-6338)
- from ARLINGTON (Green Line) walk N on Arlington St. four blocks to Beacon, turn left

Gore Place
52 Gore St., Waltham (781/894-2798), www.goreplace.org
- from CENTRAL (Red Line) take bus 70 (Cedarwood or Watertown Sq.-University Park) or 70A (N. Waltham-University Park)

Hancock-Clarke House
See "Lexington Historical Society"

Harrison Gray Otis House
141 Cambridge St., Boston (617/227-3956), www.spnea.org
- BOWDOIN (Blue Line)
- GOVERNMENT CTR (Green or Blue Line)
- CHARLES/MGH (Red Line)

Harvard Museum of Natural History

⊕ p. 40; 26 Oxford St., Harvard University, Cambridge (617/495-3045), www.hmnh.harvard.edu
- HARVARD (Red Line)
- bus 68 or 69 to Quincy St.
- bus 86 to Divinity Ave.

Harvard Semitic Museum

⊕ p. 40; 6 Divinity Ave., Harvard University, Cambridge (617/495-4631), www.fas.harvard.edu/~semitic
See "Harvard University," p. 74

Higgins Armory Museum

100 Barber Ave., Worcester (508/853-6015), www.higgins.org
- CR Framingham/Worcester Line to WORCESTER; walk to City Hall Plaza (Main St. side) to take WRTA bus 30N (Summit/W. Boylston/Holden) to Barber
- Peter Pan Bus Lines to Worcester Bus Terminal; walk four blocks N on Southbridge and Main Sts. to City Hall Plaza, take WRTA bus 30N

Hooper-Lee-Nichols House

159 Brattle St., Cambridge (617/547-4252), www.cambridgehistory.org
- from HARVARD (Red Line) walk up Brattle St. seven blocks

House of Seven Gables

54 Turner St., Salem (978/744-0991)
- CR Newburyport/Rockport Line to SALEM; 13-block walk S on Washington and E on Derby Sts.
- A.C. Cruise Lines (seasonal) from Boston to Salem Ferry Landing; walk one block west

Institute of Contemporary Art

955 Boylston St., Boston (617/266-5152), www.icaboston.org
- HYNES/ICA (Green Line-B, C, or D)
- bus **39** (toward Back Bay only) to Dalton & Boylston Sts.

Isaac Royall House

15 George St., Medford (781/396-9032)
- from SULLIVAN SQ (Orange line) take bus 101 (Malden Center-Sullivan) to George St.
- from HARVARD (Red Line) take bus 96 (Medford Sq.-Harvard) to George St.

Isabella Stewart Gardner Museum

⊕ p. 34; 280 The Fenway, Boston (617/566-1401), www.isgm.org
- from MUSEUM OF FINE ARTS (Green Line-E) walk N on Louis Prang St. (Texaco station at corner) 1.5 blocks
- bus 8 (Harbor Pt./UMass-Kenmore) or 47 (Central-Albany St.) to corner of Ave. Louis Pasteur and the Fenway; walk one block S
- bus **39** (Forest Hills-Back Bay) to Ruggles St.; walk N on Louis Prang St. 1.5 blocks

The Jackson Homestead

527 Washington St., Newton (617/552-7238), www.ci.newton.ma.us/jackson
- bus 52 (Dedham Mall-Watertown Sq.) or **57** (Watertown Sq.-Kenmore) to Newton Corner; walk 10min W on Washington St.
- bus 553, 554, 556, or 558 to Walnut Pk.

John Fitzgerald Kennedy Birthplace National Historic Site

83 Beals St., Brookline (617/566-7937), www.nps.gov/jofi
- from COOLIDGE CORNER (Green Line-C) walk four blocks N on Harvard St., right one block on Beals St.
- bus **66** (Harvard-Dudley) to Beals St.

John F. Kennedy Library and Museum

Columbia Point, Dorchester (617/929-4523), www.cs.umb.edu/jfklibrary
See "University of Massachusetts, Boston," p. 79

Lawrence Heritage State Park

Jackson St., Lawrence (508/794-1655), www.mass.gov/dem
- CR Haverhill Line to LAWRENCE; cross Casey Bridge over river, turn right on Canal St., two blocks

Lexington Historical Society

1332 Massachusetts Ave., Lexington (781/862-1703), www.lexingtonhistory.org
- from ALEWIFE (Red Line) take bus 62 (Bedford V.A. Hospital-Alewife) or 76 (Hanscom AFB-Alewife) to Lexington Center (Depot Sq.)

*Frequent bus routes in **bold***

List Visual Arts Center

Massachusetts Institute of Technology, 20 Ames St., Cambridge (617/253-4680), web.mit.edu/lvac

• from KENDALL/MIT (Red Line) walk E on Main St. one block, turn left on Ames, one block

Longfellow National Historic Site

⊕ p. 40; 105 Brattle St., Cambridge (617/876-4491), www.nps.gov/long

• from HARVARD (Red Line) walk up Brattle St. six blocks

Longyear Museum

1125 Boylston St., Chestnut Hill (800/27-8943), www.longyear.org

• from CHESTNUT HILL (Green Line-D) walk S (away from parking) via footpath by fence, cross Middlesex Rd. to Dunster Rd., straight one block

Lowell National Historical Park

⊕ p. 45; 246 Market St., Lowell (978/970-5000), www.nps.gov/lowe

• CR Lowell Line to LOWELL; take local LRTA Downtown Shuttle to Market St.

Lyman Estate, "The Vale"

185 Lyman St., Waltham (781/891-4882 x244), www.spnea.org

• from DOWNTOWN CROSSING (Red, Orange, or Silver Line) walk two blocks SE to Otis St. to take bus 554 (Waverley-Downtown) to Lyman & Beaver Sts.

Lynn Heritage State Park

Washington & Union Sts., Lynn (781/598-1974), www.mass.gov/dem

• CR Newburyport/Rockport Line to LYNN; exit to Munroe St., turn right to corner (Washington), right one block
• bus 426, 429, 431, 435, 436, 439, 441, 442, 455, 456, or 459 to Central Sq.; walk S one block

Lynn Museum

125 Green St., Lynn (781/592-2465), www.lynnmuseum.org

• CR Newburyport/Rockport Line to LYNN; exit to Market St., turn left to corner, turn left again on Broad St., seven blocks
• bus 426, 429, 431, 435, 436, 439, 455, 456, or 459 to Central Sq.; walk E on

Central St. two blocks, turn left on Broad St., three blocks
• bus 441, 442, 448, or 449 to Green St.

The Mapparium

See "Christian Science Center."

Massachusetts State House

⊕ p. 30; Beacon St., Boston (617/727-3676), www.mass.gov/sec/trs

• from PARK STREET (Red or Green Line) walk N one block
• from BOWDOIN (Blue Line) walk S up Bowdoin St. two blocks

McMullen Museum of Art

Devlin Hall, Boston College (617/552-8100), www.bc.edu/artmuseum
See "Boston College," p. 72

Milton Art Museum

44 Edge Hill Rd., Milton (617/696-1145)

• from QUINCY CTR (Red Line) take bus 245 (Quincy Ctr.-Mattapan)

The Mineralogical and Geological Museum

See "Harvard Museum of Natural History"

MIT Museum

265 Mass. Ave., Cambridge (617/253-4444), web.mit.edu/museum

• from CENTRAL (Red Line) walk five blocks S on Mass. Ave.
• bus 1 (Harvard-Dudley) to Sidney St. (Dudley-bound) or Windsor St. (Harvard-bound)

Mogan Cultural Center

⊕ p. 45; 40 French St., Lowell (978/934-4998)

• CR Lowell Line to LOWELL; take local LRTA Downtown Shuttle bus to Boarding House Park

Munroe Tavern

See "Lexington Historical Society"

Museum for Afro American History/Black Heritage Trail

⊕ p. 30; 8 Smith Ct. (behind 46 Joy St.), Boston (617/739-1200), www.afroammuseum.org

• from BOWDOIN (Blue Line) walk four blocks W on Cambridge St.
• from CHARLES/MGH (Red Line) walk seven blocks E on Cambridge St.

Museum of Comparative Zoology
See "Harvard Museum of Natural History"

Museum of Fine Arts
⊕ p. 34; 465 Huntington Ave., Boston
(617/267-9300), www.mfa.org
• MUSEUM OF FINE ARTS (Green Line-E)
• bus 8, **39**, 47, CT2, or CT3 to Ruggles
St. & Huntington Ave.

Museum of Science
Science Park, Boston (617/723-2500),
www.mos.org
• SCIENCE PARK (Green Line)
• from CHARLES/MGH (Red Line) walk E
along the Charles River

Museum of the National Center of Afro-American Artists
300 Walnut Ave., Roxbury
(617/442-8614), www.ncaaa.org
• bus **22** (Ashmont-Ruggles) to Seaver
St. and Elm Hill Ave.
• bus 44 (Jackson Sq.-Ruggles) to
Walnut Ave. and Seaver St.

Museum of Transportation
Larz Anderson Park, 15 Newton St.,
Brookline (617/522-6547), www.mot.org
• from RESERVOIR (Green Line-D)
or FOREST HILLS (Orange Line) or
ROSLINDALE VILLAGE (CR Needham
Line) take bus 51 (Cleveland Cir.-Forest
Hills) to Newton and Clyde Sts.; walk E
on Newton St. 10min
• bus 14, 30, 34, 34E, 35, 36, 37, 40, or
50 to Roslindale Sq.; transfer to bus
51, as above

National Heritage Museum
33 Marrett Rd., Lexington
(617/861-6559), www.monh.org
• from ALEWIFE (Red Line) take bus 62
(Bedford V.A. Hospital-Alewife) or 76
(Hanscom AFB-Alewife) to Mass. Ave.
& Marrett Rd.

New Bedford Art Museum
⊕ p. 47; 608 Pleasant St., New Bedford
(508/961-3072),
www.newbedfordartmuseum.org
• American Eagle bus to New Bedford
Transit Terminal; walk S on Pleasant St.
1.5 blocks

New Bedford Whaling Museum
⊕ p. 47; 18 Johnny Cake Hill,
New Bedford (508/997-0046),
www.whalingmuseum.org
• American Eagle bus to New Bedford
Transit Terminal; walk S to corner, turn
left on William St., six blocks

New Bedford Whaling National Historical Park
⊕ p. 47; 33 William St., New Bedford
(508/996-4095), www.nps.gov/nebe
• American Eagle bus to New Bedford
Transit Terminal; walk S to corner, turn
left on William St., four blocks

New England Aquarium
⊕ p. 31; Central Wharf, Boston
(617/973-5200), www.neaq.org
• AQUARIUM (Blue Line)
• Inner Harbor Ferry from Charlestown
Navy Yard to Long Wharf
• Commuter Boat from Hull and Quincy
to Long Wharf
• Commuter Boat from Hingham to
Rowes Wharf; walk N along waterfront
one block

New England Folklife Center
See "Boott Cotton Mills Museum"

New England Quilt Museum
⊕ p. 45; 18 Shattuck St., Lowell
(978/452-4207), www.nequiltmuseum.org
• CR Lowell Line to LOWELL; take local
LRTA Downtown Shuttle to Market St.

Newton Museum & Historical Society
See "The Jackson Homestead"

Nichols House Museum
55 Mt. Vernon St., Boston (617/227-6993)
• BOWDOIN (Blue Line)
• PARK STREET (Red or Green Line)

"Old Ironsides"
See "U.S.S. *Constitution*"

Old North Church (Christ Church)
⊕ p. 29; 193 Salem St., Boston
(617/523-6676), www.oldnorth.com
• from HAYMARKET (Green or Orange
Line) cross under the Central Artery
and walk five blocks up Salem St.

Old South Meeting House
⊕ p. 31; 310 Washington St., Boston
(617/482-6439), www.oldsouth.org
• STATE (Orange or Blue Line)
• DOWNTOWN CROSSING (Red, Orange,
  or Silver Line)

Old State House Museum
⊕ p. 31; 206 Washington St., Boston
(617/720-1713), www.bostonhistory.org
• STATE (Orange or Blue Line)
• from GOVERNMENT CTR (Green or Blue
  Line) walk E on Court St. one block

Paul Revere House
⊕ p. 29; 19 North Sq., Boston (617/
523-2338), www.paulreverehouse.org
• from HAYMARKET (Green or Orange
  Line) cross under the Central Artery
  and follow the Freedom Trail (red line
  on sidewalk) N up Hanover St.

Peabody Essex Museum
⊕ p. 51; East India Square, Salem
(978/745-9500), www.pem.org
• CR Newburyport/Rockport Line to
  SALEM; five-block walk via Washington
  St. and Essex St. pedestrian mall
• A.C. Cruise Lines (seasonal) from
  Boston to Salem Ferry Landing; walk
  eight blocks west

Peabody Museum of Archaeology & Ethnology
⊕ p. 40; Harvard University, 11 Divinity
Ave., Cambridge (617/496-1027),
www.peabody.harvard.edu
See "Harvard University," p. 74

Photographic Resource Center
602 Commonwealth Ave., Boston
(617/353-0700)
• BLANDFORD ST (Green Line-B)

Pilgrim Hall Museum
75 Court St., Plymouth (508/746-1620),
www.pilgrimhall.org
• CR Plymouth Line to PLYMOUTH; take
  hourly local PAL Liberty Link bus to
  Chilton St. (return to station via PAL
  Freedom Link bus)
• CR Kingston Line to KINGSTON; take
  local PAL Puritan Link bus to Chilton St.

Plimoth Plantation
Route 3A, Plymouth (508/746-1622),
www.plimoth.org

• CR Plymouth Line to PLYMOUTH; take
  hourly local PAL Liberty Link bus to
  CVS Pharmacy on Main St. (return to
  station via PAL Freedom Link bus),
  transfer to bi-hourly PAL Mayflower
  Link bus
• CR Kingston Line to KINGSTON; take
  hourly local PAL Puritan Link bus to
  CVS Pharmacy on Main St., transfer to
  bi-hourly PAL Mayflower Link bus

Plymouth Antiquarian Society
126 Water St., Plymouth (508/746-0012)
• CR Plymouth Line to PLYMOUTH; take
  hourly local PAL Liberty Link bus to
  Chilton St. (return to station via PAL
  Freedom Link bus), walk E one block
• CR Kingston Line to KINGSTON; take
  local PAL Puritan Link bus to Chilton
  St., walk E one block

Plymouth Rock
Water St., Plymouth
• CR Plymouth Line to PLYMOUTH; take
  hourly local PAL Liberty Link bus to
  North St. (return to station via PAL
  Freedom Link bus), walk E one block
• CR Kingston Line to KINGSTON; take
  local PAL Puritan Link bus to North St.,
  walk E one block

Prudential Skywalk
⊕ p. 27; 50th floor of Prudential Tower,
800 Boylston St., Boston (617/859-0648)
• PRUDENTIAL (Green Line-E)
• HYNES/ICA (Green Line-B, C, or D)

Quincy Historical Society
8 Adams St., Quincy (617/773-1144)
• QUINCY CTR (Red Line-Braintree)

Robert S. Peabody Museum for Archaeology
175 Main St., Andover (978/749-4490),
www.andover.edu/rspeabody
• CR Haverhill Line to ANDOVER; take
  local MVRTA bus 22 (Ballardvale) to
  Phillips Academy

Rose Art Museum
Brandeis University, 415 South
St., Waltham (781/736-3434),
www.brandeis.edu/rose
See "Brandeis University," p. 72

USING TRANSIT

DESTINATIONS

ROUTE DETAILS

INDEX

Rotch-Jones-Duff House and Garden Museum

396 County St., New Bedford
(508/997-1401), www.rjdmuseum.org

• American Eagle bus to New Bedford Transit Terminal; walk S on Sixth St. two blocks, turn right on Union St., left on Seventh St., then five blocks

Roxbury Heritage State Park

⊕ p. 37; John Eliot Sq., Roxbury
(617/445-3399), www.mass.gov/dem

• ROXBURY CROSSING (Orange Line)
• DUDLEY STA (Silver Line)
• bus **28**, 41, or 46 to John Eliot Sq.
• bus **66** (Harvard-Dudley) to Madison Park High School

Sackler Museum

⊕ p. 40; 485 Broadway, Cambridge
(617/495-9400),
www.artmuseums.harvard.edu
See "Harvard University," p. 74

Salem Maritime National Historic Site

⊕ p. 51; 193 Derby St., Salem
(978/740-1660), www.nps.gov/sama

• CR Newburyport/Rockport Line to SALEM; 10-block walk S on Washington and E on Derby Sts.
• A.C. Cruise Lines (seasonal) from Boston to Salem Ferry Landing; walk four blocks west

Saugus Ironworks National Historic Site

244 Central St., Saugus (781/233-0050), www.nps.gov/sair

• from MALDEN CTR (Orange Line) take bus 430 (Appleton St., Saugus-Malden Ctr.) to entrance

Society for the Preservation of New England Antiquities (SPNEA)

See "Harrison Gray Otis House"

The Somerville Museum

1 Westwood Rd., Somerville
(617/666-9810)

• from KENDALL/MIT (Red Line) take bus 85 (Spring Hill-Kendall/MIT) to Avon & Central Sts. (end of line); museum is across Central St.

Spellman Museum of Stamps and Postal History

235 Wellesley St., Regis College, Weston
(781/768-8367), www.spellman.org
See "Regis College," p. 77

The Sports Museum of New England

Boston
⊕ p. 29; FleetCenter, 5th and 6th floors, 150 Causeway St., Boston
(617/624-1235), www.sportsmuseum.org

• NORTH STA (Green or Orange Line or CR)

Lowell
⊕ p. 45; 25 Shattuck St., Lowell (978/452-6775), www.sportsmuseum.org

• CR Lowell Line to LOWELL; take local LRTA Downtown Shuttle to Market St.

Swan Boats

See "Public Garden," p. 63

Trinity Church

Copley Sq., Boston (617/536-0944)

• COPLEY (Green Line)
• BACK BAY STA (Orange Line)
• bus **9, 10, 39**, 55, or 502 to Copley Sq.

U.S. Naval Shipbuilding Museum

U.S.S. *Salem,* 739 Washington St., Quincy (617/479-7900), www.uss-salem.org

• from QUINCY CTR (Red Line-Braintree) take bus 220, 221, or 222 to rotary at foot of Fore River Bridge
• Commuter Boat from Long Wharf (Boston) to Quincy Shipyard

U.S.S. *Constitution* (Old Ironsides)

⊕ p. 29; Charlestown Navy Yard, Charlestown (617/242-2308), www.ussconstitution.navy.mil
See "Charlestown Navy Yard"

U.S.S. *Constitution* Museum

⊕ p. 29; Charlestown Navy Yard, Charlestown (617/426-1812), www.ussconstitutionmuseum.org
See "Charlestown Navy Yard"

Whistler House Museum of Art
⊕ p. 45; 243 Worthen St., Lowell
(978/452-7641)
• CR Lowell Line to LOWELL; take local
LRTA Downtown Shuttle to Market St.

Worcester Art Museum
55 Salisbury St., Worcester
(508/799-4406), www.worcesterart.org
• CR Framingham/Worcester Line to
WORCESTER; walk to City Hall Plaza
(Main St. side) to take WRTA bus 6N
(Holden/Ararat) or 30N (Summit/W.
Boylston/Holden), or continue two

blocks N on Main to Foster St. to take
WRTA bus 32 (Holden/Jefferson)
• Peter Pan Bus Lines to Worcester
Bus Terminal; walk four blocks N on
Southbridge and Main Sts. to City Hall
Plaza, take local WRTA buses, as above

Worcester Historical Museum
⊕ p. 52; 30 Elm St., Worcester (508/
753-8278), www.worcesterhistory.org
• CR Framingham/Worcester Line to
WORCESTER
• Peter Pan Bus Lines to Worcester Bus
Terminal

Beaches and Parks

Arnold Arboretum
125 Arborway, Jamaica Plain (617/
524-1718), www.arboretum.harvard.edu
• FOREST HILLS (Orange Line)
• bus 38 (Wren St.-Forest Hills) or **39**
(Forest Hills-Back Bay Station) to
Custer St.; walk W to end of Custer
and across the Arborway

Back Bay Fens
⊕ p. 27, 34; between Park Dr. &
The Fenway, Boston
• from HYNES/ICA (Green Line-B, C, or
D or bus **39**) turn S on Mass Ave. to
corner, right on Boylston St. two blocks
• from MUSEUM OF FINE ARTS (Green
Line-E) walk N one block, cross the
Fenway
• bus 55 (Jersey & Queensberry Sts.-
Park & Tremont Sts.) to Queensberry
St. (end of line), turn right on Jersey
St. one block

Belle Isle Marsh Reservation
Bennington St., East Boston
(617/727-5350), www.mass.gov/mdc
• from SUFFOLK DOWNS (Blue Line) exit
to Bennington St., turn left

Blue Hills Reservation
Braintree, Canton, Milton, Quincy,
and Randolph (617/698-1802),
www.mass.gov/mdc
• from MATTAPAN (Red Line-
Mattapan) take JBL Bus Lines bus
716 (Mattapan-Canton) to Trailside
Museum
• from ASHMONT (Red Line-Ashmont)

take bus 240 (Avon Line or Holbrook/
Randolph Commuter Rail Sta.-
Ashmont) to Chickatawbut Rd.
• from QUINCY CTR (Red Line-Braintree)
take bus 238 (Quincy Center-
Holbrook/Randolph Commuter Rail
Sta.) to Shea Rink on Willard St.

Blue Hills Trailside Museum
1904 Canton Ave., Milton (617/
333-0690), www.massaudubon.org
• from MATTAPAN (Red Line-Mattapan)
take JBL Bus Lines bus 716
(Mattapan-Canton) to museum parking

Boston Common
⊕ p. 30; Tremont, Boylston, Charles,
Beacon, and Park St., Boston (events
line: 617/635-3445)
• BOYLSTON (Green or Silver Line)
• PARK STREET (Red or Green Line)

Boston Harbor Islands National Park Area
Discovery Center, U.S. Courthouse,
Northern Ave., Boston (617/223-8666),
www.bostonislands.com
Note: all boat service is seasonal

George's Island
Transfer point to interisland water taxi
• from AQUARIUM (Blue Line) take
Boston Harbor Cruises at Long Wharf
• Boston Harbor Cruises from Hingham
Shipyard at Hewitt's Cove, Hingham
• Boston Harbor Cruises from Salem
Ferry Landing, Blaney St., Salem
• Boston Harbor Cruises from Squantum
Point pier, Marina Bay, Quincy

Thompson Island
- from AQUARIUM (Blue Line) four-block walk S to iron pedestrian-only Old Northern Ave. bridge to Fan Pier, take Thompson Island Outward Bound Ferry (seasonal, weekly; 617/328-3900 x918)

Little Brewster Island (Boston Light)
- from AQUARIUM (Blue Line) four-block walk S to iron pedestrian-only Old Northern Ave. bridge to Fan Pier, take M/V *Hurricane* (seasonal, weekly; 617/223-8666)
- from JFK/UMASS (Red Line) take free wheelchair-accessible UMass-Kennedy Library shuttle bus (#2) to Fallon State Pier, take M/V *Hurricane* (seasonal, weekly; 617/223-8666)

Boston Nature Center
450B Walk Hill St., Mattapan (617/983-8500), www.massaudubon.org
- from JACKSON SQ (Orange Line) or DUDLEY STA (Silver Line) or ROSLINDALE VILLAGE (CR Needham Line) take bus 14 (Roslindale Sq.-Heath St.) to American Legion Hwy. & Walk Hill Ave.; walk 10min SE

Carson Beach
Day Blvd., South Boston
- from JFK/UMASS (Red Line) walk 10min E past rotary

Castle Island
Day Blvd., South Boston (617/727-5250), www.mass.gov/mdc
- from BROADWAY (Red Line) take bus 11 (City Point-Downtown) to Day Blvd., walk N then E 20min to park
- bus 3, 5, **7, 9,** 10, or **11** to City Pt. (end of line); less pleasant walk E 20min

Charles River Basin and Esplanade
⊕ p. 27; Science Park to B.U. Bridge, Boston and Cambridge (617/727-4708), www.mass.gov/mdc
- from ARLINGTON or COPLEY (Green Line) walk four blocks N
- from HYNES/ICA or KENMORE (Green Line-B, C, D) walk three-four blocks N
- from BLANDFORD ST, BU EAST, or BU CENTRAL (Green Line-B) walk two blocks N
- SCIENCE PARK (Green Line)
- CHARLES/MGH (Red Line)

- bus **1** (Harvard-Dudley) to Beacon St., walk N one block to river

Christian Herter Park
Soldiers Field Rd., Allston, www.mass.gov/mdc
- from CLEVELAND CIR (Green Line-C) take bus 86 (Sullivan-Cleveland Circle) to Everett St.; walk one block north
- from CENTRAL (Red Line) take bus 70 (Cedarwood or Watertown Sq.-Univ. Park) or 70A (N. Waltham-Univ. Park) to Everett St.; walk as above

Commonwealth Ave. Mall
⊕ p. 27; Commonwealth Ave. between Arlington St. & Charlesgate East, Boston
- from COPLEY or ARLINGTON (Green Line) two-block walk N

Constitution Beach
Bennington St., East Boston
- from ORIENT HEIGHTS (Blue Line) walk one block W on Bennington St.

Dorchester Shores Reservation
Savin Hill Ave. to Tenean St., Dorchester (617/727-6034), www.mass.gov/mdc
- from SAVIN HILL (Red Line-Ashmont) walk two blocks E on Savin Hill Ave. to Playstead St., turn right

Emerald Necklace
See "Arnold Arboretum," "Back Bay Fens," "Boston Common," "Commonwealth Ave. Mall," "Franklin Park," "Jamaica Pond," "Olmsted Park," "Public Garden," and "The Riverway"

The Esplanade
See "Charles River Basin & Esplanade"

Franklin Park
Blue Hill Ave., Morton St., Seaver St., Roxbury (617/635-4505), www.cityofboston.gov/parks
- from GREEN ST (Orange Line) turn right upon exiting, walk four blocks uphill to footpath entrance
- from FOREST HILLS (Orange Line) or ANDREW (Red Line) take bus 16 (Forest Hills-Andrew) which makes many stops in the park, or walk from FOREST HILLS
- from DUDLEY STA (Silver Line) or RUGGLES (Orange Line) take bus 45 (Franklin Park Zoo-Ruggles) to Peabody Circle

*Frequent bus routes in **bold***

• bus 14 (Roslindale Sq.-Heath St.) or **28** (Mattapan-Ruggles) to American Legion Hwy. & Blue Hill Ave. or Franklin Park Dr.
• bus **22** (Ashmont-Ruggles) or 29 (Mattapan-Jackson Sq.) to Walnut Ave., Humboldt Ave., or Franklin Park Dr.

Jamaica Pond
Jamaicaway, Perkins St., & Parkman Dr., Jamaica Plain (boathouse: 617/ 522-6258), www.cityofboston.gov/parks
• bus **39** (Forest Hills-Back Bay) to Pond St.; two-block walk NW on Pond

L and M Street Beaches
Day Blvd., South Boston
• from JFK/UMASS (Red Line) 20-minute walk E past rotary
• from BROADWAY (Red Line) take bus **11** (City Point-Downtown) to any stop on E. 8th St., then walk two blocks S

Malibu Beach
See "Dorchester Shores Reservation"

Middlesex Fells Reservation
Malden, Medford, Melrose, Stoneham, and Winchester (617/662-5230), www.mass.gov/mdc

Bellevue Pond
• from WELLINGTON (Orange Line) take bus 100 (Elm St.-Wellington) to Roosevelt Circle.; circle rotary counterclockwise to S. Border Rd., turn right, 4min walk

Sheepfold Picnic Area
• from WELLINGTON (Orange Line) take bus 100 to end of line (Elm St.); walk 20min N on Fellsway West (Rte. 28) to entrance on left (beyond overpass)

Nahant Beach
See "Lynn (Rec. Excursion)," p. 46

Olmsted Park
The Riverway between Rte. 9 & Perkins St., Jamaica Plain and Brookline
• from BROOKLINE VILLAGE (Green Line-D) walk S one block to Rte. 9, turn left two blocks
• from RIVERWAY (Green Line-E) walk W on Rte. 9 one block under the Riverway overpass, turn left
• bus **66** (Harvard-Dudley) to Riverway overpass; walk around to SW side

Public Garden
⊕ p. 30; Boylston, Charles, Beacon, and Arlington Sts., Boston, www.cityofboston.gov/parks
• ARLINGTON (Green Line)

Revere Beach
Revere Beach Blvd., Revere
• from REVERE BEACH or WONDERLAND (Blue Line) walk one block E

The Riverway
The Riverway between Park Dr. & Rte. 9, Boston and Brookline
• from FENWAY (Green Line-D) ascend stairs and cross Park Dr. (eastern end)
• LONGWOOD (Green Line-D) (middle)
• from BROOKLINE VILLAGE (Green Line-D) one-block walk E to Brookline Ave. (western end)

Savin Hill Beach
See "Dorchester Shores Reservation"

Singing Beach
See "Manchester-by-the-Sea (Recommended Excursion)," p. 46

Stony Brook Reservation
Turtle Pond Parkway, West Roxbury (617/727-5114), www.mass.gov/mdc
• from FOREST HILLS (Orange Line) take bus 34 (Dedham Line-Forest Hills) to Turtle Pond Parkway

Walden Pond State Reservation
Walden St. (Rte. 126), Concord (978/369-3254), www.mass.gov/dem
• CR Fitchburg/South Acton Line to CONCORD; walk E on Thoreau St. to end, turn right on Walden St., 35min (1.7 miles) total

Winthrop Beach
Winthrop Shore Dr., Winthrop
• from ORIENT HEIGHTS (Blue Line) exit Winthrop side to take Paul Revere Bus 712 or 713

Wollaston Beach
Quincy Shore Dr., Quincy, www.mass.gov/mdc
• from ASHMONT (Red Line-Ashmont) or WOLLASTON (Red Line-Braintree) take bus 217 (Ashmont-Wollaston Beach)
• from WOLLASTON (Red Line-Braintree) walk 30min (1.5 miles) E on Beach St.

Cinemas and Performing Arts Venues

Cinemas

Allston-Bombay Cinema
214 Harvard Ave., Allston (617/277-2140)
- from HARVARD AVE (Green Line-B) walk one block S on Harvard Ave.
- bus **66** (Harvard-Dudley) to Commonwealth Ave. (northbound) or Verndale St. (southbound)

AMC Chestnut Hill Cinema
27 Boylston St., Chestnut Hill (617/277-2500), www.moviewatcher.com
- from CHESTNUT HILL (Green Line-D) walk S on Hammond St. two blocks to Boylston, turn right

AMC Fenway Theatre
⊕ p. 34; 201 Brookline Ave., Boston (617/424-6266), www.moviewatcher.com
- FENWAY (Green Line-D)
- bus 8, 60, or 65 to Park Dr. & Brookline Ave.

Belmont Studio Cinema
376 Trapelo Rd., Belmont (617/484-1706), www.studiocinema.com
- bus **73** (Waverley Sq.-Harvard) to Beech St.

Boston Film & Video Foundation
1126 Boylston St., Boston (617/596-1540), www.bfvf.org
- from HYNES/ICA (Green Line-B, C, or D) walk S to traffic light, turn right

Brattle Theatre
⊕ p. 40; 40 Brattle St., Cambridge (617/876-6837), www.brattlefilm.org
- HARVARD (Red Line)

Capitol Theatre
204 Massachusetts Ave., Arlington (781/648-4340), www.capitoltheatreonline.com
- bus **77** (Arlington Heights-Harvard) or 79 (Arlington Heights-Alewife) to Lake St.

Circle Cinemas
⊕ p. 39; Cleveland Cir., Boston (617/566-4040)
- CLEVELAND CIR (Green Line-C)
- RESERVOIR (Green Line-D)
- bus 86 (Sullivan-Cleveland Circle) or 51 (Cleveland Circle-Forest Hills)

Coolidge Corner Theatre
290 Harvard St., Brookline (617/734-2500), www.coolidge.org
- COOLIDGE CORNER (Green Line-C)
- bus **66** (Harvard Sta-Dudley Sta) to Coolidge Corner

Dedham Community Theatre
580 High St., Dedham (781/326-1463), www.dedhamcommunitytheatre.com
- bus 34E (Walpole Center-Forest Hills) to Dedham Square

Harvard Film Archive
⊕ p. 40; Carpenter Center, 28 Quincy St., Cambridge (617/496-6064), www.harvardfilmarchive.org
See "Harvard University," p. 74

Landmark's Embassy Cinema
16 Pine St., Waltham (781/893-2500), www.landmarktheatres.com
- CR Fitchburg/South Acton Line (or bus 70, 70A, 505, 553, 554, 556, or 558) to WALTHAM Central Sq.; two-block walk S over Charles River to Pine St., turn left

Landmark's Kendall Square Cinema
1 Kendall Sq., Cambridge (617/494-9800)
- from KENDALL/MIT (Red Line) take free shoppers' shuttle (The Wave), or 12min walk: through lobby of Marriott Hotel to Broadway, turn left three blocks, turn right on Hampshire St. then right again at the One Kendall restaurant-retail-office complex (the cinema is at the very back next to the parking garage)
- bus 64 (Oak Sq.-Kendall/MIT, *not* Oak Sq.-University Park) or 68 (Harvard-Kendall) to Broadway & Hampshire St.
- bus 85 (Spring Hill-Lechmere) to Hampshire & Portland Sts.

Loews Cineplex Boston Common
175 Tremont St., Boston (617/423-3499), www.loewscineplex.com
- BOYLSTON (Green or Silver Line)
- from CHINATOWN (Orange or Silver Line) walk W on Boylston St. one block, turn right on Tremont

Loews Cineplex Copley Place
100 Huntington Ave., Boston
(617/266-1300)
• COPLEY (Green Line)
• BACK BAY STA (Orange Line)
• bus **9**, 10, **39**, 55, or 502 to Copley Sq.

Loews Cineplex Fresh Pond
Fresh Pond Plaza, Fresh Pond Pkwy.,
Cambridge (617/661-2900)
• from ALEWIFE (Red Line) walk S on
  bridge over tracks

Loews Cineplex Harvard Square Theatre
⊕ p. 40; 10 Church St., Cambridge
(617/864-4580)
• HARVARD (Red Line)

Mugar Omni Theatre
Museum of Science, Science Park
(617/723-2500)
• SCIENCE PARK (Green Line)

Regent Theatre
7 Medford St., Arlington (781/646 4TIX),
www.regenttheatre.com
• bus 67, **77**, 79, 80, 87, or 350 to
  Arlington Ctr.; walk SE (toward Boston)
  one block to Medford St., turn left

Simons IMAX Theatre
⊕ p. 31; New England Aquarium,
Central Wharf, Boston (866/815-IMAX)
See "New England Aquarium"

Somerville Theatre
⊕ p. 43; 55 Davis Sq., Somerville
(617/625-5700),
www.somervilletheatreonline.com
• DAVIS (Red Line)

Theater, Dance and Performance Art

Actors Workshop Theatre
327 Summer St., Studio 4, Boston
(617/423-7313),
www.actorsworkshopboston.com
• from SOUTH STA (Red Line or CR)
  three-block walk E on Summer St.,
  over Fort Point Channel

Agassiz Theatre
⊕ p. 40; 10 Garden St., Cambridge

(Harvard box office: 617/496-2222),
www.fas.harvard/~ofa
• HARVARD (Red Line)

American Repertory Theatre
⊕ p. 40; 64 Brattle St., Cambridge (box
office 617/547-8300), www.amrep.org
• HARVARD (Red Line)

Back Alley Theatre
1253 Cambridge St., Cambridge
(617/576-1253)
• from SULLIVAN SQ (Orange Line) take
  bus 91 (Sullivan-Central) to Inman Sq.,
  walk E on Cambridge St.
• from CENTRAL (Red Line) take bus 83
  (Rindge Ave.-Central) or 91 (Sullivan-
  Central) to Inman Sq., as above
• from HARVARD (Red Line) take bus 69
  (Harvard-Lechmere) to Inman Sq., as
  above

Ballet Theatre of Boston
⊕ p. 40; Sanctuary Theatre (Old
Cambridge Baptist Church), 440
Harvard St., Cambridge (617/354-7467),
www.btb.org
• HARVARD (Red Line)
• bus **1,** 68, or 69 to Quincy St.

Berwick Research Institute
14 Palmer St., Roxbury (617/532-4527),
www.berwickinstitute.org
• DUDLEY STA (Silver Line)

Blue Man Group
See "Charles Playhouse"

Boston Baked Theatre
The Garfield School, 140 Garfield Ave.,
Revere (781/289-5065)
• from REVERE BEACH (Blue Line) exit
  Shirley Ave. side, turn left through Orr
  Sq. walk up Garfield St. three blocks

Boston Lyric Opera
See "Shubert Theatre;" www.blo.org

Boston Center for the Arts
539 Tremont St., Boston (617/426-5000)
• from ARLINGTON (Green Line) exit to
  Berkeley St. and walk S eight blocks to
  Tremont St., turn right
• from BACK BAY STA (Orange Line) exit
  to Clarendon, turn right five blocks to
  Tremont St., then left
• from UNION PARK ST (Silver Line)

walk N on Union Park two blocks to Tremont, turn right
- bus **9** (City Point-Copley Sq.) to E. Berkeley St.
- bus 10 (City Point-Copley Sq.) to W. Dedham & Tremont Sts.; walk NE on Tremont one block
- bus **43** (Ruggles-Park St.) to Clarendon St.

Boston Children's Theatre
321 Columbus Ave., Boston (617/424-6634), www.bostonchildrenstheatre.org
- from BACK BAY STA (Orange Line) exit to Clarendon, turn right to corner of Columbus, then right again

Boston Conservatory Dance Theater
31 Hemenway St., Boston (617/536-3063)
- from HYNES/ICA (Green Line-B, C, or D) walk S to corner, right on Boylston one block, left on Hemenway

Boston Playwrights' Theatre
949 Commonwealth Ave., Boston (617/353-5443)
- PLEASANT ST (Green Line-B)

Boston University Theatre
See "Huntington Theatre Company"

C. Walsh Theatre
55 Temple St., Boston (617/573-8680)
See "Suffolk University," p. 78

Cabot Street Theater
286 Cabot St., Beverly (978/927-3677)
- CR Newburyport/Rockport Line to BEVERLY DEPOT; walk three blocks E on Broadway to Cabot St., turn left, five blocks
- CR Newburyport/Rockport Line to SALEM; take bus 451 (North Beverly-Salem Depot) to theatre

Cambridge Multicultural Arts Center
41 Second St., Cambridge (617/577-1400)
- LECHMERE (Green Line)

Charles Playhouse
74 Warrenton St., Boston (617/426-6912)
- from BOYLSTON (Green or Silver Line)

walk S on Tremont to Stuart, right on Stuart, left on Warrenton St.
- from NE MEDICAL CTR (Orange or Silver Line) exit to Washington St., walk N to corner of Stuart St., turn left two blocks to Warrenton, turn left

Charlestown Working Theater
442 Bunker Hill St., Charlestown (617/242-3285), www.charlestownworkingtheater.org
- from SULLIVAN SQ (Orange Line) walk NE under highway overpass to Bunker Hill St., then three blocks
- bus 92 (Assembly Sq. Mall-Downtown) to Armory St.; walk N on Armory one block to Bunker Hill
- bus **93** (Sullivan-Downtown) to Baldwin St.

Colonial Theatre
106 Boylston St., Boston (617/426-9366)
- BOYLSTON (Green or Silver Line)
- from CHINATOWN (Orange or Silver Line) walk W on Boylston St. two blocks

Copley Theatre at The New England
225 Clarendon St., Boston (617/266-7262)
- from COPLEY (Green Line) walk one block E on Boylston St. to Clarendon
- from BACK BAY STA (Orange Line) exit to Clarendon St., turn left, four blocks
- bus **9, 39,** or 55 to Clarendon St. & Boylston Ave.

Elm Street Theater
⊕ p. 43; 255 Elm St., Somerville (617/628-9555), www.elmstreettheater.com
- DAVIS (Red Line)

Emerson Majestic Theatre
219 Tremont St., Boston (617/824-8000)
- BOYLSTON (Green or Silver Line)
- CHINATOWN or NE MEDICAL CTR (Orange or Silver Line)

The Foothills Theatre Company
⊕ p. 52; Worcester Common Outlet Mall, 100 Front St., Worcester (508/754-4015), www.foothillstheatre.org
- CR Framingham/Worcester Line to WORCESTER
- Peter Pan Bus Lines to Worcester Bus Terminal

*Frequent bus routes in **bold***

Footlight Club
7A Eliot St., Jamaica Plain
(617/524-3200), www.footlight.org
• bus 37, 37/38, **39**, 41, or 48 to
  Monument Sq.; Eliot St. is on N side of
  "square"

Hasty Pudding Theatre
⊕ p. 40; 12 Holyoke St., Cambridge
(617/496-8400)
• HARVARD (Red Line)
• bus **1**, 68, or 69 to Harvard-Holyoke
  Gate (last stop)
• bus 86 (Sullivan-Cleveland Circle) to
  Harvard-Johnston Gate

Huntington Theatre Company
264 Huntington Ave., Boston
(617/266-0800)
• SYMPHONY (Green Line-E)
• MASSACHUSETTS AVE (Orange Line)
• bus **1** (Harvard-Dudley) to Mass Ave.,
• bus **39** (Forest Hills-Back Bay).

The Improv Asylum
216 Hanover St., Boston (617/263-6887)
• from HAYMARKET (Green or Orange
  Line) cross under the Central Artery to
  Hanover St.

ImprovBoston
See "Back Alley Theatre"

Jewish Theatre of New England
Leventhal-Sidman Jewish Community
Center, 333 Nahanton St., Newton
Centre (box office: 617/965-5226)
• from NEWTON CENTRE (Green Line-D)
  take bus 52 (Dedham Mall or Charles
  River Loop-Watertown Sq.) via Centre
  & Winchester Sts. (*not* via Parker or
  Meadowbrook) to Community Ctr.

Jose Mateo's Ballet Theatre
See "Ballet Theatre of Boston"

Le Grand David & His Own
Spectacular Magic Company
See "Cabot Street Theater"

Loeb Drama Center
See "American Repertory Theatre".

Lyric Stage Company of Boston
YWCA, 140 Clarendon St., Boston
(617/437-7172)
• from COPLEY (Green Line) walk E
  on Boylston one block, turn right on
  Clarendon, three blocks
• from BACK BAY STA (Orange Line) exit
  to Clarendon, turn left
• bus **9** (City Point-Copley Sq.) to
  Berkeley & Stuart Sts.; walk W on Stuart
  one block, turn left on Clarendon
• bus 10 (City Point-Copley Sq.) to Dartmouth & Stuart Sts.; walk E on Stuart
  one block, turn right on Clarendon

Merrimack Repertory Theatre
⊕ p. 45; 50 E. Merrimack St., Lowell
(978/454-3926), www.mrtlowell.com
• CR Lowell Line to LOWELL; take local
  LRTA Downtown Shuttle; two-block
  walk E from downtown bus station

Mobius
354 Congress St., Boston
(617/542-7416), wwwmobius.org
• from SOUTH STA (Red Line or CR)
  walk NE one block on Atlantic Ave.,
  right on Congress, then three blocks

New Repertory Theatre
54 Lincoln St., Newton Highlands
(617/332-1646)
• NEWTON HIGHLANDS (Green Line-D)

The Nora Theatre Company
(617/491-2026)
See "Boston Playwrights' Theatre"

North Shore Music Theatre
62 Dunham Rd., Beverly
(978/922-8220), www.nsmt.org
• CR Newburyport/Rockport Line to
  NORTH BEVERLY; walk 20min S
  via Budleigh and Brimbal Aves. to
  Dunham Rd., last left before Rte. 128

Omega Theatre
Carriage House Studio, 83 Elm
St., Jamaica Plain (617/522-8300),
www.omegatheatre.org
• from GREEN ST (Orange Line) exit left
  one block to light, left again one block,
  bear right at fork on Elm
• bus **39** (Forest Hills-Back Bay) to
  Eliot St. or Greenough St., follow
  Greenough St. two blocks to end, turn
  left on Elm

Pilgrim Theatre Research and Performance Collaborative

(413/628-0112), www.pilgrimtheatre.org
See "Boston Center for the Arts"

Puppet Showplace Theater

🌐 p. 38; 32 Station St., Brookline
(617/731-6400)
• BROOKLINE VILLAGE (Green Line-D)

Quincy Dinner Theater

1170 Hancock St., Quincy (781/
843-5862), www.quincydinnertheater.com
• QUINCY CTR (Red Line-Braintree)

Riverside Theatre Works

French's Opera House, 45 Fairmount
Ave., Hyde Park (617/363-7024),
www.riversidetheatreworks.org
• from MATTAPAN (Red Line-Mattapan)
take bus 24 (Wakefield Ave. & Truman
Pkwy.-Mattapan) or 33 (Dedham Line-
Mattapan) to Logan Sq., walk SE on
Fairmount one block
• CR Fairmount Line to FAIRMOUNT; walk
NW 1.5 blocks

Shear Madness

See "Charles Playhouse"

Shubert Theatre

270 Tremont St., Boston (617/482-9393)
• BOYLSTON (Green or Silver Line)
• NE MEDICAL CTR (Orange or Silver Line)

Sorenson Center for the Arts

Park Manor South, Babson
College, Wellesley (781/239-5682),
www.babson.edu
See "Babson College," p. 71

SpeakEasy Stage Company

(617/427-7731),
www.speakeasystage.com
See "Boston Center for the Arts"

Spingold Theater Arts Center

415 South St., Brandeis University,
Waltham (781/736-3400),
www.brandeis.edu/theater
See "Brandeis University," p. 72

The Súgán Theater Company

(781/497-5134), www.sugan.org
See "Boston Center for the Arts"

Tremont Theatre (Chinese Culture Institute)

276 Tremont St., Boston (617/542-4599)
• BOYLSTON (Green or Silver Line)
• NE MEDICAL CTR (Orange or Silver Line)

Theatre Cooperative

277 Broadway, Somerville (617/
625-1300), www.theatrecoop.org
• from SULLIVAN SQ (Orange Line) take
bus 89 (Clarendon Hill-Sullivan Sq.) or
101 (Malden Ctr.-Sullivan Sq.) to Star
Market

The Theater Offensive

(617/542-4214),
www.thetheateroffensive.org
See "Boston Center for the Arts"

Theatre1

Bates Art Resource Center, 731
Harrison Ave., Boston (617/859-7480),
www.theatre1.org
• from NEWTON ST (Silver Line) walk SE
on East Newton St. one block
• bus **1** (Harvard-Dudley) to Mass. Ave.
& Harrison Ave.; walk NE on Harrison
three blocks
• bus 8, 10, 47, CT1, or CT3 to East
Newton St.; walk NW to corner

TheatreZone

189 Winnisimmet St., Chelsea
(617/887-2321), www.theatrezone.org
• from MAVERICK (Blue Line) take bus
114, 116, or 117 to Chelsea Sq.,
walk W on Park St. one block to
Winnisimmet, turn sharp right
• from HAYMARKET (Green or Orange
Line) take bus **111** (Woodlawn or
Broadway & Park Ave.-Haymarket) to
Chelsea Sq., as above
• from WELLINGTON (Orange Line) take
bus 112 (Wellington-Wood Island) to
Chelsea Sq., as above
• CR Newburyport/Rockport Line to
CHELSEA; walk S on Washington Ave.
two blocks, bear right on Broadway,
four blocks, Winnisimmet forks to left

Trinity Repertory Theater

🌐 p. 48; 201 Washington St.,
Providence, RI (401/351-4242)
• Amtrak or CR Attleboro Line to
PROVIDENCE; exit to Gaspee St. to
take Providence LINK Gold Line trolley

• Bonanza Bus Lines to Kennedy Plaza; take South Side-bound Providence LINK Gold Line trolley or Federal Hill-bound Green Line trolley, or seven-block walk SW on Washington St.

Underground Railway Theater
41 Foster St., Arlington (781/643-6916)
• from HARVARD (Red Line) take bus **77** (Arlington Heights-Harvard Sta.) to Foster St.

Wang Center for the Performing Arts
270 Tremont St., Boston (617/482-9393)
• BOYLSTON (Green or Silver Line)
• NE MEDICAL CTR (Orange or Silver Line)

Wheelock Family Theater
⊕ p. 34; 200 The Riverway, Boston (box office 617/734-4760), www.wheelock.edu/wft
See "Wheelock College," p. 80

Wilbur Theatre
246 Tremont St., Boston (617/423-7440)
• BOYLSTON (Green or Silver Line)
• NE MEDICAL CTR (Orange or Silver Line)

Auditoriums

Berklee Performance Center
⊕ p. 27; 136 Massachusetts Ave., Boston (617/226-7455)
See "Berklee College of Music," p. 72

Boston University School for the Arts Concert Hall
855 Commonwealth Ave., Boston (617/353-3349)
• BU WEST (Green Line-B)

Community Music Center of Boston
See "Boston Center for the Arts," p. 65

Converse Hall
Tremont Temple, 88 Tremont St., Boston (617/523-7320)
• PARK STREET (Red or Green Line)

Cyclorama
See "Boston Center for the Arts," p. 65

Faneuil Hall
⊕ p. 31; Merchants Row, Boston

(617/951-2555)
• from STATE (Orange or Blue Line) walk N
• from GOVERNMENT CTR (Green or Blue Line) walk E past City Hall
• from HAYMARKET (Green or Orange Line) walk S

Fleet Boston Pavilion
Northern Ave., South Boston
• from SOUTH STA (Red Line or CR) take bus 3 (City Point-Bedford & Chauncy Sts.) or 6 (Boston Marine Industrial Park-Haymarket) to entrance
• Inner Harbor Ferry from Lovejoy Wharf to World Trade Center
• Quincy Commuter Boat directly to Pavilion pier (limited service)

FleetCenter
⊕ p. 29; 150 Causeway St., Boston (617/227-3200), www.fleetcenter.com
• NORTH STA (Green, Orange Line or CR)

Hatch Memorial Shell
⊕ p. 27; Charles River Esplanade, Mugar Way, Boston (617/727-5215)
• from ARLINGTON (Green Line) walk N on Arlington to Fiedler Footbridge
• CHARLES/MGH (Red Line)

John Hancock Hall
180 Berkeley St., Boston (617/572-7700)
• ARLINGTON (Green Line)
• BACK BAY STA (Orange Line)

Jordan Hall
30 Gainsborough St., Boston (617/536-2412), www.newenglandconservatory.edu
• SYMPHONY (Green Line-E)
• MASSACHUSETTS AVE (Orange Line)
• bus 39 (Forest Hills-Back Bay)

Jorge Hernandez Cultural Center at Villa Victoria
65 W. Newton St., Boston (617/867-9191), www.jhcconline.org
• from PRUDENTIAL (Green Line-E) walk four blocks S on W. Newton St.
• from NEWTON ST (Silver Line) walk two blocks N
• bus 8 (Harbor Pt./UMass-Kenmore) or 10 (City Pt.-Copley Sq.) to W. Newton St.; walk N
• bus 43 (Ruggles-Park St.) to W. Newton St.; walk S

Killian Hall
160 Memorial Dr., Massachusetts Institute of Technology, Cambridge
- from KENDALL/MIT (Red Line) upon exiting, walk N to Ames St., turn left one long block to Amherst St., turn right on walkway into enclosed courtyard, Killian Hall is to left past the giant Alexander Calder sculpture
- bus **1** (Harvard-Dudley) to Memorial Dr.

Kresge Auditorium
48 Massachusetts Ave., Massachusetts Institute of Technology, Cambridge (617/253-4720)
- bus **1** (Harvard-Dudley) to MIT main entrance at 77 Massachusetts Ave.

Lowell Memorial Auditorium
⊕ p. 45; 50 E. Merrimack St., Lowell (978/454-3926), www.mrtlowell.com
- CR Lowell Line to LOWELL; take local LRTA Downtown Shuttle to Kearney Sq., two-block walk E

Mechanics Hall
⊕ p. 52; 321 Main St., Worcester (508/752-5608), www.mechanicshall.org
- CR Framingham/Worcester Line to WORCESTER
- Peter Pan Bus Lines to Worcester Bus Terminal

New England Hall
See "Copley Theatre at The New England," p. 66

Orpheum Theatre
Hamilton Place, Boston (617/482-0650)
- from PARK STREET (Red or Green Line) walk E on Tremont St. 50yds, turn right on Hamilton

Paine Concert Hall
⊕ p. 40; Harvard University, Cambridge
See "Harvard University," p. 74

Pickman Concert Hall
⊕ p. 40; Longy School of Music, 1 Follen St., Cambridge (617/876-0952)
See "Longy School of Music," p. 75

Sanders Theatre
⊕ p. 40; Memorial Hall, Kirkland St., Cambridge (617/496-2222)
See "Harvard University," p. 74

Strand Theatre
543 Columbia Rd., Uphams Corner, Dorchester (617/282-8000)
- bus **15**, 16, 17, or 41 to Uphams Corner
- from JFK/UMASS (Red Line) 15min walk W on Columbia Rd., or special shuttle bus from JFK/UMASS to some events
- CR Fairmount Line to UPHAMS CORNER; five-block walk E to Columbia Rd.

Symphony Hall
⊕ p. 27; 301 Massachusetts Ave., Boston (888-266-1200 or 617/266-1492), www.bso.org
- SYMPHONY (Green Line-E)
- from MASSACHUSETTS AVE (Orange Line) three-block walk N
- bus **1** (Harvard-Dudley) to Huntington Ave.
- bus **39** (Forest Hills-Back Bay) to Gainsborough St.; walk NE one block

Tsai Performance Center
655 Commonwealth Ave., Boston University, Boston (617/353-8724)
- BU CENTRAL or BU EAST (Green Line-B)
- bus 47 (Central-Albany St.)

Tweeter Center
S. Main St. (Rte. 140), Mansfield (508/339-2333), www.tweetercenter.com
- CR Attleboro Line to MANSFIELD; three-mile walk or taxi ride S on N. Main and S. Main Sts.

Orpheum Theatre and back entrance to the Corner Mall in Downtown Crossing.

Colleges, Universities, Seminaries, and Conservatories

Andover-Newton Theological School
210 Herrick Rd., Newton Centre
(617/964-1100), www.ants.edu
• NEWTON CENTRE (Green Line-D)
• bus 52 (Dedham Mall-Watertown)

The Art Institute of Boston at Lesley University
700 Boylston St., Boston
(617/262-1223), www.aiboston.edu
• KENMORE (Green Line-B, C, or D)

Arthur D. Little School of Management
194 Beacon St., Chestnut Hill
(617/552-2877), www.adlsom.edu
• from CHESTNUT HILL (Green Line-D)
10min walk N on Hammond St. to
Beacon St.

Assumption College
500 Salisbury St., Worcester
(508/767-7000), www.assumption.edu
• CR Framingham/Worcester Line to
WORCESTER; walk to City Hall Plaza
(Front St. side) to take WRTA bus 21
(Highland/Assumption College) or
CC3 (College Consortium Route—only
during school year)
• Peter Pan Bus Lines to Worcester
Bus Terminal; take WRTA bus CC3
(College Consortium Route—only
during school year), or walk four
blocks N on Southbridge and Main
Sts. to City Hall Plaza to take WRTA
bus 21, as above

Babson College
Forest St. & Wellesley Ave., Wellesley
(781/235-1200), www.babson.edu
• from WOODLAND (Green Line-D) take
Babson College shuttle bus Fri-Sun
(schedule: 781/239-4330)
• CR Framingham/Worcester Line to
WELLESLEY HILLS; walk 20min S on
Forest St.

Baptist Bible College East
950 Metropolitan Ave., Hyde Park
(617/364-3510), www.bbceast.edu
• from MATTAPAN (Red Line-Mattapan)

take bus 24 (Wakefield Ave. & Truman
Pkwy.-Mattapan) to Metropolitan Ave.
• CR Fairmount Line to FAIRMOUNT; take
bus 24 or walk SE on Fairmount Ave.
one block, left on Beacon St. three
blocks, then right on Metropolitan

Bay State College
122 Commonwealth Ave., Boston
(617/236-8000), www.baystate.edu
• COPLEY (Green Line)

Becker College
Leicester
3 Paxton St., Leicester (877/BECKER or
508/791-9241), www.beckercollege.edu
• CR Framingham/Worcester Line to
WORCESTER; walk to City Hall Plaza
(Main St. side) to take WRTA bus 19S
(Cherry Valley/Leicester Center)
• Peter Pan Bus Lines to Worcester Bus
Terminal; walk NW on Madison St. two
blocks to Main St. to take WRTA bus
19S, as above

Worcester
61 Sever St., Worcester (877/BECKER or
508/791-9241), www.beckercollege.edu
• CR Framingham/Worcester Line to
WORCESTER; walk to City Hall Plaza
(Front St. side) to take WRTA bus 21
(Highland/Assumption College) or
CC3 (College Consortium Route—only
during school year), or continue two
blocks N on Main to Foster St. to take
WRTA bus 5W (June/Mill)
• Peter Pan Bus Lines to Worcester Bus
Terminal; take WRTA bus CC3 (College
Consortium Route—only during
school year), or walk four blocks N on
Southbridge and Main Sts. to City Hall
Plaza to take other local WRTA buses,
as above

Benjamin Franklin Institute of Technology
41 Berkeley St., Boston (617/423-4630),
www.bfit.edu
• from BACK BAY STA (Orange Line)
walk S on Clarendon St. two blocks,
left on Chandler St., right on Berkeley
• from ARLINGTON (Green Line) walk S
on Berkeley St. six blocks

Bentley College
Forest & Beaver Sts., Waltham
(781/891-2000); www.bentley.edu
- from DOWNTOWN CROSSING (Red, Orange, or Silver Line) walk two blocks SE to Otis St. to take bus 554 (Waverley-Downtown)
- CR Fitchburg/South Acton Line to WAVERLEY or WALTHAM; take bus 554 (Waverley-Downtown)
- from HARVARD (Red Line) take Bentley College shuttle bus (nights and weekends during school year, schedule 781/891-2148)

Berklee College of Music
1140 Boylston St., Boston
(617/266-1400), www.berklee.edu
- HYNES/ICA (Green Line-B, C, or D)

Boston Architectural Center
320 Newbury St., Boston (617/262-5000), www.the-bac.edu
- HYNES/ICA (Green Line-B, C, or D)

Boston Center for Adult Education
5 Commonwealth Ave., Boston
(617/267-4430), www.bcae.org
- ARLINGTON (Green Line)

Boston College
140 Commonwealth Ave., Chestnut Hill
(617/552-8000), www.bc.edu
- BOSTON COLLEGE (Green Line-B) (end of line, on north edge of campus)
- from CLEVELAND CIR (Green Line-C) take Boston College shuttle on Chestnut Hill Ave., daily (schedule 617/552-3060)
- from CHESTNUT HILL (Green Line-D) 10min walk N on Hammond St. to south edge of campus

Newton Campus
885 Centre St., Newton (617/552-8550)
- from NEWTON CENTRE (Green Line-D) take bus 52 (Dedham Mall or Charles River Loop-Watertown Sq.)

Boston Conservatory
8 The Fenway, Boston (617/536-6340), www.bostonconservatory.edu
- HYNES/ICA (Green Line-B, C, or D)

Boston Graduate School of Psychoanalysis
1581 Beacon St., Brookline
(617/277-3915), www.bgsp.edu
- WASHINGTON SQ (Green Line-C)

Boston University
Charles River Campus
Commonwealth Ave., Boston
(617/353-2000), www.bu.edu
- BLANDFORD ST, BU EAST, BU CENTRAL, BU WEST, SAINT PAUL ST, PLEASANT ST, or BABCOCK ST (Green Line-B or bus **57**)
- bus 47 (Central-Broadway) or CT2 (Sullivan-Ruggles) to Commonwealth Ave. or Mountfort St.

Medical School
88 E. Newton St., Boston (617/638-8000)
See "Boston Medical Center" p. 84

Brandeis University
415 South St., Waltham (781/736-2000), www.brandeis.edu
- express bus 553 (Roberts-Downtown Boston) to campus
- from CENTRAL (Red Line) take bus 70 (Cedarwood or Watertown Sq.-University Park) to Cedarwood Ave.; walk up Cedarwood three blocks, turn left on Thornton Rd.
- CR Fitchburg/South Acton Line to BRANDEIS/ROBERTS
- local Waltham CitiBus 17

Bridgewater State College
100 State St., Bridgewater
(508/697-1200), www.bridgew.edu
- CR Middleborough/Lakeville Line to BRIDGEWATER; stop is next to campus
- Interstate Coach (Boston-Middleborough)

Brown University
45 Prospect St., Providence, RI
(401/863-1000), www.brown.edu
- Amtrak or CR Attleboro Line to PROVIDENCE; exit to Park Row and walk three blocks S on Exchange St. to Kennedy Plaza to take local RIPTA buses listed below, or exit to Gaspee St. and catch any RIPTA bus or trolley across the street to Kennedy Plaza to transfer to RIPTA buses, below
- Bonanza Bus Lines to Kennedy Plaza; take local RIPTA bus 35 (Rumford), 40 (Butler-Elmgrove-Tunnel), 42 (Hope-Tunnel), or Providence LINK Green Line trolley to Tunnel & Thayer St.

Bunker Hill Community College

New Rutherford Ave., Charlestown
(617/228-2000), www.bhcc.state.ma.us
• COMMUNITY COLLEGE (Orange Line)

Cambridge Center for Adult Education

⊕ p. 40; 42 Brattle St., Cambridge
(617/547-6789)
• HARVARD (Red Line)

Cambridge College

⊕ p. 40; 1000 Mass. Ave., Cambridge
(617/868-1000), www.cambridge.edu
• HARVARD (Red Line)
• bus **1** (Harvard-Dudley Sq.) to Mass.
Ave. & Dana St.

Clark University

950 Main St., Worcester (508/793-7711),
www.clarku.edu
• CR Framingham/Worcester Line to
WORCESTER; walk to City Hall Plaza
(Main St. side) to take WRTA bus
19S, 26S, 30S, or 33, or to Front St.
side to take WRTA bus CC2 (College
Consortium Route—school year only)
• Peter Pan Bus Lines to Worcester
Bus Terminal; take WRTA bus CC2
(College Consortium Route—only
during school year), or walk NW on
Madison St. two blocks to Main St. to
take WRTA bus 19S, 26S, 30S, or 33

College of the Holy Cross

College Hill, Worcester (508/793-2011),
www.holycross.edu
• CR Framingham/Worcester Line to
WORCESTER; walk to City Hall Plaza
(Franklin St. side) to take WRTA bus
10 (College Hill), or to Front St. side
to take WRTA bus CC2 (College
Consortium Route—school year only)
• Peter Pan Bus Lines to Worcester Bus
Terminal; take WRTA bus 10 (College
Hill) or CC2 (College Consortium
Route—school year only)

Curry College

1071 Blue Hill Ave., Milton
(617/333-0500), www.curry.edu
• from MATTAPAN (Red Line-Mattapan)
take JBL Bus Lines bus 716
(Mattapan-Canton) to college entrance

Dean College

99 Main St., Franklin (508/541-1900),
www.dean.edu
• CR Franklin Line to FRANKLIN/DEAN
COLLEGE

Eastern Nazarene College

23 E. Elm Ave., Wollaston (Quincy)
(800/883-6288 or 617/773-6350),
www.enc.edu
• from WOLLASTON (Red Line-Braintree)
take bus 217 (Wollaston-Ashmont), or
10min walk E via Beale and Beach Sts.
to Gould St., turn right four blocks
• from QUINCY CTR (Red Line-Braintree)
take bus 212 (Quincy Ctr.-N. Quincy)

Emerson College

120 Boylston St., Boston
(617/824-8500), www.emerson.edu
• BOYLSTON (Green or Silver Line)

Emmanuel College

⊕ p. 34; 400 The Fenway, Boston
(617/277-9340), www.emmanuel.edu
• FENWAY (Green Line-D)
• bus 8 (Harbor Pt./UMass-Kenmore) or
47 (Central-Albany St.) to Ave. Louis
Pasteur & the Fenway
• bus 60 (Chestnut Hill-Kenmore) or 65
(Brighton Ctr.-Kenmore) to Brookline
Ave. & the Fenway
• bus CT2 (Sullivan-Ruggles) or CT3
(Beth Israel-Andrew) to Beth Israel
Hosp. or Ave. Louis Pasteur
• LMA Shuttle M2 (Cambridge-Harvard
Medical School)

Episcopal Divinity School

⊕ p. 40; 99 Brattle St., Cambridge
(617/868-3450), www.episdivschool.edu
• from HARVARD (Red Line) walk up
Brattle St. six blocks

Fisher College

⊕ p. 27, 118 Beacon St., Boston
(617/236-8800), www.fisher.edu
• ARLINGTON (Green Line)

Forsyth School of Dental Hygienists

⊕ p. 34; 140 The Fenway, Boston
(617/262-5200), www.forsyth.org
• NORTHEASTERN (Green Line-E)
• bus **39** (Forest Hills-Back Bay) to
Forsyth Way & Huntington Ave.

Framingham State College
100 State St., Framingham
(508/620-1220), www.frc.mass.edu
- CR Framingham/Worcester Line to
FRAMINGHAM; walk E to Concord St.,
take local LIFT bus 2 or 3

Harvard University
⊕ p. 40; Harvard Sq., Cambridge
(617/495-1000), www.harvard.edu
- HARVARD (Red Line)
- LMA Shuttle M2 (Cambridge-Harvard
Medical School)

Business School
Soldiers Field Rd., Allston
(617/495-6800)
- from HARVARD (Red Line) 10min walk
SW on JFK St. across river, or take bus
66 or 86
- bus **66** (Harvard-Dudley) or 86
(Sullivan-Cleveland Circle) to Harvard
Stadium Gate 2
- bus 70 (Cedarwood or Watertown Sq.-
University Park) to B-School parking lot
on Western Ave.

Medical School and School of Public Health and School of Dental Medicine
⊕ p. 34; 25 Shattuck St., Boston
(617/432-1000)
- BRIGHAM CIR or LONGWOOD/
HOSPITALS (Green Line-E)
- bus 8 (Harbor Pt./UMass-Kenmore) or
47 (Central-Broadway) to Children's
Hospital or Ave. Louis Pasteur
- bus **39** (Forest Hills-Back Bay) or CT2
(Sullivan-Ruggles) to Longwood &
Huntington Ave.
- bus **66** (Harvard-Dudley) to Brigham
Circle
- LMA Shuttle M2 (Cambridge-Harvard
Medical School)

Hebrew College
160 Herrick Rd., Newton Centre
(800/866-4814 or 617/559-8600),
www.hebrewcollege.edu
- from NEWTON CENTRE (Green Line-D)
walkway from platform to Herrick Rd.,
left three blocks

Hellenic College/Holy Cross Greek Orthodox School of Theology
50 Goddard Ave., Brookline
(617/731-3500), www.hchc.edu

- from RESERVOIR (Green Line-D)
or FOREST HILLS (Orange Line) or
ROSLINDALE VILLAGE (CR Needham
Line) take bus 51 (Cleveland Cir.-
Forest Hills) to Newton and Clyde Sts.;
walk E on Newton St. and bear left on
Goddard Ave., 20min
- bus 14, 30, 34, 34E, 35, 36, 37, 40, or
50 to Roslindale Sq.; transfer to bus
51, as above

Johnson & Wales University
Downtown
⊕ p. 48; 8 Abbot Park Place,
Providence, RI (800/DIAL-JWU or
410/598-1000), www.jwu.edu
- Amtrak or CR Attleboro Line to
PROVIDENCE; exit to Gaspee St. to
take Providence LINK Gold Line trolley
to Chestnut & Weybosset Sts., then
walk E one block to JWU Admissions
or four to JWU Quad; or exit to Park
Row, then eight-block walk S to Quad
- Bonanza Bus Lines to Kennedy Plaza;
four-block walk SE to Quad, or take
South Side-bound Providence LINK
Gold Line trolley, as above

Harborside
265 Harborside Blvd., Providence, RI
(401/598-1892)
- Amtrak or CR Attleboro Line to
PROVIDENCE; exit to Gaspee St. to
take Providence LINK Gold Line trolley
to Kennedy Plaza and take local RIPTA
buses, below, or exit to Park Row and
walk three blocks S on Exchange St.
to Kennedy Plaza and take local RIPTA
buses, below
- Bonanza Bus Lines to Kennedy Plaza;
take local RIPTA bus 1 (Eddy St.) or 11
(Broad St.) to Broad/City Line, walk NE
one block
- Free college inter-campus shuttle from
Weybosset St. side of downtown JWU
Quad (year-round)

Katherine Gibbs School
126 Newbury St., Boston (617/578-7100),
www.kgibbsboston.com
- from COPLEY (Green Line) walk one
block N on Dartmouth St., turn right on
Newbury St.

Laboure College
2120 Dorchester Ave., Dorchester
(617/296-8300), www.labourecollege.org
- from FOREST HILLS (Orange Line)

take bus 21 (Ashmont-Forest Hills) to Gallivan Blvd. & Dorchester Ave., turn right (S) on Dorchester, two blocks
• from ASHMONT (Red Line-Ashmont) take bus 27, 217, or 240 to Carney Hospital, or walk 10min S on Dorchester Ave.
• bus 215 (Quincy Ctr.-Ashmont) to Gallivan Blvd. & Dorchester Ave., turn S on Dorchester

Lasell College
1844 Commonwealth Ave., Newton (617/243-2000), www.lasell.edu
• from RIVERSIDE (Green Line-D), walk 10min E on Grove St., turn right on Woodland Rd. to back of campus

Lesley University
Main Campus
⊕ p. 40; 29 Everett St., Cambridge (617/868-9600), www.lesley.edu
• from HARVARD (Red Line) walk three blocks N on Mass. Ave. to Everett St.
• bus 77, 77A, or 96 to Everett St.

The Art Institute of Boston
700 Boylston St., Boston (617/262-1223), www.aiboston.edu
• KENMORE (Green Line-B, C, or D)

Longy School of Music
⊕ p. 40; 1 Follen St., Cambridge (617/876-0956), www.longy.edu
• HARVARD (Red Line)
• bus 72, 74, or 78 to Garden St.

Massachusetts Bay Community College
50 Oakland St., Wellesley (781/239-3000), www.mbcc.mass.edu
• from RIVERSIDE (Green Line-D) take college shuttle, Mon-Fri only, Sept-May

Massachusetts College of Art
⊕ p. 34; 621 Huntington Ave., Boston (617/879-7000), www.massart.edu
• LONGWOOD/HOSPITALS (Green Line-E)
• bus 8 (Harbor Pt./UMass-Kenmore) or 47 (Central-Broadway) to Ruggles St. & Huntington Ave.
• bus 39 (Forest Hills-Back Bay) or CT2 (Sullivan-Ruggles) to Longwood & Huntington Ave.
• bus 66 (Harvard-Dudley) to Brigham Circle

Massachusetts College of Pharmacy and Health Sciences
⊕ p. 34; 179 Longwood Ave., Boston (617/732-2800), www.mcp.edu
• LONGWOOD/HOSPITALS (Green Line-E)
• bus 8 (Harbor Pt./UMass-Kenmore) or 47 (Central-Broadway) to Ave. Louis Pasteur
• bus 39 (Forest Hills-Back Bay) or CT2 (Sullivan-Ruggles) to Longwood & Huntington Ave.
• bus 66 (Harvard-Dudley) to Brigham Circle
• bus CT3 (Beth Israel-Andrew) to Children's Hospital or Ave. Louis Pasteur
• LMA Shuttle M2 (Cambridge-Harvard Medical School)

Massachusetts Communications College
⊕ p. 38; 10 Brookline Place West, Brookline (617/739-1700), www.masscomm.edu
• BROOKLINE VILLAGE (Green Line-D)

Massachusetts Institute of Technology (MIT)
77 Massachusetts Ave., Cambridge (617/253-1000), www.mit.edu
• KENDALL/MIT (Red Line) (at east edge of campus)
• bus 1 (Harvard-Dudley) or CT1 (Central Sq.-B.U. Medical Ctr.) to main entrance
• bus CT2 (Sullivan-Ruggles) to Vassar St. & Mass. Ave.
• LMA Shuttle M2 (Cambridge-Harvard Medical School)

Massasoit Community College
1 Massasoit Blvd., Brockton (508/588-9100), www.massasoit.mass.edu
• CR Middleborough/Lakeville Line to BROCKTON; take BAT bus 6 (Massasoit via Crescent)

MGH Institute of Health Professions
101 Merrimac St., Boston (617/726-3140), www.mghihp.edu
• from NORTH STA (Green or Orange Line or CR) walk SE to Lancaster St., turn left to end of block

Middlesex Community College
Bedford
Springs Rd., Bedford (781/280-3200),
www.middlesex.cc.ma.us
- from ALEWIFE (Red Line) Mon-Fri take
  bus 62 (Bedford V.A. Hospital-Alewife)
  or Saturday take bus 62/76 (Bedford
  V.A. Hospital-Alewife via Hanscom) to
  V.A. Hospital, college shuttle meets
  each bus (info: 781/280-3528)

Lowell
- ⊕ p. 45; 33 Kearney Sq., Lowell (978/
  656-3200), www.middlesex.cc.ma.us
- CR Lowell Line to LOWELL; take local
  LRTA Downtown Shuttle to Kearney Sq.

Montserrat College of Art
41 Essex St., Beverly (978/922-8222),
www.montserrat.edu
- CR Newburyport/Rockport Line to
  BEVERLY DEPOT; walk three blocks E
  on Broadway to Cabot St., turn left, two
  blocks, bear right at fork onto Essex,
  main bldg. faces town common
- CR Newburyport/Rockport Line to
  SALEM; take bus 451 (North Beverly-
  Salem Depot) to Beverly Sq. (foot of
  Essex St./town common)

Mount Ida College
777 Dedham St., Newton Centre
(617/969-7000), www.mountida.edu
- from NEWTON CENTRE (Green Line-
  D) during school year take Mount Ida
  Shuttle Bus from Starbucks or Cypress
  St. parking lot (schedule: 617/
  928-4588), or take bus 52 (Dedham
  Mall or Charles River Loop-Watertown
  Sq.)

Mount Wachusett Community College
444 Green St., Gardner (978/632-6600),
www.mwcc.mass.edu
- CR Fitchburg Line to FITCHBURG;
  take MART Mt. Wachusett Community
  College Express (weekdays only)

The New England College of Finance
1 Lincoln Plaza, Boston (617/951-2350),
www.finance.edu
- from SOUTH STA (Red Line or CR) walk
  S on Atlantic Ave. to first right on Essex
  St., two blocks to Lincoln St.

New England College of Optometry
424 Beacon St., Boston (617/266-2030),
www.ne-optometry.edu
- from HYNES/ICA (Green Line-B, C or
  D) walk N on Mass. Ave. three or four
  blocks to Beacon St., right, one block
- bus 1 (Harvard-Dudley) to Beacon St.

New England Conservatory of Music
290 Huntington Ave., Boston
(617/585-1100),
www.newenglandconservatory.edu
- from SYMPHONY (Green Line-E) walk
  SW one block
- from MASSACHUSETTS AVE (Orange
  Line) walk N two blocks to Huntington
  Ave., turn left, one block
- bus 39 (Forest Hills-Back Bay) to
  Gainsborough St.

New England School of Acupuncture
40 Belmont St., Watertown
(617/926-1788), www.nesa.edu
- from HARVARD (Red Line) take bus 73
  (Waverley Sq.-Harvard Sta.) to Cushing
  St.
- bus 71 (Watertown Sq.-Harvard Sta.) to
  Mt. Auburn Bridge; turn up.Belmont St.
  two blocks

New England School of Law
154 Stuart St., Boston (617/451-0010),
www.nesl.edu
- from BOYLSTON (Green or Silver Line)
  walk S on Tremont St. one block, right
  on Stuart
- from NE MEDICAL CTR (Orange or
  Silver Line) exit to Tremont St., walk N
  one block, turn left on Stuart
- bus 43 (Ruggles-Park & Tremont Sts.)
  to Stuart St.

Newbury College
129 Fisher Ave., Brookline
(617/730-7000), www.newbury.edu
- from RESERVOIR (Green Line-D) take
  college shuttle van Mon-Fri during
  school year, or six-block walk, left upon
  exiting station onto Chestnut Hill Ave.,
  left again at first light (Clinton Rd.), then
  first right onto Fisher Ave., to top of hill

*Frequent bus routes in **bold***

Northeastern University
⊕ p. 34, 37; 360 Huntington Ave., Boston (617/437-2000), www.neu.edu
- NORTHEASTERN (Green Line-E)
- RUGGLES (Orange Line)
- bus 1 (Harvard-Dudley) to Huntington Ave.

North Shore Community College
Beverly
Cummings Center, Beverly (978/927-9374), www.northshore.edu
- CR Newburyport/Rockport Line to SALEM; take bus 451 (North Beverly-Salem Depot) to Cummings Center

Lynn
300 Broad St., Lynn
- CR Newburyport/Rockport Line to LYNN; exit to Market St., turn left to corner, cross Broad St.
- bus 426, 429, 431, 435, 436, 439, 441, 442, 455, 456, or 459 to Central Sq.; walk S on Union two blocks, cross Broad St.

(Franklin W.) Olin College of Engineering
1735 Great Plain Ave., Needham (781/292-2222), www.olin.edu
- CR Needham Line to HERSEY; walk SE on Great Plain Ave. 20min, to just across I-95

Perkins School for the Blind
175 N. Beacon St., Watertown (617/924-3434), www.perkins.org
- from CENTRAL (Red Line) take bus 70 (Cedarwood or Watertown Sq.-University Park) or 70A (N. Waltham-University Park)

Pine Manor College
400 Heath St., Chestnut Hill (617/731-7000), www.pmc.edu
- from CHESTNUT HILL (Green Line-D) take college shuttle bus
- bus 60 (Chestnut Hill-Kenmore) to Randolph Rd.; walk up Randolph to Heath St.

Providence College
549 River Ave., Providence, RI (401/865-1000), www.providence.edu
- Amtrak or CR Attleboro Line to PROVIDENCE; exit to Park Row and walk three blocks S on Exchange St. to Kennedy Plaza to take local RIPTA bus 50, as below, or exit to Gaspee St. and catch any RIPTA bus or trolley across the street to Kennedy Plaza to transfer to RIPTA bus 50, as below
- Bonanza Bus Lines to Kennedy Plaza; take local RIPTA bus 50 (Douglas Ave.) to Admiral St. & River Ave.

Quincy College
34 Coddington St., Quincy (617/984-1600), www.quincycollege.edu
- from QUINCY CTR (Red Line-Braintree) exit to Quincy St., turn up Washington St. one block to Coddington

Quinsigamond Community College
670 W. Boylston St., Worcester (508/853-2300), www.qcc.mass.edu
- CR Framingham/Worcester Line to WORCESTER; walk to City Hall Plaza (Main St. side) to take WRTA bus 19N (Burncoat) or 30N (Summit/W. Boylston/Holden) to college entrance
- Peter Pan Bus Lines to Worcester Bus Terminal; walk four blocks N on Southbridge and Main Sts. to City Hall Plaza, take local WRTA buses, as above

Regis College
235 Wellesley St., Weston (781/893-1820), www.regiscollege.edu
- from RIVERSIDE (Green Line-D) connect to daily shuttle (school year only, schedule 781/768-7135)

Rhode Island College
600 Mt. Pleasant Ave., Providence, RI (401/456-8000), www.ric.edu
- Amtrak or CR Attleboro Line to PROVIDENCE; exit to Park Row and walk three blocks S on Exchange St. to Kennedy Plaza to take local RIPTA bus 26 or 27, as below, or exit to Gaspee St. to take local RIPTA bus 56 (selected runs only—ask driver), or catch any RIPTA bus or trolley across the street to Kennedy Plaza to transfer to RIPTA bus 26 or 27, as below
- Bonanza Bus Lines to Kennedy Plaza; take local RIPTA bus 26 (Atwells-Academy-RI College), 27 (Broadway Manton), or 56 (Chalkstone-Mt. Pleasant, selected runs only—ask driver) to college entrance

Rhode Island School of Design

⊕ p. 48; 2 College St., Providence, RI
(401/454-6100), www.risd.edu

- Amtrak or CR Attleboro Line to
PROVIDENCE; exit to Park Row, three-
block walk SE, or exit to Gaspee St.
and catch any RIPTA bus or trolley
across the street to Kennedy Plaza to
transfer to Providence LINK Green Line
trolley, as below
- Bonanza Bus Lines to Kennedy Plaza;
three-block walk E, or take East Side-
bound Providence LINK Green Line
trolley to N. Main St.

Roxbury Community College

⊕ p. 37; 1234 Columbus Ave., Roxbury
(617/445-1927), www.rcc.mass.edu

- ROXBURY CROSSING (Orange Line)
- bus 41 (Centre & Eliot Sts.-JFK/UMass)
to Roxbury St.; walk W on Roxbury two
blocks

Saint John's Seminary

127 Lake St., Brighton (617/254-2610),
www.sjs.edu

- BOSTON COLLEGE (Green Line-B)

Salem State College

352 Lafayette St., Salem (978/741-6000),
www.salemstate.edu

- bus 455 (Salem-Haymarket) or 459
(Salem-Downtown)

School of the Museum of Fine Arts

⊕ p. 34; 230 The Fenway, Boston
(617/267-6100), www.smfa.edu

- from MUSEUM OF FINE ARTS (Green
Line-E) walk N on Museum Rd. one
block, turn left
- bus 8 (Harbor Pt./UMass-Kenmore)
or 47 (Central-Albany St.) to corner of
Ave. Louis Pasteur and the Fenway;
walk two blocks S
- bus **39** (Forest Hills-Back Bay) to
Ruggles St.; walk N on Louis Prang St.
one block, turn right

Simmons College

⊕ p. 34; 300 The Fenway, Boston
(617/521-2000), www.simmons.edu

Dormitories

- from FENWAY (Green Line-D) cross
Park Dr. & the Riverway
- bus 8, 47, 60, 65, CT2, or CT3 to Beth
Israel Hospital

Academic buildings

- from MUSEUM OF FINE ARTS (Green
Line-E) walk N on Louis Prang St.
(Texaco station at corner) two blocks
- bus 8 (Harbor Pt./UMass-Kenmore) or
47 (Central-Albany St.) to Ave. Louis
Pasteur & the Fenway
- bus 60 (Chestnut Hill-Kenmore) or 65
(Brighton Ctr.-Kenmore) to Brookline
Ave. & the Fenway
- bus CT2 (Sullivan-Ruggles) or CT3
(Beth Israel-Andrew) to Ave. Louis
Pasteur
- LMA Shuttle M2 (Cambridge-Harvard
Medical School)

Stonehill College

320 Washington St. (Rte. 138), Easton
(508/238-1081), www.stonehill.edu

- CR Middleborough/Lakeville Line to
BROCKTON; take BAT bus 9 (Pearl via
W. Elm & Torrey St.)

Suffolk University

⊕ p. 30; 41 Temple St., Boston
(617/573-8000), www.suffolk.edu

- from PARK STREET (Red or Green Line)
walk N one block to Beacon, turn right
and then left on Bowdoin one block to
back of State House, left on Derne St.,
right on Temple
- from BOWDOIN (Blue Line) walk W one
block on Cambridge St., turn left up
brick-paved Temple St.

Tufts University

Boston Ave., Medford (781/628-5000),
www.tufts.edu

- from DAVIS (Red Line) take Joseph
Transportation campus shuttle (from
plaza in front of Davis Square's
Somerville Theatre), or Medford-bound
bus 94 and 96 (see below), or walk
15min via College Ave.
- bus 80 (Arlington Ctr.-Lechmere), 94
(Medford Sq.-Davis), or 96 (Medford
Sq.-Harvard) to east campus entrance
on College Ave. or north edge of
campus on Boston Ave.
- bus 89 (Clarendon Hill-Sullivan Sq.)
to Powder House Square (edge of
campus athletic fields)

Medical School

136 Harrison Ave., Boston
(617/956-7000)
See "New England Medical Ctr." p. 86

UMass Boston and Kennedy Library (far right) set against the Boston skyline.

University of Massachusetts Boston (UMass Boston)
100 Morrissey Blvd., Dorchester
(617/287-5000), www.umb.edu
- from JFK/UMASS (Red Line) take daily UMass shuttle bus #1 (schedule: 617/287-5040)
- bus 8 (Harbor Pt./UMass-Kenmore)
- bus 16 (Forest Hills-UMass, *not* Forest Hills-Andrew), rush hours only

For John F. Kennedy Library and Museum, Commonwealth Museum, or Massachusetts Archives, take UMass shuttle bus #2 or walk from campus.

University of Massachusetts Dartmouth (UMass Dartmouth)
285 Old Westport Rd., N. Dartmouth
(508/999-8000), www.umassd.edu
- American Eagle commuter bus to New Bedford Transit Terminal; local SRTA bus 9 (New Bedford-Dartmouth)

University of Massachusetts Lowell (UMass Lowell)
North Campus
1 University Ave., Lowell (978/934-4000), www.uml.edu
- CR Lowell Line to LOWELL; take local LRTA Downtown Shuttle bus to downtown Transit Center, transfer to LRTA bus 11 (Pawtucketville)

South Campus
Broadway and Wilder St., Lowell
- CR Lowell Line to LOWELL; take local LRTA Downtown Shuttle bus to downtown Transit Center, transfer to LRTA bus 10 (UMass Lowell S.)

West Campus
Princeton Blvd., Lowell
- CR Lowell Line to LOWELL; take local LRTA bus NC (N. Chelmsford)

University of Massachusetts at Worcester
55 Lake Ave. N., Worcester
(508/856-0011), www.umassmed.edu
- CR Framingham/Worcester Line to WORCESTER; walk to City Hall Plaza (Main St. side) to take WRTA bus 12, 15, or 24, or to Front St. side to take WRTA bus 28 (Lakeshore)
- Peter Pan Bus Lines to Worcester Bus Terminal; walk four blocks N on Southbridge and Main Sts. to City Hall Plaza, take local WRTA buses, as above

University of Rhode Island, Providence (URI)
College of Continuing Education
⊕ p. 48; 80 Washington St., Providence, RI (401/277-5000), www.uri.edu
- Amtrak or CR Attleboro Line to PROVIDENCE; exit to Gaspee St. to take Providence LINK Gold Line trolley to Washington & Aborn Sts., walk back two blocks E; or exit to Park Row, six-block walk SW
- Bonanza Bus Lines to Kennedy Plaza; two-block walk W

Urban College of Boston
178 Tremont St., Boston (617/292-4723), www.urbancollegeofboston.org
- BOYLSTON (Green or Silver Line)
- from CHINATOWN (Orange or Silver Line) walk W on Boylston St. one block to Tremont, turn right

Wellesley College
106 Central St., Wellesley
(781/283-1000), www.wellesley.edu
- CR Framingham/Worcester Line to
  WELLESLEY SQ, 10min walk W
- Wellesley and MIT operate a bus
  between the schools for cross-
  registered students, Mon-Fri.
  Others from the Wellesley and MIT
  communities may ride if space is
  available (info: 617/253-1668).
- from HARVARD (Red Line),
  Massachusetts Institute of Technology
  (MIT), Mass. Ave. & Beacon St., or
  WOODLAND (Green Line-D) take
  G&W Transportation bus Fri night-Sun
  (schedule & tickets: 781/341-4447)

Wentworth Institute of Technology
⊕ p. 34, 37; 550 Huntington Ave.,
Boston (617/442-9010), www.wit.edu
- MUSEUM OF FINE ARTS (Green Line-E)
- RUGGLES (Orange Line)
- bus 8 (Harbor Pt./UMass-Kenmore),
  39 (Forest Hills-Back Bay), 47 (Central
  Sq.-Broadway), CT2 (Sullivan-Ruggles),
  or CT3 (Beth Israel-Andrew) to Ruggles
  St. & Huntington Ave.

Weston Jesuit School of Theology
⊕ p. 40; 3 Phillips Place, Cambridge
(617/492-1960), www.wjst.edu
- HARVARD (Red Line)
- bus 72, 74, or 78 to Garden St.; walk S
  on Garden to corner of Mason St., turn
  right, one block

Wheaton College
26 E. Main St., Norton (508/286-7722),
www.wheatonma.edu
- CR Attleboro Line to ATTLEBORO;
  take GATRA bus 18 (Attleboro-Norton-
  Taunton), Mon-Sat
- CR Attleboro Line to MANSFIELD; take
  GATRA bus (Norton-Mansfield Rte.
  140), Mon-Fri
- Wheaton College shuttle bus from
  Copley Sq., Boston, Fri. night and Sat.
  afternoon (info: 508/286-3816)

Wheelock College
⊕ p. 34; 200 The Riverway, Boston
(617/734-5200), www.wheelock.edu
- FENWAY or LONGWOOD (Green Line-D)

- bus 8, 47, 60, 65, CT2, or CT3 to Beth
  Israel Hospital

Women's Educational and Industrial Union
356 Boylston St., Boston (617/536-5651),
www.weiu.org
- from ARLINGTON (Green Line) walk W
  on Boylston 50yds
- bus **9** (City Pt.-Copley Sq.) or 55 (Jersey
  & Queensberry Sts.-Park & Tremont
  Sts.) to Arlington & Boylston Sts.
- bus 10 (City Point-Copley Sq.) to Copley
  Sq.; walk E on Boylston three blocks
- bus **39** (Forest Hills-Back Bay) to
  Clarendon & Boylston Sts.; walk E on
  Boylston two blocks

Worcester Polytechnic Institute
100 Institute Rd., Worcester
(508/831-5000). www.wpi.edu
- CR Framingham/Worcester Line to
  WORCESTER; walk to City Hall Plaza
  (Main St. side) to take WRTA bus
  6N (Holden/Ararat), or to Front St.
  side to take WRTA bus 21 (Highland/
  Assumption College) or CC3 (College
  Consortium Route—only during school
  year), or continue two blocks N on
  Main to Foster St. to take WRTA bus
  5W (June/Mill) or 32 (Holden/Jefferson)
- Peter Pan Bus Lines to Worcester Bus
  Terminal; take WRTA bus CC3 (College
  Consortium Route—only during
  school year), or walk four blocks N on
  Southbridge and Main Sts. to City Hall
  Plaza, take other local WRTA buses, as
  above

Worcester State College
486 Chandler St., Worcester
(508/793-8000), www.worcester.edu
- CR Framingham/Worcester Line to
  WORCESTER; walk to City Hall Plaza
  (Franklin St. side) to take WRTA bus 6S
  (Chandler), or continue two blocks N
  on Main to Foster St. to take WRTA bus
  5W (June/Mill)
- Peter Pan Bus Lines to Worcester Bus
  Terminal; take WRTA bus CC3 (College
  Consortium Route—only during
  school year), or walk four blocks N on
  Southbridge and Main Sts. to City Hall
  Plaza, take other local WRTA buses, as
  above

Convention Centers and Meeting Halls

Bayside Exposition Center
200 Mt. Vernon St., Dorchester
(617/825-5151), www.baysidexpo.com
• from JFK/UMASS (Red Line) three-block walk
• bus 8 (Harbor Pt./UMass-Kenmore)
• Special shuttle bus from JFK/UMASS to some events

Dunkin' Donuts Center
🜨 p. 48; 1 LaSalle Sq., Providence, RI
(401/331-6700), www.provcc.com
• Amtrak or CR Attleboro Line to PROVIDENCE; exit to Park Row, four-block walk SW, or exit to Gaspee St. to take Providence LINK Gold Line trolley to Kennedy Plaza, transfer to local RIPTA buses listed below
• Bonanza Bus Lines to Kennedy Plaza; three-block walk W or take local RIPTA bus 26 (Atwells-Academy-RI College), 27 (Broadway-Manton), 28 (Broadway-Hartford), or Providence LINK Green Line trolley to entrance

Exchange Conference Center
1 Fish Pier (Northern Ave.), South Boston (617/790-1900)
• from SOUTH STA (Red Line or CR) take free Boston Coach shuttle bus (6am-8pm weekdays) to World Trade Center (WTC), then SE to adjacent pier; or walk 15min SE on Summer St. to Viaduct, turn left two blocks to WTC, as above
• bus **7** (City Point-Otis & Summer Sts.) to WTC, walk S as above
• Inner Harbor Ferry from Lovejoy Wharf to WTC, walk S as above

Hynes Convention Center
🜨 p. 27; 900 Boylston St., Boston
(617/954-2000), www.mccahome.com
• HYNES/ICA (Green Line-B, C, or D)

Park Plaza Castle
Arlington St., Boston (617/426-2000)
• from ARLINGTON (Green Line) walk two blocks S on Arlington St.

Providence Civic Center
See "Dunkin' Donuts Center"

Rhode Island Convention Center
🜨 p. 48; 1 Sabin St., Providence, RI
(401/458-6000), www.riconvention.com
• Amtrak or CR Attleboro Line to PROVIDENCE; exit to Park Row, three-block walk SW, or exit to Gaspee St. to take Providence LINK Gold Line trolley to the Westin Hotel
• Bonanza Bus Lines to Kennedy Plaza; two-block walk W or take local RIPTA bus 26 (Atwells-Academy-RI College), 27 (Broadway-Manton), 28 (Broadway-Hartford), or Providence LINK Green Line trolley to entrance

Worcester Centrum Centre
🜨 p. 52; 50 Foster St., Worcester
(508/755-6800)
• CR Framingham/Worcester Line to WORCESTER; cross street to parking garage, walk 5min N
• Peter Pan Bus Lines to Worcester Bus Terminal; 10min walk N

World Trade Center
Commonwealth Pier, 164 Northern Ave., Boston (617/385-5000), www.wtcb.com
• from SOUTH STA (Red Line) take free Boston Coach shuttle bus (6am-8pm weekdays), or walk 15min S on Summer St. to Viaduct, turn left
• bus 3, 4, 6, **7**, 448, 449, or 459
• Inner Harbor Ferry from Lovejoy Wharf to World Trade Center

Government Buildings

Boston City Hall
🜨 p. 31; 1 City Hall Plaza
(617/635-4000), www.cityofboston.com
• GOVERNMENT CTR (Green or Blue Line)

Brookline Town Hall
🜨 p. 38; 333 Washington St., Brookline
(617/730-2000)
• BROOKLINE VILLAGE (Green Line-D)

Cambridge City Hall
⊕ p. 42; 795 Mass. Ave., Cambridge
(617/349-4000)
• CENTRAL (Red Line)
• bus **1** (Harvard-Dudley)

Internal Revenue Service
See "John F. Kennedy Federal Bldg."

John Adams Courthouse
Pemberton Square, Boston (617/725-8787)
• GOVERNMENT CTR (Green or Blue Line)

John F. Kennedy Federal Bldg.
⊕ p. 31; Cambridge St., Boston
• GOVERNMENT CTR (Green or Blue Line)

John Joseph Moakley Courthouse
See "U.S. Courthouse"

Mass. Civil Service Commission
1 Ashburton Pl., Boston (617/727-8371,
or -3777 for exam information)
• GOVERNMENT CTR (Green or Blue Line)

Mass. Commission for the Blind
88 Kingston St., Boston (800/392-6450
or 617/727-5550)
• CHINATOWN (Orange or Silver Line)
• DOWNTOWN CROSSING (Red, Orange,
or Silver Line)
• bus **11** (City Point-Downtown)

Mass. Department of Revenue
51 Sleeper St., Boston (800-392-6089 or
617/887-6367)
• from SOUTH STA (Red Line or CR)
walk three blocks NE via Congress St.
Bridge, past the Children's Museum

Massachusetts Division of Employment and Training
Charles F. Hurley Bldg., 19 Staniford St.,
Boston (617/727-6560)
• GOVERNMENT CTR (Green or Blue Line)
• NORTH STA (Green, Orange Line or CR)

Massachusetts State House
⊕ p. 30; Beacon St., Boston
(617/727-3676), www.mass.gov/sec/trs
• from PARK STREET (Red or Green Line)
walk N one block
• from BOWDOIN (Blue Line) walk S up
Bowdoin St. two blocks

Mass. State Office of Minority & Women's Business Assistance
10 Park Plaza, Boston (617/727-8692)
• ARLINGTON (Green Line)

Middlesex County Courthouse
*Family, Housing, Juvenile, and
Superior Courts; Cambridge Jail*
40 Thorndike St., Cambridge
(617/494-4000)
• from LECHMERE (Green Line) walk
one block S on First St., turn right on
Thorndike, two blocks

Moakley Courthouse
See "U.S. Courthouse"

Newton City Hall
1000 Commonwealth Ave., Newton
(617/796-1200), www.ci.newton.ma.us
• from RIVERSIDE (Green Line-D)
or AUBURNDALE (CR Worcester/
Framingham Line) take local Newton
Nexus bus 1

Old Middlesex County Courthouse
Probate Court, Registry of Deeds
208 Cambridge St., Cambridge
(617/494-4500)
• from LECHMERE (Green Line) two-
block walk W on Cambridge St.

Old Suffolk County Courthouse
See "John Adams Courthouse"

Registry of Motor Vehicles
All offices (800/858-3926 or
617/351-4500), www.mass.gov/rmv

Beverly
176 Cabot St.
• bus 451 (North Beverly-Salem Depot)
to Wallis St.

Boston
630 Washington St.
• CHINATOWN (Orange or Silver Line)

Cambridge
Galleria Mall, 100 CambridgeSide Pl.
• LECHMERE (Green Line)

Melrose
40 Washington St.
• OAK GROVE (Orange Line) walk N on
Washington 10min or take bus 132
(Redstone Shopping Ctr.-Malden Ctr.)

*Frequent bus routes in **bold***

Quincy
76 Ross Way (behind Hancock St.)
• from QUINCY CTR (Red Line-Braintree) walk 5min S on Hancock St., turn right to rear buildings

Roslindale
8 Cummins Hwy.
• CR Needham Line to ROSLINDALE VILLAGE; walk SE on South St. two blocks to Roslindale Sq.
• bus 14, 30, 34, 34E, 35, 36, 37, 40, or 50 to Roslindale Sq.

Watertown
Watertown Mall, 550 Arsenal St.
• from CENTRAL (Red Line) take bus 70 (Cedarwood or Watertown Sq.-Univ. Park) or 70A (N. Waltham-Univ. Park)

Social Security Administration
All offices (800/772-1213), www.ssa.gov

Boston
See "Thomas P. O'Neill Federal Bldg."

Brookline
209 Harvard St.
• COOLIDGE CORNER (Green Line-C)
• bus **66** (Harvard-Dudley) to Coolidge Corner

Chelsea
80 Everett Ave.
• from WOOD ISLAND (Blue Line) or WELLINGTON (Orange Line) take bus 112 (Wellington-Wood Island) to Everett St. & Revere Beach Pkwy.

Dorchester
540 Gallivan Blvd.
• from ASHMONT (Red Line-Ashmont) take bus 215 (Quincy Ctr.-Ashmont) to Gallivan & Granite Ave., short walk E
• from FIELDS CORNER (Red Line-Ashmont) take bus 20 (Fields Corner)

Roslindale
4200 Washington St.
• CR Needham Line to ROSLINDALE VILLAGE; walk SE on South St. two blocks to Roslindale Sq.
• bus 14, 30, 34, 34E, 35, 36, 37, 40, or 50 to Roslindale Sq.

Roxbury
⊕ p. 37; 10 Malcolm X Blvd.
• DUDLEY STA (Silver Line)

Somerville
⊕ p. 43; Marks Bldg., 240 Elm St.
• DAVIS (Red Line)

Somerville City Hall
93 Highland Ave., Somerville (617/625-6600)
• from LECHMERE (Green Line) take bus 88 (Clarendon Hill-Lechmere) to City Hall/High School
• from WELLINGTON or SULLIVAN (Orange Line) take bus 90 (Davis Sq.-Wellington) to City Hall/High School
• from DAVIS (Red Line) take bus 88 (Clarendon Hill-Lechmere) or 90 (Davis Sq.-Wellington) to City Hall/High School

Suffolk County Courthouse
Family, Housing, Juvenile, Probate, and Superior Courts; Registry of Deeds
⊕ p. 31; New Chardon St., Boston (617/788-8000)
• NORTH STA (Green or Orange Line or CR)
• HAYMARKET (Green or Orange Line)

Thomas P. O'Neill Federal Bldg.
⊕ p. 29; 10 Causeway St., Boston
• NORTH STA (Green or Orange Line or CR)
• Inner Harbor ferries from Charlestown Navy Yard or World Trade Center to Lovejoy Wharf; walk S to corner of Causeway St., turn right, two blocks

U.S. Courthouse
Court of Appeals, Massachusetts District Court
⊕ p. 31; Fan Pier, 12 Northern Ave., South Boston (617/261-2440)
• from SOUTH STA (Red Line or CR) walk 10 min NE
• bus 4 (North Station-World Trade Center) or **7** (City Pt.-Downtown) to courthouse
• Inner Harbor Ferry F5 (Lovejoy Wharf-Fan Pier)

U.S. Passport Agency
See "Thomas P. O'Neill Federal Bldg."

U.S. Post Office
24-hour General Mail Facility
25 Dorchester Av., Boston (617/654-5327)
• SOUTH STA (Red Line or CR)

Hospitals

Angell Memorial Animal Hospital
350 S. Huntington Ave., Jamaica Plain (617/522-7282)
• bus 39 (Forest Hills-Back Bay) to Perkins St. (Call the MBTA for current pet policy)

Beth Israel Deaconess Medical Center
East Campus
⊕ p. 34; 330 Brookline Ave., Boston (617/667-7000)
• LONGWOOD (Green Line-D)
• bus 8, 47, 60, 65, CT2, or CT3 to Beth Israel Hospital
• LMA Shuttle M2 (Cambridge-Harvard Medical School)
West Campus
⊕ p. 34; 185 Pilgrim Rd., Boston (617/752-2200)
• LONGWOOD (Green Line-D)
• bus 8 (Harbor Pt./UMass-Kenmore) or 47 (Central-Broadway) to Longwood and Brookline Ave.
• bus 60 (Chestnut Hill-Kenmore) or 65 (Brighton Ctr.-Kenmore) to Deaconess Rd.
• bus CT2 (Sullivan-Ruggles) or CT3 (Beth Israel-Andrew) to Beth Israel Hospital
• LMA Shuttle M2 (Cambridge-Harvard Medical School)

Boston Medical Center
One Boston Medical Center Pl., Boston (617/638-8000)
• from MASSACHUSETTS AVE (Silver Line) walk SE on Mass. Ave. one block
• bus 1 (Harvard-Dudley) to Mass. Ave. & Harrison Ave.
• bus 8, 10, 47, CT1, or CT3 to any of several stops around the Center

Brigham and Women's Hospital
⊕ p. 34; 75 Francis St., Boston (617/732-5500)
• BRIGHAM CIR (Green Line-E)
• bus **39,** 60, 65, or **66** to Francis St.
• LMA Shuttle M2 (Cambridge-Harvard Medical School)

Ambulatory Care Center
850 Boylston St., Chestnut Hill (617/278-0880)
• bus 60 (Chestnut Hill-Kenmore) to Eliot St.

Cambridge Health Alliance
See "Cambridge Hospital," "Somerville Hospital," and "Whidden Mem. Hospital"

Cambridge Hospital
1493 Cambridge St., Cambridge (617/498-1000)
• bus 69 (Harvard-Lechmere)
• bus 83 (Rindge Ave.-Central) to Beacon & Cooney Sts.; one-block walk

Carney Hospital
2100 Dorchester Ave., Dorchester (617/296-4000)
• from FOREST HILLS (Orange Line) take bus 21 (Ashmont-Forest Hills) to Gallivan Blvd. & Dorchester Ave., turn right on Dorchester, two blocks
• from ASHMONT (Red Line-Ashmont) take bus 27, 217, or 240 to hospital entrance, or walk 10min S on Dorchester Ave.
• bus 215 (Quincy Ctr.-Ashmont) to Gallivan Blvd. & Dorchester Ave., turn S on Dorchester, two blocks

Children's Hospital
⊕ p. 34; 300 Longwood Ave., Boston (617/335-6000)
• LONGWOOD (Green Line-D)
• LONGWOOD/HOSPITALS (Green Line-E)
• bus 8, 47, CT2, or CT3 to Children's Hospital
• bus 60 (Chestnut Hill-Kenmore) or 65 (Brighton Ctr.-Kenmore) to Longwood and Brookline Ave.
• LMA Shuttle M2 (Cambridge-Harvard Medical School)

Dana-Farber Cancer Institute
⊕ p. 34; 44 Binney St., Boston (617/632-3000)
• LONGWOOD (Green Line-D)
• bus 8 (Harbor Pt./UMass-Kenmore) or 47 (Central-Broadway) to Longwood and Brookline Ave.
• bus 60 (Chestnut Hill-Kenmore) or 65 (Brighton Ctr.-Kenmore) to Deaconess

*Frequent bus routes in **bold***

Rd.
- bus CT2 (Sullivan-Ruggles) or CT3 (Beth Israel-Andrew) to Beth Israel Hospital
- LMA Shuttle M2 (Cambridge-Harvard Medical School)

Deaconess-Glover Hospital
148 Chestnut St., Needham (781/453-3000)
- CR Needham Line to NEEDHAM JCT or NEEDHAM CTR; walk 5min S (from NEEDHAM CTR) or 10min N (from NEEDHAM JCT) on Chestnut St.
- bus 59 (Needham Jct.-Watertown)

Deaconess-Waltham Hospital
Hope Ave., Waltham (781/647-6000)
- from DOWNTOWN CROSSING (Red, Orange, or Silver Line) walk two blocks SE to Otis St. to take bus 553 (Roberts-Downtown Boston)
- CR Fitchburg/South Acton Line to WALTHAM; walk 15min, or take bus 553 (Roberts)
- bus 70 (Cedarwood or Watertown Sq.-University Park) to Main & South Sts.; walk S on South St. to Hope Ave. 10min
- local Waltham CitiBus 17

Faulkner Hospital
1153 Centre St., Jamaica Plain (617/983-7000)
- bus 38 (Wren St.-Forest Hills)

The Fernald Center (Mass. Dept. of Mental Retardation)
200 Trapelo Rd., Waltham (781/894-3600)
- from ALEWIFE (Red Line) connect Mon-Fri to Fernald shuttle bus (schedule: 781/894-3600 x2175)
- CR Fitchburg/South Acton Line or bus 73 (Waverley-Harvard) or 554 (Waverley-Downtown) to WAVERLEY; take local Waltham CitiBus 14 (Waltham Center-Waverley Sq.) to Trapelo Rd. entrance, or take Fernald shuttle bus, as above

Franciscan Children's Hospital and Rehabilitation Center
30 Warren St., Brighton (617/254-3800)
- from WARREN ST (Green Line-B) two-block walk
- bus 57 (Watertown-Kenmore) to Warren St.; one-block walk

Hallmark Health System
See "Lawrence Memorial Hospital," "Malden Hospital," "Melrose-Wakefield Hospital," or "Whidden Mem. Hospital"

Hebrew Rehabilitation Center for the Aged
1200 Centre St., Roslindale (617/325-8000)
- bus 38 (Wren St.-Forest Hills)

Jewish Memorial Hospital & Rehabilitation Center
59 Townsend St., Roxbury (617/442-8760)
- bus 42 (Forest Hills-Ruggles) to Townsend St.

Joslin Diabetes Center
⊕ p. 34; 1 Joslin Pl. (off 437 Brookline Ave.), Boston (617/732-2400)
- LONGWOOD (Green Line-D)
- bus 8 (Harbor Pt./UMass-Kenmore) or 47 (Central-Broadway) to Longwood and Brookline Ave.
- bus 60 (Chestnut Hill-Kenmore) or 65 (Brighton Ctr.-Kenmore) to Deaconess Rd.
- bus CT2 (Sullivan-Ruggles) or CT3 (Beth Israel-Andrew) to Beth Israel Hospital
- LMA Shuttle M2 (Cambridge-Harvard Medical School)

Kindred Hospital Boston
1515 Commonwealth Ave., Brighton (617/254-1100)
- WASHINGTON ST (Green Line-B)
- bus 65 (Brighton Ctr.-Kenmore)

Lahey Clinic at Arlington
39 Hospital Rd., Arlington (781/646-1500)
- bus 67 (Turkey Hill-Alewife) to Hospital Rd.
- bus 77 (Arlington Hts.-Harvard) to Brattle St.; walk 10min up hill

Lahey Clinic
Medical Center
41 Mall Rd., Burlington (781/273-5100)
- from HAYMARKET (Green or Orange Line) take bus 353 (Burlington Industrial Area-Haymarket)
- from ALEWIFE (Red Line) take bus 350 (Burlington-Alewife)

Northshore clinic
One Essex Center Dr., Peabody

(978/538-4000)

- CR Newburyport/Rockport Line to LYNN; take bus 435 (Liberty Tree Mall-Central Sq., Lynn) or 436 (Liberty Tree Mall-Central Sq., Lynn) to North Shore Shopping Center, clinic is at S edge
- CR Newburyport/Rockport Line to SALEM; take bus 465 (Salem Depot-Liberty Tree Mall) to North Shore Shopping Center, as above

Lawrence Memorial Hospital
170 Governors Ave., Medford (781/306-6000)

- bus 95 (West Medford-Sullivan Sq.), 101 (Malden Center-Sullivan Sq.), 134 (N. Woburn-Wellington), or 326 (W. Medford-Haymarket) to Medford Sq., transfer to A&A Metro Transportation bus 710 (North Medford) to hospital

Lemuel Shattuck Hospital
170 Morton St., Jamaica Plain (617/522-8110)

- from FOREST HILLS (Orange Line) 10min walk
- bus 21 (Ashmont-Forest Hills) or **31** (Mattapan-Forest Hills)

Malden Hospital
100 Hospital Rd., Malden (781/338-7575)

- from WELLINGTON (Orange Line) take bus 99 (Boston Regional Medical. Ctr.-Wellington)

Mass. Eye and Ear Infirmary
243 Charles St., Boston (617/523-7900)
- CHARLES/MGH (Red Line)

Mass. General Hospital (MGH)
32 Fruit St., Boston (617/726-2000)
- CHARLES/MGH (Red Line)

McLean Hospital
115 Mill St., Belmont (617/855-2000)

- CR Fitchburg/South Acton Line to WAVERLEY; take free shuttle (schedule 617/855-2121)
- bus **73** (Waverley-Harvard) or 554 (Waverley-Newton Corner) to Waverley Sq.; transfer to shuttle as above

Hospital is 5min walk up a steep hill from Waverley Sq. Do not follow the signs "To McLean Hospital"; this is the considerably longer auto route.

Melrose-Wakefield Hospital
585 Lebanon St., Melrose (781/979-3000)

- CR Haverhill/Reading Line to MELROSE/CEDAR PARK; 10min
- bus 106 (some trips), 131, or 136/137

Milton Hospital
92 Highland St., Milton (617/696-4600)

- from ASHMONT (Red Line-Ashmont) take bus 240 (Avon Line or Holbrook/Randolph Commuter Rail Sta.-Ashmont) to hospital entrance
- from MATTAPAN (Red Line-Mattapan) or QUINCY CTR (Red Line-Braintree) take bus 245 (Quincy Center-Mattapan) to hospital entrance (Mon-Fri only)

Mount Auburn Hospital
330 Mt. Auburn St., Cambridge (617/492-3500)

- bus **71** (Watertown-Harvard) or **73** (Waverley-Harvard)

New England Baptist Hospital
125 Parker Hill Ave., Roxbury (617/754-5800)

- from BRIGHAM CIR (Green Line-E) take Mission Hill Link bus to entrance
- from MISSION PARK (Green Line-E) walk up Parker Hill Ave. (very steep)
- bus **39** (Forest Hills-Back Bay) or **66** (Harvard-Dudley) to Parker Hill Ave.
- from ROXBURY CROSSING (Orange Line) take Mission Hill Link bus (rush hour service only) to entrance

New England Medical Center
750 Washington St., Boston (617/956-5000)

- NE MEDICAL CTR (Orange or Silver Line)
- from BOYLSTON (Green or Silver Line) four-block walk
- bus **11** (City Pt.-Downtown) or **43** (Ruggles-Park St.)

New England Rehabilitation Hospital
2 Rehabilitation Way, Woburn (781/935-5050)

- bus 350 (Burlington-Alewife)

Newton-Wellesley Hospital
2014 Washington St., Newton Lower Falls (617/243-6000)

- WOODLAND (Green Line-D)

*Frequent bus routes in **bold***

Quincy Medical Center
114 Whitwell St., Quincy (617/773-6100)
• from QUINCY CTR (Red Line-Braintree) exit to Burgin Pkwy to take free QMC shuttle bus (Mon-Fri, 617/773-6100)
• bus 245 (Quincy Ctr.-Mattapan) Mon-Sat (see bus 215 for Sun)

Rogers Memorial Veterans Hospital
200 Springs Rd., Bedford (781/275-7500)
• from ALEWIFE (Red Line) take bus 62 (Bedford V.A.-Alewife), before 7pm only

St. Elizabeth's Medical Center
736 Cambridge St., Brighton (617/789-3000)
• from KENMORE (Green Line-B, C, or D) take bus 57 (Watertown-Kenmore) or 65 (Brighton Ctr.-Kenmore)
• bus 86 (Sullivan-Cleveland Circle) to Brighton Ctr.; three-block walk E on Washington St.
• express bus 501 (Downtown Boston-Brighton Ctr.)

Sancta Maria Nursing Facility
799 Concord Ave., Cambridge (617/868-2200)
• bus 74/75 (Belmont Ctr.-Harvard Sta.), trips "via Concord Ave." only
• bus 78 (Park Cir.-Harvard Sta.)

Shriners Burns Institute and Hospital for Crippled Children
51 Blossom St., Boston (617/722-3000)
• CHARLES/MGH (Red Line)

Somerville Hospital
230 Highland Ave., Somerville (617/666-4400)
• bus 88 (Clarendon Hill-Lechmere) or 90 (Davis-Wellington)

Spaulding Rehabilitation Hospital
125 Nashua St., Boston (617/573-7000)
• SCIENCE PARK (Green Line)
• NORTH STA (Green or Orange Line or CR)

Tufts-New England Medical Ctr.
See "New England Medical Center"

Union Hospital
500 Lynnfield St., Lynn (781/581-9200)
• bus 434 (Peabody Sq.-Haymarket) or 436 (Liberty Tree Mall-Central Sq., Lynn)

Veterans Administration Clinic
251 Causeway St., Boston (617/248-1010)
• NORTH STA (Green or Orange Line or CR)

Veterans Administration Medical Center
150 S. Huntington Ave., Jamaica Plain (617/232-9500)
• HEATH ST (Green Line-E)
• bus 39 (Forest Hills-Back Bay)
• bus 14 (Roslindale-Heath St.)

Veterans Administration Hospital
1400 V.F.W. Parkway, West Roxbury (617/323-7700)
• from FOREST HILLS (Orange Line) take bus 36 (Charles River Loop or VA Hospital-Forest Hills)

Whidden Memorial Hospital
103 Garland St., Everett (617/389-6270)
• bus 110 (Wonderland-Wellington) to Woodlawn St.; 10min walk via Woodlawn St., left on Garland St.

Winthrop Community Health Center
495 Pleasant St., Winthrop (617/539-5000)
• from ORIENT HEIGHTS (Blue Line) take Paul Revere bus 712 (Point Shirley-Orient Heights via Highlands) or Paul Revere bus 713 (Point Shirley-Orient Heights via Center) to Main & Pleasant Sts.

Youville LifeCare
1575 Cambridge St., Cambridge (617/876-4344)
• bus 69 (Harvard-Lechmere)

Libraries and Archives

American Antiquarian Society
185 Salisbury St., Worcester
(508/755-5221)
www.americanantiquarian.org
- CR Framingham/Worcester Line to WORCESTER; walk to City Hall Plaza (Main St. side) to take WRTA bus 6N (Holden/Ararat), or continue two blocks N on Main to Foster St. to take WRTA bus 32 (Holden/Jefferson)
- Peter Pan Bus Lines to Worcester Bus Terminal; walk four blocks N on Southbridge and Main Sts. to City Hall Plaza, take local WRTA buses, as above

American Jewish Historical Society
160 Herrick Rd., Hebrew College, Newton (617/559-8880), www.ajhs.org
See "Hebrew College," p. 74

Armenian Library and Museum of America
65 Main St., Watertown (617/926-2562), www.almainc.org
- bus 59, 70, 70A, or **71** to Watertown Sq.; walk NW on Main St. one block
- bus 52, **57**, 502, or 504 to Watertown Yard; cross Charles River then left on Main St. one block

Boston Athenæum
10½ Beacon St., Boston (617/227-0270), www.bostonathenaeum.org
- from BOWDOIN (Blue Line) two-block walk S up Bowdoin St., cross Beacon
- from PARK STREET (Red or Green Line) walk N one block to Beacon, turn right

Boston Public Library
⊕ p. 27; 700 Boylston St., Boston (617/536-5400), www.bpl.org
- COPLEY (Green Line)
- from BACK BAY STA (Orange Line) walk N on Dartmouth St. two blocks

The Bostonian Society
15 State St., 3rd floor, Boston (617/720-3285 x12), www.bostonhistory.org
- STATE (Orange or Blue Line)

French Library & Cultural Center
53 Marlborough St., Boston
(617/266-4351)

- from ARLINGTON (Green Line) walk N on Arlington St. three blocks, turn left on Marlborough, two blocks

Goethe-Institut inter Nationes
170 Beacon St., Boston (617/262-6050), www.goethe.de/boston
- from COPLEY or ARLINGTON (Green Line) walk N four blocks to Beacon St. then right (from Copley) or left (from Arlington) 1.5 blocks

John F. Kennedy Library
Columbia Point, Dorchester (617/929-4523), www.cs.umb.edu/jfklibrary
See "University of Mass., Boston," p. 79

Mary Baker Eddy Library
See "Christian Science Center," p. 54

Massachusetts Archives
220 Morrissey Blvd., Dorchester (617/727-2816), www.mass.gov/sec/arc
See "University of Mass., Boston," p. 79

Massachusetts Historical Society
1154 Boylston St., Boston
(617/536-1608)
- from HYNES /ICA (Green Line-B, C, or D) walk S to corner, turn right on Boylston, two blocks

National Archives—New England Region
380 Trapelo Rd., Waltham (781/536-5740)
- CR Fitchburg/South Acton Line or bus **73** (Waverley-Harvard) or 554 (Waverley-Downtown) to WAVERLEY; take local Waltham CitiBus 14 (Waltham Center-Waverley Sq.)

New England Historical Genealogical Society
101 Newbury St., Boston (617/536-5740), www.newenglandancestors.org
- from COPLEY (Green Line) walk N on Dartmouth St. one block, turn right on Newbury just over one block
- from BACK BAY STA (Orange Line) exit to Clarendon St., turn left, walk four blocks, turn right on Newbury
- bus **9, 39,** or 55 to Clarendon St. & Boylston Ave.; walk N on Clarendon one block, turn right on Newbury

Shopping Centers

The Arsenal Marketplace
485 Arsenal St., Watertown
- from CENTRAL (Red Line) take bus 70 (Cedarwood or Watertown Sq.-Univ. Park) or 70A (N. Waltham-Univ. Park)

Assembly Square Mall
133 Middlesex Ave., Somerville
- from SULLIVAN (Orange Line) take bus 95 (W. Medford-Sullivan)
- from DAVIS (Red Line) take bus 90 (Davis-Wellington)
- bus 92 (Assembly Sq.-Downtown)

The Atrium
Boylston St. (Rte. 9), Newton
- from CHESTNUT HILL (Green Line-D) walk S on Hammond St. and right on Boylston St. (10min)
- bus 60 (Chestnut Hill-Kenmore)

Burlington Mall
Rte. 128 & Middlesex Tpk., Burlington
- from ALEWIFE (Red Line) take bus 350 (Burlington-Alewife)
- bus 62 (Bedford V.A. Hospital-Alewife) or 76 (Hanscom AFB-Alewife) to Depot Sq.; transfer to Lexpress bus 5 (Depot Sq.-Malls)

CambridgeSide Galleria
First St., Cambridge
- LECHMERE (Green Line)
- from KENDALL/MIT (Red Line) take free shuttle bus (The Wave)
- bus 64 (Oak Sq.-Kendall/MIT, *not* Oak Sq.-University Park) to KENDALL/MIT; take free shuttle as above

Chestnut Hill Shopping Center
27 Boylston St. (Rte. 9), Newton
- from CHESTNUT HILL (Green Line-D) walk S on Hammond St. and right on Boylston St. (10min)
- bus 60 (Chestnut Hill-Kenmore)

The Mall at Chestnut Hill
199 Boylston St. (Rte. 9), Newton
- bus 60 (Chestnut Hill-Kenmore) to end of line at Hammond Pond Pkwy.; 1.5-block walk, stairs to parking on right

Copley Place
⊕ p. 27; 100 Huntington Ave., Boston
- COPLEY (Green Line)
- BACK BAY STA (Orange Line)
- bus **9**, 10, **39**, 55, or 502 to Copley Sq.

Dedham Mall
300 V.F.W. Pkwy. (Rte. 1), Dedham
- from FOREST HILLS (Orange Line) take bus 34E (Walpole Ctr.-Forest Hills) or 35 (Dedham Mall-Forest Hills)
- bus 52 (Dedham Mall-Watertown)

Dedham Plaza
725 Providence Hwy. (Rte. 1), Dedham
- bus 34E (Walpole Ctr.-Forest Hills). Bus stops at back entrance to plaza

Downtown Crossing
⊕ p. 31; Summer and Washington Sts., Boston
- STATE (Orange or Blue Line)
- PARK STREET (Red or Green Line)
- DOWNTOWN CROSSING (Red, Orange, or Silver Line)

Endicott Plaza
Endicott St., Danvers
- CR Newburyport/Rockport Line to SALEM; take bus 465 (Salem Depot-Liberty Tree Mall) to mall entrance

Faneuil Hall Marketplace
⊕ p. 31; Congress St., Boston
- from AQUARIUM (Blue Line) exit to State St., head W away from harbor, turn right at next corner
- from GOVERNMENT CTR (Green or Blue Line) walk E past City Hall
- from STATE (Orange or Blue Line) walk N on New Congress St.
- from HAYMARKET (Green or Orange Line) walk S

Fresh Pond Mall
186 Alewife Brook Pkwy., Cambridge
- from ALEWIFE (Red Line) 5min walk
- from HARVARD (Red Line) take bus 74 (Belmont Ctr.-Harvard), trips "via Concord Ave." only, or 78 (Arlmont-Harvard)

Liberty Tree Mall
Independence Way, Danvers
- CR Newburyport/Rockport Line to LYNN; take bus 435 (Liberty Tree Mall-Central Sq., Lynn) or 436 (Liberty Tree Mall-Central Sq., Lynn)
- CR Newburyport/Rockport Line to SALEM; take bus 465 (Salem Depot-Liberty Tree Mall)

Marketplace Center
200 State St., Boston
- from AQUARIUM (Blue Line) exit to State St., head W away from harbor, turn right at next corner
- from GOVERNMENT CTR (Green or Blue Line) walk E past City Hall and through Faneuil Hall Marketplace to far end
- from STATE (Orange or Blue Line) walk E on State three blocks, turn left on Commercial St.
- from HAYMARKET (Green or Orange Line) walk S on New Congress St., turn left through Faneuil Hall Marketplace to far end

Meadow Glen Mall
3850 Mystic Valley Pkwy., Medford
- from WELLINGTON (Orange Line) take bus 134 (N. Woburn-Wellington) to Locust St.; two-block walk
- bus 94, 95, 96, 101, 134, or 325 to Medford Sq., transfer to A&A Metro bus 710 (Meadow Glen Mall)

Mystic Mall
166 Everett Ave., Chelsea
- from WOOD ISLAND (Blue Line) or WELLINGTON (Orange Line) take bus 112 (Wellington-Wood Island)
- CR Newburyport/Rockport Line to CHELSEA; exit to Sixth & Arlington Sts., walk SW on Arlington to Fourth St., turn right one block and cross Everett Ave.

Natick Mall
1245 Worcester St. (Rte. 9), Natick
- CR Framingham/Worcester Line to FRAMINGHAM; walk E to Concord St. to take local LIFT bus 2 or 3
- CR Framingham/Worcester Line to NATICK; walk one block N to catch Natick Neighborhood Bus

Newbury Street
⊕ p. 27; Back Bay, Boston
- ARLINGTON, COPLEY or HYNES/ICA

(Green Line)
- from BACK BAY STA (Orange Line) turn N from any exit, four blocks
- bus **9**, 10, **39**, or 55 to any Boylston St. stop; walk N one block

Northgate Shopping Center
Squire Rd., Revere
- bus 119 (Northgate-Beachmont) or 429 (Northgate-Central Sq., Lynn) to mall entrance

North Shore Mall
Rte. 128 at Rte. 114, Peabody
- CR Newburyport/Rockport Line to LYNN; take bus 435 (Liberty Tree Mall-Central Sq., Lynn) or 436 (Liberty Tree Mall-Central Sq., Lynn)
- CR Newburyport/Rockport Line to SALEM; take bus 465 (Salem Depot-Liberty Tree Mall)

Porter Square Shopping Center
Mass. Ave. & White St., Cambridge
- PORTER (Red Line)

Quincy Market
See "Faneuil Hall Marketplace"

Sherwood Plaza
Worcester St. (Rte. 9), Natick
- CR Framingham/Worcester Line to FRAMINGHAM; walk E to Concord St. to take local LIFT bus 2 or 3
- CR Framingham/Worcester Line to NATICK; walk one block N to catch Natick Neighborhood Bus

Shoppers World
1 Worcester Rd. (Rte. 9), Framingham
- from SOUTH STA (Red Line or CR) take Peter Pan Bus Lines (Boston-Framingham express)
- CR Framingham/Worcester Line to FRAMINGHAM; walk E to Concord St.; take local LIFT bus 2 or 3
- CR Framingham/Worcester Line to NATICK; walk one block N to catch Natick Neighborhood Bus

Shops at Prudential Center
⊕ p. 27; 800 Boylston St., Boston
- COPLEY, PRUDENTIAL, or HYNES/ICA (Green Line)
- from BACK BAY STA (Orange Line) go through Copley Place and the Huntington Ave. skybridge

North Market Building at Faneuil Hall Marketplace (a.k.a. Quincy Market), a short walk from four rapid transit stations. For directions see page 89. Additional description appears on page 33.

ANDREW RUBEL

• bus **9** (City Point-Copley Sq.) or 10 (City Point-Copley Sq.) to Ring Rd.
• bus **39** (Forest Hills-Back Bay) or 55 (Jersey & Queensberry Sts.-Park & Tremont Sts.) to Prudential Center

Silver City Galleria
2 Galleria Drive at Rte. 24, Taunton
• from SOUTH STA (Red Line or CR) take either American Eagle commuter bus (Boston-New Bedford) to Galleria parking lot, or Bloom Bus Lines commuter bus (Boston-Taunton) to Taunton, transfer to local GATRA bus 2 (East Taunton-Plain & Hart) or 3 (Silver City Galleria-East Taunton P.O.)

Solomon Pond Mall
601 Donald Lynch Blvd., Marlborough
• CR Framingham/Worcester Line to FRAMINGHAM; take local LIFT bus 7 (Mon-Fri) or Gulbankian bus (Sat)

South Bay Shopping Center
Newmarket Sq., Boston
• from ANDREW (Red Line) take free shuttle bus
• bus 8 (Harbor Pt./UMass-Kenmore) or 10 (City Pt.-Copley Sq.)

South Shore Plaza
250 Granite St., Braintree
• from QUINCY CTR (Red Line-Braintree) take bus 236 (Quincy Ctr.-South Shore Plaza) or 238 (Quincy Ctr.-Holbrook/Randolph CR sta.)

Square One Mall
1205 Broadway (Rte. 1), Saugus
• from MALDEN CTR (Orange Line) take

bus 430 (Appleton St., Saugus-Malden Ctr.)
• CR Newburyport/Rockport Line to LYNN; take bus 429 (Central Sq., Lynn-Northgate)

Swampscott Mall
450 Paradise Rd., Swampscott
• bus 439 (some trips), 441, 448, 455, or 459 to Vinnin Sq.

Twin City Plaza
264 O'Brien Hwy., Cambridge
• from LECHMERE (Green Line) walk E on Monsignor O'Brien Hwy. four blocks
• bus 80 (Arlington Ctr.-Lechmere), 87 (Arlington Ctr.-Lechmere), or 88 (Clarendon Hill-Lechmere) to plaza
• bus 69 (Harvard-Lechmere) to Lambert St., one-block walk N

Watertown Mall
550 Arsenal St., Watertown
• from CENTRAL (Red Line) take bus 70 (Cedarwood or Watertown Sq.-Univ. Park) or 70A (N. Waltham-Univ. Park)

Woburn Mall
300 Mishawum Rd., Woburn
• from HAYMARKET (Green or Orange Line) or STATE (Orange or Blue Line) take express bus 355 (Mishawum Station-Boston)

Wrentham Village Premium Outlets
1 Premium Outlets Blvd. (I-495 Exit 15), Wrentham (508/384-0600)
• Private van from downtown Boston via Back Bay Coach (info: 877/404-9909)

Sports Arenas, Stadiums, and Racetracks

Boston Breakers (WUSA Women's Soccer)
Nickerson Field, Gaffney St., Boston
(866/462-7325)
• PLEASANT ST (Green Line-B)

Boston Bruins (NHL)
⊕ p. 29; FleetCenter, 150 Causeway St.,
Boston (617/227-3206)
• NORTH STA (Green or Orange Line or
CR)

Boston Cannons (Major League Lacrosse)
Cawley Memorial Stadium, 508
Douglas Rd., Lowell (888/847-9700),
www.bostoncannons.com
• CR Lowell Line to LOWELL; take
local LRTA Downtown Shuttle bus to
downtown Transit Center, transfer to
LRTA bus 02 (Belvidere)

Boston Celtics (NBA)
⊕ p. 29; FleetCenter, 150 Causeway St.,
Boston (617/523-6050)
• NORTH STA (Green or Orange Line or
CR)

Boston Red Sox (AL)
⊕ p. 27; Fenway Park, Boston
(617/267-8661)
• KENMORE (Green Line-B, C, or D)
• FENWAY (Green Line-D)
• CR Framingham/Worcester Line to
YAWKEY STA

Lowell Lock Monsters (AHL)
Tsongas Arena, Father Morissette Blvd.,
Lowell (978/458-PUCK)
• CR Lowell Line to LOWELL; take local
LRTA Downtown Shuttle to Main Post
Office; arena is one block behind P.O.

Lowell Spinners (Minor League Baseball A)
LeLacheur Stadium, Aiken St., Lowell
(978/459-1702)
• CR Lowell Line to LOWELL; take local
LRTA Downtown Shuttle, transfer to
LRTA bus 11 (Pawtucketville) to Aiken St.

New England Patriots (NFL)
Gillette Stadium, Foxborough
(800-543-1776), www.patriots.com

• Special CR trains to all games from
SOUTH STA via BACK BAY STA, DEDHAM
CORPORATE CTR, and NORWOOD
CENTRAL. Also from Providence, RI
Amtrak Station via SOUTH ATTLEBORO,
ATTLEBORO, and MANSFIELD; easy
walk to stadium from trains

New England Revolution (MLS)
Gillette Stadium, Foxboro (877-GET-
REVS), www.nerevolution.com
No transit to Revolution games

Providence Bruins (AHL)
⊕ p. 48; Dunkin' Donuts Center, LaSalle
Sq., Providence, RI (401/273-5000),
www.provbruins.com
• Amtrak or CR Attleboro Line to
PROVIDENCE; exit to Park Row, four-
block walk SW, or exit to Gaspee St. to
take Providence LINK Gold Line trolley
to Kennedy Plaza, transfer to local
RIPTA buses listed below
• Bonanza Bus Lines to Kennedy Plaza;
three-block walk W or take local RIPTA
bus 26 (Atwells-Academy-RI College),
27 (Broadway-Manton), **28** (Broadway-
Hartford), or Providence LINK Green
Line trolley to entrance

Raynham Greyhound Park
Raynham (508/824-4071)
• from SOUTH STA (Red Line or CR)
take Bloom Bus Lines commuter bus
(Boston-Taunton) to dog track

Suffolk Downs Racetrack
111 Waldemar Ave., East Boston
(617/567-3900)
• SUFFOLK DOWNS (Blue Line)

Wonderland Greyhound Park
V.F.W. Parkway, Revere (781/284-1300)
• WONDERLAND (Blue Line)
• **bus 441/442** (Marblehead-Haymarket)

Worcester IceCats (AHL)
⊕ p. 52; Worcester's Centrum Centre,
50 Foster St., Worcester (800/830-CATS
or 508/798-5400)
• CR Framingham/Worcester Line to
WORCESTER
• Peter Pan Bus Lines to Worcester Bus
Terminal

*Frequent bus routes in **bold***

Chapter 7:
Cities and Towns

This chapter gives you a complete list of transit services for every major neighborhood in Boston, virtually every city and town in Eastern Massachusetts, many cities and towns in Central Massachusetts, and Providence, RI. For transit options outside this area, including Western Massachusetts and Cape Cod, see Chapter 13, "New England and Beyond" or look for the town in the index on page 175. Details for transit routes below can be found in Chapters 8-11 (MBTA routes) and Chapter 12 (non-MBTA routes); more options to and from Logan Airport are listed in Chapter 14, "Regional Airports."

MBTA Commuter Rail and rapid transit station names are upper case, and all buses are MBTA buses unless noted. Additionally, "CR" denotes "Commuter Rail," ♻ indicates a multi-use trail or bicycle path, ⊕ refers to a map elsewhere in the book, and ⊞ indicates a selected park-and-ride lot (for park-and-ride information see Chapter 3, "More Local Transportation").

Abington
• CR Plymouth/Kingston Line to ABINGTON
• JBL Bus Lines commuter bus (Boston-Whitman) to Abington Ctr. and N. Abington *(Rtes. 139 & 58)*

Acton
• CR Fitchburg/South Acton Line to SOUTH ACTON
• Yankee Line commuter bus (Boston-Acton) to Hoyt Cinemas *(Rtes 2A & 119)*
See LRTA in Chapter 12
⊞ Off Main St. (Rte. 27), S. Acton *(S of Rtes. 2 & 111)*

Acushnet
See SRTA in Chapter 12

Allston (Boston)
• Green Line-B, serves Commonwealth Ave.
• **bus 57** (Watertown Sq.-Kenmore)
• bus 64 (Oak Sq.-Univ. Park or Kendall/MIT)
• **bus 66** (Harvard Sta.-Dudley)
• bus 70 (Cedarwood or Watertown Sq.-Univ. Park)
• bus 70A (North Waltham-Univ. Park)
• bus 86 (Sullivan Sq.-Reservoir/Cleveland Cir.)
Union Sq.: buses **57**, 64, **66**
Western Ave.: buses 70, 70A, 86
♻ Dr. Paul Dudley White Bike Path

Amesbury
• The Coach Co. commuter bus (Boston-Amesbury), rush hour only
• Flight Line Seacoast Service from Logan Airport
See MVRTA in Chapter 12

Amherst
See Western Massachusetts, Chapter 13

Andover
• CR Haverhill Line to BALLARDVALE and ANDOVER
• MVRTA (Lawrence-Andover-Boston)
• Flight Line from Logan Airport
See local MVRTA service in Chapter 12

Arlington
• bus 62 (Bedford VA Hospital-Alewife)
• bus 62/76 (Bedford VA Hospital-Alewife), Sat. only
• bus 67 (Turkey Hill-Alewife)
• **bus 77** (Arlington Hghts.-Harvard Sta.)
• bus 78 (Arlmont Village-Harvard Sta.)
• bus 79 (Arlington Heights-Alewife)
• bus 80 (Arlington Ctr.-Lechmere)
• bus 84 (Arlmont Village-Alewife)
• bus 87 (Arlington Ctr.-Lechmere)
• bus 350 (North Burlington-Alewife)
Arlington Ctr.: buses 67, **77**, 79, 80, 87, 350
Arlington Heights: buses 62, **77**, 79
♻ Minuteman Commuter Bikeway

Ashland
- CR Framingham/Worcester Line to ASHLAND
- LIFT 5 local bus (Framingham-Hopkinton), serving Rte. 135
- LIFT 6 local bus (Framingham-Milford), serving Rte. 126

Attleboro
- CR Attleboro Line to ATTLEBORO and SOUTH ATTLEBORO

See GATRA in Chapter 12

🚗 Main St. (Rte. 152), S of Rte. 123

Auburn
See WRTA in Chapter 12

Auburndale (Newton)
- CR Framingham/Worcester Line to AUBURNDALE
- x-bus 505 (Central Sq., Waltham-Downtown), rush hour only
- x-bus 558 (Auburndale-Downtown)
- Green Line-D to RIVERSIDE; 10min walk
- Newton Nexus local bus
- Waltham CitiBus 16 local bus

Avon
- bus 240 (Avon Line or Holbrook/Randolph Sta.-Ashmont)
- Red Line (Ashmont) to ASHMONT; connect to BAT 12 local bus (Ashmont-Brockton)

Ayer
- CR Fitchburg Line to AYER

Back Bay (Boston)
⊕ p. 27
- Green Line (all branches) to Arlington and Copley
- Green B, C, and D Line to HYNES/ICA
- Green E Line to PRUDENTIAL and SYMPHONY
- Orange Line to BACK BAY STA and MASSACHUSETTS AVE
- **bus 1** (Harvard-Dudley)
- **bus 9** (City Point-Copley Sq.)
- bus 10 (City Point-Copley Sq.)
- **bus 39** (Forest Hills-Back Bay Sta.)
- **bus 55** (Jersey & Queensberry Sts.-Copley Sq. or Park & Tremont Sts.)
- x-bus 502 (Watertown-Copley)
- bus CT1 (Central Sq., Cambridge-Boston Medical Center)
- Cavalier Coach (Boston-Northborough)

to Stuart & Dartmouth Sts.
- Gulbankian Bus Lines (Boston-Hudson) to Stuart & Dartmouth Sts.
- MVRTA (Lawrence-Andover-Boston) to Copley Sq.
- Peter Pan Bus Lines (Boston-Worcester and -Framingham) to Copley Sq.
- Yankee Line commuter bus (Boston-Acton) to Copley Sq. *(St. James Ave.)*

🚲 Dr. Paul Dudley White Bike Path; Southwest Corridor Bike Path

Ballardvale (Andover)
See **Andover**

Bay Village (Boston)
- Green Line to ARLINGTON
- Orange Line to NE MEDICAL CTR
- **bus 9** (City Point-Copley Sq.)
- **bus 43** (Ruggles-Park & Tremont Sts.)
- bus 55 (Jersey & Queensberry Sts.-Copley Sq. or Park & Tremont Sts.)
- Cavalier Coach (Boston-Northborough) to Park Sq.
- Gulbankian Bus Lines (Boston-Hudson) to Park Sq.
- Interstate Coach commuter bus (Boston-Middleboro/Bridgewater) to Park Sq.
- MVRTA (Lawrence-Andover-Boston) to Park Sq.
- Trombly Commuter Lines (Boston-Methuen) to Park Sq.
- Peter Pan Bus Lines (Boston-Worcester and -Framingham) to Park Sq.
- Plymouth & Brockton (Boston-Cape Cod; -Duxbury; -Plymouth; -Rockland; and -Scituate) to Park Sq., Mon-Fri only

Beacon Hill (Boston)
⊕ p. 30
- Blue Line to BOWDOIN
- Green Line to PARK STREET
- Red Line to CHARLES/MGH and PARK STREET
- **bus 43** (Ruggles-Park & Tremont Sts.)
- bus 55 (Jersey & Queensberry Sts.-Copley Sq. or Park & Tremont Sts.)
- Gulbankian Bus Lines (Boston-Hudson) to the State House
- Peter Pan Bus Lines (Boston-Worcester and -Framingham) to the State House

Bedford
- bus 62 (Bedford VA Hospital-Alewife)
- bus 62/76 (Bedford VA Hospital-

*Frequent bus routes in **bold**; "x-bus" denotes express bus*

Alewife), Sat. only
• bus 76 (Hanscom AB-Alewife)
• bus 170 (Oak Park-Dudley Sq.), rush hour "reverse commute" only
• x-bus 351 (Oak Park-Alewife)
• Bedford Local Transit
• Minuteman Commuter Bikeway

Bellingham
See **Franklin** for CR service

Belmont
• CR Fitchburg/South Acton Line to BELMONT and WAVERLEY
• bus 72/75 (Belmont Ctr.-Harvard Sta.)
• **bus 73** (Waverley Sq.-Harvard Sta.)
• bus 74/75 (Belmont Ctr.-Harvard Sta.)
• bus 78 (Arlmont Village-Harvard Sta.)
• x-bus 554 (Waverley Sq.-Downtown)
• Waltham CitiBus 14 local bus

Berlin
I-495 Exit 26 (Rte. 62)

Beverly
• CR Rockport Line to BEVERLY, MONTSERRRAT, PRIDES CROSSING, and BEVERLY FARMS
• Newburyport Line to BEVERLY and NORTH BEVERLY
• bus 451 (N. Beverly-Salem Depot)
• Beverly Shoppers' Shuttle

Billerica
• CR Lowell Line to NORTH BILLERICA
• Flight Line from Logan Airport
See LRTA in Chapter 12

Boston
🌐 pp. 27, 29, 30-31, 34, 37, 39
Below are services that terminate in downtown Boston (Financial District, Government Ctr., and Downtown Crossing); services that stop elsewhere are summarized under the following Boston neighborhoods: **Allston, Back Bay, Bay Village, Beacon Hill, Brighton, Charlestown, Chinatown/ Leather District, Dorchester, East Boston, Fenway/Kenmore Sq., Fort Point Channel, Hyde Park, Jamaica Plain, Mattapan, Mission Hill, North End, Roslindale, Roxbury, South Boston, South End,** and **West Roxbury**
• Red Line and south CR Lines to SOUTH STA

• Red, Orange, and Silver Lines to DOWNTOWN CROSSING
• Green and Blue Lines to GOVERNMENT CTR
• Orange and Blue Lines to STATE
• bus 3 (City Point-Chinatown)
• bus 6 (Marine Ind. Park-Haymarket)
• **bus 7** (City Point-Otis & Summer Sts.)
• **bus 11** (City Point-Downtown)
• bus 92 (Assembly Sq.-Downtown)
• **bus 93** (Sullivan Sq.-Downtown)
• x-bus 352 (Burlington-State)
• x-bus 354 (Woburn-State)
• x bus 355 (Mishawum Sta.-Boston)
• x-bus 448 (Marblehead-Downtown)
• x-bus 449 (Marblehead-Downtown)
• x-bus 459 (Salem Depot-Downtown)
• x-bus 500 (Riverside-Downtown)
• x-bus 501 (Brighton Ctr.-Downtown)
• x-bus 504 (Watertown-Downtown)
• x-bus 505 (Central Sq., Waltham-Downtown)
• x-bus 553 (Roberts-Downtown)
• x-bus 554 (Waverley Sq.-Downtown)
• x-bus 556 (Waltham Highlands-Downtown)
• x-bus 558 (Auburndale-Downtown)
• Cavalier Coach (Boston-Northborough) to Government Ctr./JFK Bldg.
• The Coach Co. (Boston-Newburyport and -Haverhill) to GOVERNMENT CTR and PARK STREET
• Gulbankian Bus Lines (Boston-Hudson) to PARK STREET and Federal & Matthews Sts.
• MVRTA (Lawrence-Andover-Boston) to PARK STREET, GOVERNMENT CTR, and Essex St.
• Peter Pan Bus Lines (Boston-Framingham and -Worcester) to Post Office Sq.
• Trombly Commuter Lines (Boston-Methuen) to PARK STREET and Government Ctr./100 Cambridge St.

See Chapter 5, "Popular Sights and Excursions," for an overview of Boston neighborhood attractions
See Chapter 14, "Regional Airports," for service to Logan International and other nearby airports

Boxborough
• Zebra Shuttle from Logan Airport

Boxford
- The Coach Co. commuter bus (Boston-Haverhill)
- Flight Line Seacoast Service from Logan Airport

Bradford (Haverhill)
See **Haverhill**

Braintree
- Red Line (Braintree) to BRAINTREE
- CR Plymouth/Kingston and Middleborough/Lakeville Lines to BRAINTREE
- bus 225 (Quincy Ctr.-Weymouth Landing), serves Quincy Ave.
- bus 230 (Quincy Ctr.-Montello Sta.), serves Washington St.
- bus 236 (Quincy Ctr.-South Shore Plaza)
- bus 238 (Quincy Ctr.-Holbrook/Randolph Sta.), serves Granite and Pond Sts.
- JBL Bus Lines commuter bus (Weymouth-Braintree) to BRAINTREE
- JBL Bus Lines commuter bus (Whitman-Boston) to Church & Elm Sts.
- Logan Express from Logan Airport to Forbes Rd., off Granite St.
- Plymouth & Brockton (Marshfield-Hanover-Braintree) to BRAINTREE

E. Braintree: bus 236

Bridgewater
- CR Middleborough/Lakeville Line to BRIDGEWATER
- Interstate Coach commuter bus (Boston-Middleboro/Bridgewater) to Winter Place, Bridgewater Ctr., Kingswood, High St., and Rte. 104 & 24 park-and-ride lot.

Brighton (Boston)
⊕ p. 39 (Cleveland Circle)
- Green Line-B, serves Commonwealth Av.
- Green Line-C to CLEVELAND CIR
- Green Line-D to RESERVOIR
- **bus 57** (Watertown Sq.-Kenmore)
- bus 64 (Oak Sq.-Univ. Park or Kendall/MIT)
- bus 65 (Brighton Ctr.-Kenmore)
- bus 70 (Cedarwood or Watertown Sq.-Univ. Park)
- bus 70A (North Waltham-Univ. Park)
- bus 86 (Sullivan Sq.-Reservoir/Cleveland Cir.)

- x-bus 501 (Brighton Ctr.-Downtown)
Brighton Ctr.: buses **57,** 65, 86, 501
Oak Sq.: buses **57,** 64, 501
Western Ave.: buses 70, 70A, 86
🚲 Dr. Paul Dudley White Bike Path

Brockton
- CR Middleborough Line to MONTELLO, BROCKTON, and CAMPELLO
- bus 230 (Quincy Ctr.-Montello Sta.)
- BAT buses 12 and 12X (Ashmont-Brockton) from ASHMONT (Red Line-Ashmont)
- Plymouth & Brockton (Boston-Brockton) from Park Plaza and SOUTH STA

See BAT in Chapter 12
🚐 Westgate Mall by Cinema 1 & 2, Rte. 27 at Rte. 24 Exit 18A

Brookline
⊕ p. 38 (Brookline Village)
- Green Line-B, serves Commonwealth Ave. along Allston/Brighton boundary
- Green Line-C, serves SAINT MARY'S ST, HAWES ST, KENT ST, SAINT PAUL ST, COOLIDGE CORNER, WINCHESTER/SUMMIT, BRANDON HALL, FAIRBANKS ST, WASHINGTON SQ, TAPPAN ST, DEAN RD, and ENGLEWOOD AVE
- Green Line-D to LONGWOOD, BROOKLINE VILLAGE, BROOKLINE HILLS, BEACONSFIELD, and RESERVOIR
- bus 51 (Reservoir-Forest Hills)
- bus 60 (Chestnut Hill-Kenmore)
- bus 65 (Brighton Ctr.-Kenmore)
- **bus 66** (Harvard Sta.-Dudley)
- bus 86 (Sullivan Sq.-Reservoir/Cleveland Cir.)

Beacon St.: entire above-ground portion of Green C Line
Boylston St. (Rte. 9): bus 60
Harvard St.: **bus 66**
Washington St.: bus 65
🚲 Muddy River Bike Path

Burlington
- bus 170 (Oak Park-Dudley Sq.), rush hour "reverse commute" only
- bus 350 (North Burlington-Alewife)
- x-bus 351 (Bedford Woods-Alewife)
- x-bus 352 (Burlington-Boston), rush hour only
- Lexpress (Lexington-Burlington Mall)
- Burlington B Line local bus

Frequent bus routes in bold; "x-bus" denotes express bus

Buzzards Bay (Wareham)
- Bonanza Bus Lines (Boston-Woods Hole) from SOUTH STA to Main St.

See OWL in Chapter 12

Byfield (Newbury)
- The Coach Co. (Boston-Amesbury), rush hour only

Cambridge
⊕ p. 40 (Harvard Square) and p. 42 (Central Square)
- Green Line to LECHMERE
- Red Line to KENDALL/MIT, CENTRAL, HARVARD, PORTER, ALEWIFE
- CR Fitchburg/South Acton Line to PORTER SQ
- **bus 1** (Harvard-Dudley)
- bus 47 (Central Sq.-Broadway)
- bus 62 (Bedford VA Hospital-Alewife)
- bus 62/76 (Bedford VA Hospital-Alewife), Sat. only
- bus 64 (Oak Sq.-Univ. Park or Kendall/MIT)
- **bus 66** (Harvard Sta.-Dudley)

- bus 67 (Turkey Hill-Alewife)
- bus 68 (Harvard-Kendall/MIT)
- bus 69 (Harvard-Lechmere)
- bus 70 (Cedarwood or Watertown Sq.-Univ. Park)
- bus 70A (North Waltham-Univ. Park)
- **bus 71** (Watertown Sq.-Harvard Sta.)
- bus 72 (Huron Ave.-Harvard Sta.)
- bus 72/75 (Belmont Ctr.-Harvard Sta.)
- **bus 73** (Waverley Sq.-Harvard Sta.)
- bus 74/75 (Belmont Ctr.-Harvard Sta.)
- bus 76 (Hanscom AB-Alewife)
- **bus 77** (Arlington Hghts.-Harvard Sta.)
- bus 77A (N. Cambridge-Harvard Sta.)
- bus 78 (Arlmont Village-Harvard Sta.)
- bus 79 (Arlington Heights-Alewife)
- bus 80 (Arlington Ctr.-Lechmere)
- bus 83 (Rindge Ave.-Central Sq.)
- bus 84 (Arlmont Village-Alewife)
- bus 85 (Spring Hill-Kendall/MIT)
- bus 86 (Sullivan Sq.-Reservoir/Cleveland Cir.)
- bus 87 (Arlington Ctr. or Clarendon Hill-Lechmere)

Harvard Square, Cambridge
Drawing by George Kelso; reproduced with permission from the artist.

- bus 88 (Clarendon Hill-Lechmere)
- bus 91 (Sullivan Sq.-Central Sq.)
- bus 96 (Medford Sq.-Harvard Sta.)
- bus 350 (North Burlington-Alewife)
- x-bus 351 (Oak Park-Alewife)
- bus CT1 (Central Sq., Cambridge-Boston Medical Center)
- bus CT2 (Sullivan Sq.-Ruggles)

Central Sq.: Red Line (CENTRAL); buses **1**, 47, 64, 70, 70A, 83, 91, CT1

E. Cambridge: Green Line (LECHMERE) and bus 69

Harvard Sq.: Red Line (HARVARD); buses **1, 66**, 68, 69, **71**, 72, 72/75, **73**, 74/75, **77**, 77A, 78, 86, 96

Inman Sq.: buses 69, 83, 91

Mass. Ave.: Red Line (CENTRAL, HARVARD, PORTER); buses **1** (lower half) and **77** (upper half)

Kendall Sq: Red Line (KENDALL/MIT); buses 64, 68, 85, CT2

Mt. Auburn St.: buses **71, 73**

N. Cambridge: Red Line (PORTER, DAVIS, ALEWIFE); CR; and buses **77** and 83

Porter Sq.: Red Line and CR (PORTER); buses **77**, 77A, 83, 96

🚗 Rte. 2, junction Rte. 16 and US 3 (Alewife)

🚲 Minuteman Commuter Bikeway

Canton

- CR Stoughton Line to CANTON JCT and CANTON CTR
- CR Attleboro Line to CANTON JCT
- Interstate Coach commuter bus (Boston-Canton Commerce Center) from SOUTH STA and Park Square
- JBL Bus Lines 716 (Mattapan-Canton) from MATTAPAN (Red Line-Mattapan)

Charlestown (Boston)
⊕ p. 29

- Orange Line to COMMUNITY COLLEGE and SULLIVAN SQ
- bus 86 (Sullivan Sq.-Reservoir/Cleveland Cir.)
- bus 89 (Clarendon Hill-Sullivan Sq.)
- bus 90 (Davis Sq.-Wellington)
- bus 91 (Sullivan Sq.-Central Sq.)
- bus 92 (Assembly Sq.-Downtown)
- **bus 93** (Sullivan Sq.-Downtown)
- bus 95 (W. Medford-Sullivan Sq.)
- bus 101 (Malden Ctr.-Sullivan Sq.)
- bus 104 (Malden Ctr.-Sullivan Sq.)

- bus 104 (Malden Ctr.-Sullivan Sq.)
- bus 109 (Linden Sq.-Sullivan Sq.)
- **bus 111** (Woodlawn or Broadway & Park Ave.-Haymarket)
- MBTA Inner Harbor Ferry Long Wharf and Lovejoy Wharf
- Navy Yard Shuttle Bus

Bunker Hill St.: bus 93

Main St.: bus 92

Charlestown Navy Yard: Inner Harbor Ferry and bus **93**

Chelmsford
See **Lowell** for CR service

- Flight Line from Logan Airport
See LRTA in Chapter 12

Chelsea
- CR Newburyport/Rockport Line to CHELSEA
- **bus 111** (Woodlawn or Broadway & Park Ave.-Haymarket)
- bus 112 (Wellington-Wood Island)
- bus 114 (Bellingham Sq.-Maverick)
- bus 116 (Wonderland-Maverick) via Revere St.
- bus 117 (Wonderland-Maverick) via Beach St.

Chestnut Hill (Brookline/Newton)
- Green Line-B to BOSTON COLLEGE
- Green Line-D to CHESTNUT HILL
- bus 51 (Reservoir-Forest Hills)
- bus 60 (Chestnut Hill-Kenmore)

Chinatown/Leather District (Boston)
⊕ p. 30-31

- Orange and Silver Lines to CHINATOWN and NE MEDICAL CTR
- Green and Silver Lines to BOYLSTON, cross Tremont, walk one block on Boylston
- bus 3 (City Pt.-Bedford & Chauncy Sts.)
- **bus 11** (City Point-Downtown)
- **bus 43** (Ruggles-Park Street)
- bus 55 (Queensberry St.-Park Street)
- Cavalier Coach (Boston-Northborough) to Essex & South Sts.
- Gulbankian Bus Lines (Boston-Hudson) to Essex & South Sts.
- Interstate Coach commuter bus (Boston-Middleboro/Bridgewater) to Beach & Lincoln Sts.
- MVRTA (Lawrence-Andover-Boston) to

Essex St.
• Trombly Commuter Lines (Boston-Methuen) to Essex & Lincoln Sts.

Cochituate (Framingham)
See **Framingham**

Cohasset
• Plymouth & Brockton (Boston-Scituate) from SOUTH STA and Park Sq. to Cohasset Common

Concord
• CR Fitchburg/South Acton Line to CONCORD and WEST CONCORD
• Yankee Line commuter bus (Boston-Acton) to Concord center *(Crosby's Market, Sudbury Rd.)*
• Concord Community Bus free local bus (Mon., Wed., and Fri. AM only)

Danvers
• bus 435 (Liberty Tree Mall-Central Sq., Lynn) via Peabody Sq.
• bus 436 (Liberty Tree Mall-Central Sq., Lynn) via Goodwins Circle
• bus 465 (Liberty Tree Mall-Salem Depot)
• bus 468 (Danvers Sq.-Salem Depot)
• Flight Line Seacoast Service from Logan Airport

Dartmouth
See SRTA in Chapter 12

Dedham
• CR Franklin Line to ENDICOTT and DEDHAM CORP CTR
• bus 34E (Walpole Ctr.-Forest Hills)
• bus 35 (Dedham Mall-Forest Hills)
• bus 52 (Dedham Mall-Watertown)
• Amtrak (Acela Express and Acela Regional, Boston-New York) from SOUTH STA and BACK BAY STA to ROUTE 128 STA
• Plymouth & Brockton (ROUTE 128 STA-Woods Hole) to park-and-ride (seasonal)
• Dedham Local Bus
Washington St. (Rte. 1A): bus 34E
🚗 Allied Dr., off rotary at Route 128/I-95 Exit 14 (Dedham Corporate Center)

Dighton
See SRTA in Chapter 12

Dorchester (Boston)
• Red Line (all branches) to JFK/UMASS
• Red Line (Ashmont) to SAVIN HILL, FIELDS CORNER, SHAWMUT, and ASHMONT
• Red Line (Mattapan) to CEDAR GROVE, BUTLER ST, MILTON, and CENTRAL AVE
• CR Fairmount Line to UPHAMS CORNER and MORTON ST
• CR Plymouth/Kingston and Middleborough/Lakeville Lines to JFK/UMASS
• bus 8 (Harbor Pt./UMass or Dudley Sta.-Kenmore)
• bus 14 (Roslindale Sq.-Heath St.)
• **bus 15** (Kane Sq. or Fields Corner-Ruggles)
• bus 16 (Forest Hills-Andrew or UMass)
• bus 17 (Fields Corner-Andrew)
• bus 18 (Ashmont-Andrew)
• bus 19 (Fields Corner-Ruggles)
• bus 20 (Fields Corner Loop via Neponset & Adams)
• bus 21 (Ashmont-Forest Hills)
• **bus 22** (Ashmont-Ruggles) via Talbot Ave.
• **bus 23** (Ashmont-Ruggles) via Washington St.
• bus 26 (Ashmont-Norfolk & Morton Belt Line)
• bus 27 (Mattapan-Ashmont)
• **bus 28** (Mattapan-Ruggles)
• bus 29 (Mattapan-Jackson Sq.)
• bus 41 (Centre & Eliot Sts.-JFK/UMass)
• bus 44 (Jackson Sq.-Ruggles)
• bus 45 (Franklin Park Ruggles)
• bus 210 (Quincy Ctr.-Fields Corner)
• bus 215 (Quincy Ctr.-Ashmont)
• bus 217 (Wollaston-Ashmont)
• bus 240 (Avon Line or Holbrook/Randolph Sta.-Ashmont)
• x-bus 275/276 (Boston Medical Ctr. or Downtown-Long Island Hospital)
• BAT bus 12 (Ashmont-Brockton) to ASHMONT
• Interstate Coach commuter bus (Boston-Middleboro/Bridgewater) to JFK/UMASS
Codman Sq.: buses **22, 23,** 26; or walk from Red Line-Ashmont (SHAWMUT), 3 blocks
Edward Everett Sq.: buses 8, 16, 17, 41; or walk from Red Line (JFK/UMASS), 4 blocks

Fields Corner: Red Line-Ashmont (FIELDS CORNER) and buses 17, 18, 19, 20, 210
Four Corners: bus **23**
Grove Hall: buses 14, 19, **23, 28,** 45
Lower Mills: Red Line-Mattapan (MILTON); buses 27, 217, 240; BAT
Meeting House Hill: buses **15,** 17
Neponset: buses 20, 210
Uphams Corner: CR (3 blocks) and buses **15,** 16, 17, 41
🚲 Neponset River Trail

Dover
See **Needham** for CR service
• Brush Hill Bus Lines (Boston-Milford), serving Rte. 109

Dracut
• Flight Line from Logan Airport
See LRTA in Chapter 12

Duxbury
• Plymouth & Brockton (Boston-Duxbury) from SOUTH STA and Park Sq. to Millbrook Motors *(Rtes. 3A & 139)*

East Boston (Boston)
• Blue Line to MAVERICK, AIRPORT, WOOD ISLAND, ORIENT HEIGHTS, and SUFFOLK DOWNS
• bus 112 (Wellington-Wood Island)
• bus 114 (Bellingham Sq.-Maverick)
• bus 116 (Wonderland-Maverick) via Revere St.
• bus 117 (Wonderland-Maverick) via Beach St.
• bus 120 (Orient Heights-Maverick)
• bus 121 (Wood Island-Maverick)
• bus 171 (Dudley Sta.-Logan Airport)
• x-bus 448 (Marblehead-Haymarket) via Logan Airport
• x-bus 449 (Marblehead-Downtown Crossing) via Logan Airport
• x-bus 459 (Salem Depot-Downtown) via Logan Airport
See Logan Airport in Chapter 14 for complete airport transit information

Easton
See **Stoughton** for CR service
See BAT in Chapter 12

Ellisville (Plymouth)
See **Plymouth** for CR service
See PAL in Chapter 12

Essex
See CATA in Chapter 12

Everett
• bus 97 (Malden Ctr.-Wellington)
• bus 99 (Boston Regional Medical Ctr.-Wellington)
• bus 104 (Malden Ctr.-Sullivan Sq.)
• bus 105 (Malden Ctr.-Sullivan Sq.)
• bus 106 (Lebanon St./Malden-Wellington)
• bus 109 (Linden Sq.-Sullivan Sq.)
• bus 110 (Wonderland-Wellington)
• **bus 111** (Woodlawn or Broadway & Park Ave.-Haymarket)
• bus 112 (Wellington-Wood Island)
Everett Sq.: buses 97, 104, 109, 110, 112
Glendale Sq.: buses 104, 109
Main St.: buses 99, 105, 106

Fairhaven
• American Eagle from SOUTH STA
See SRTA in Chapter 12

Fall River
• Bonanza Bus Lines (Boston-Newport, RI) from Logan Airport and SOUTH STA to SRTA Terminal *(221 Second St.)*
• Bonanza Bus Lines (Albany, NY-Hyannis; New York-Hyannis via Providence, RI) from Hyannis to SRTA Terminal
• Bloom Bus Lines (Fall River-Taunton-Boston) from SOUTH STA to SRTA Terminal
See SRTA in Chapter 12

Falmouth
See Cape Cod in Chapter 13.

Fenway/Kenmore Sq. (Boston)
⊕ p. 27 (Back Bay) and p. 34 (Longwood Medical Area)
• Green Line-B to KENMORE SQ, BLANDFORD ST, BU EAST, and BU CENTRAL
• Green Line-C to KENMORE SQ and SAINT MARY'S ST
• Green Line-D to KENMORE SQ and FENWAY
• Green Line-E to SYMPHONY, NORTHEASTERN, and MUSEUM OF FINE ARTS
• CR Framingham/Worcester Line to YAWKEY

Frequent bus routes in bold; "x-bus" denotes express bus

* bus 8 (Harbor Pt./UMass or Dudley Sta.-Kenmore)
* **bus 39** (Forest Hills-Back Bay Sta.)
* bus 47 (Central Sq.-Broadway)
* bus 55 (Jersey & Queensberry Sts.-Copley Sq. or Park & Tremont Sts.)
* bus 60 (Chestnut Hill-Kenmore)
* bus 65 (Brighton Ctr.-Kenmore)

Fitchburg
* CR Fitchburg Line to FITCHBURG
* Vermont Transit (Boston-Keene, NH; Boston-Rutland, VT) from SOUTH STA and RIVERSIDE to Fitchburg Jct. *(Bickford Restaurant, Rtes. 2 & 12)*

See MART in Chapter 12

Fort Point Channel (South Boston)
* Red Line to SOUTH STA
* bus 3 (City Pt.-Bedford & Chauncy Sts.)
* bus 6 (Haymarket-Marine Indust. Pk.)
* **bus 7** (City Point-Otis & Summer Sts.)

Foxborough
See **Sharon** for CR service
* Bonanza Bus Lines (Boston-T.F. Green Airport, RI) from SOUTH STA to Foxfield Plaza *(Rte. 140 off I-95)*
* Bonanza Bus Lines (Logan Airport-Providence, RI) from Logan Airport to Foxfield Plaza
* Mass Limousine from Logan Airport

Framingham
* CR Framingham/Worcester Line to FRAMINGHAM
* Peter Pan Bus Lines (Boston-Framingham and -Worcester) from SOUTH STA and RIVERSIDE
* Gulbankian Bus Lines (Boston-Hudson), rush hour only
* Gulbankian Bus Lines (Marlborough/Solomon Pond Mall-Framingham), Sat. only
* Amtrak (Boston-Chicago) from SOUTH STA and BACK BAY STA to FRAMINGHAM
* Natick Neighborhood Bus
* LIFT local buses to Ashland, Holliston, Hopkinton, Marlborough, Milford, and Southborough
* Framingham Logan Express from Logan Airport
* Zebra Shuttle from Logan Airport

Downtown Framingham: CR; Amtrak; and all LIFT routes

Framingham Ctr.: Peter Pan Bus Lines and LIFT local buses

Shoppers World: Peter Pan Bus Lines; Logan Express; LIFT bus 2 and 3; and Natick Neighborhood Bus
* ᗕᗑ Rte. 135, W of Rte. 126 (downtown); Rte. 9 (Shoppers World); and Rte. 9 (Mass. Pike exit 12)

Franklin
* CR Franklin Line to FRANKLIN/DEAN COLLEGE and FORGE PARK/495
* ᗕᗑ Route 140, 1/2 mile W of I-495 Exit 17 (Forge Park/495)

Freetown
See SRTA in Chapter 12
* ᗕᗑ Rte. 24 Exit 10 (Great Dean Rd.)

Georgetown
* The Coach Co. (Boston-Haverhill), rush hour only
* Flight Line Seacoast Service from Logan Airport

Gloucester
⊕ p. 44
* CR Rockport Line to WEST GLOUCESTER and GLOUCESTER
* AC Cruises Boston/Pier 1 to Rocky Neck, summer only

See CATA in Chapter 12

Grafton
* CR Worcester Line to GRAFTON

Greenfield
See Western Massachusetts, Chapter 13

Groton
See LRTA in Chapter 12

Groveland
* The Coach Co. (Boston-Haverhill) to S. Groveland
* Flight Line Seacoast Service from Logan Airport

Halifax
* CR Plymouth/Kingston Line to HALIFAX

Hamilton
* CR Newburyport Line to HAMILTON/WENHAM
* Flight Line Seacoast Service from Logan Airport

Hanover

- Plymouth & Brockton (Marshfield-Hanover-Braintree) from BRAINTREE (Red Line) to Hanover Mall *(Rte. 53 at Rte. 3 Exit 13)*
- 🚌 Rte. 53 at Rte. 3 Exit 13 (Hanover Mall)

Hanson

- CR Plymouth/Kingston Line to HANSON

Hartford, CT

See Connecticut in Chapter 13

Haverhill

- CR Haverhill Line to BRADFORD and HAVERHILL
- Amtrak (Downeaster, Boston-Portland, ME) from NORTH STA
- The Coach Co. (Boston-Haverhill), rush hour only, serves Bradford and Washington Sq.
- Flight Line from Logan Airport

See MVRTA in Chapter 12

Hingham

- Boston Harbor Cruises Commuter Boats from Boston/Rowes Wharf
- Plymouth & Brockton (Boston-Scituate) from SOUTH STA, serves Rte. 228, East St.
- bus 220 (Quincy Ctr.-Hingham)
- JBL Bus Lines bus 714 (Pemberton Point, Hull-Hingham Depot)

See **Rockland** for service to Rte. 3/228 interchange

Holbrook

See **Randolph** for CR service

- bus 230 (Quincy Ctr.-Montello Sta.)

Holliston

- LIFT 6 local bus (Framingham-Milford)

Hopkinton

- LIFT 5 local bus (Framingham-Hopkinton)

Hudson

- Gulbankian Bus Lines (Boston-Hudson), rush hour only

Hull

- bus 220 (Quincy Ctr.-Hingham); connect to JBL Bus Lines bus 714 (Pemberton Point-Hingham Depot)
- MBTA Commuter Boat (Boston-Pemberton Point) Long Wharf, year-round, rush hour only

Hyannis (Barnstable)

See Cape Cod in Chapter 13

Hyde Park (Boston)

- CR Attleboro/Stoughton and Franklin Lines to HYDE PARK
- CR Fairmount Line to FAIRMOUNT
- bus 24 (Wakefield Ave.-Mattapan)
- **bus 32** (Wolcott Sq. or Cleary Sq.-Forest Hills)
- bus 33 (Dedham Line-Mattapan)
- bus 40 (Georgetowne-Forest Hills)
- bus 50 (Cleary Sq.-Forest Hills)

Cleary Sq.: buses **32, 33, 50,** and CR (Hyde Park)

Readville: buses **32, 33,** and CR

🚲 Stony Brook Bike Path

Ipswich

- CR Newburyport Line to IPSWICH
- Flight Line Seacoast Service from Logan Airport

See CATA in Chapter 12

Jamaica Plain (Boston)

See also **Mission Hill** and **Roxbury**

- Green Line-E to BACK OF THE HILL and HEATH ST
- Orange Line to JACKSON SQ, STONY BROOK, GREEN ST, and FOREST HILLS
- CR Needham Line to FOREST HILLS
- bus 14 (Roslindale Sq.-Heath St.)
- bus 16 (Forest Hills-Andrew or UMass)
- bus 21 (Ashmont-Forest Hills)
- **bus 22** (Ashmont-Ruggles)
- bus 29 (Mattapan-Jackson Sq.)
- bus 30 (Mattapan-Forest Hills or Roslindale Sq.)
- **bus 31** (Mattapan-Forest Hills)
- **bus 32** (Wolcott Sq. or Cleary Sq.-Forest Hills)
- bus 34 (Dedham Line-Forest Hills)
- bus 34E (Walpole Ctr.-Forest Hills)
- bus 35 (Dedham Mall-Forest Hills)
- bus 36 (Charles River-Forest Hills)
- bus 37 (Baker & Vermont-Forest Hills)
- bus 37/38 (Baker & Vermont-Forest Hills), Sat. morning and Sunday only
- bus 38 (Wren St.-Forest Hills)
- **bus 39** (Forest Hills-Back Bay Sta.)
- bus 40 (Georgetowne-Forest Hills)
- bus 41 (Centre & Eliot Sts.-JFK/UMass)
- bus 42 (Forest Hills-Ruggles)
- bus 44 (Jackson Sq.-Ruggles)

*Frequent bus routes in **bold**; "x-bus" denotes express bus*

- bus 48 (Jamaica Plain Loop)
- bus 50 (Cleary Sq.-Forest Hills)
- bus 51 (Reservoir-Forest Hills)

Centre St./The Monument: buses 38, 39, 41, 48

Egleston Sq.: buses **22**, 29, 42, 44, 48

S. Huntington Ave.: Green E Line (BACK OF THE HILL, HEATH ST) and **bus 39**

Washington St.: Orange Line (GREEN ST, FOREST HILLS) and bus 42

🚲 Southwest Corridor Bike Path; Jamaicaway Bike Path

Kingston
- CR Plymouth/Kingston Line to KINGSTON
- Plymouth & Brockton (Boston-Plymouth) from SOUTH STA and Park Sq. to Kingsbury Plaza

See PAL in Chapter 12

Lakeville
- CR Middleborough Line to MIDDLEBOROUGH/LAKEVILLE

Lawrence
- CR Haverhill Line to LAWRENCE
- MVRTA (Lawrence-Andover-Boston)
- Flight Line from Logan Airport

See MVRTA in Chapter 12

Leicester
See WRTA in Chapter 12

Lenox
See Western Massachusetts, Chapter 13

Leominster
- CR Fitchburg Line to NORTH LEOMINSTER
- Vermont Transit (Boston-Keene, NH; Boston-Rutland, VT) from SOUTH STA and RIVERSIDE to Fitchburg Jct. *(Bickford Restaurant, Rtes. 2 & 12)*

See MART in Chapter 12

Lexington
- bus 62 (Bedford VA Hospital-Alewife)
- bus 62/76 (Bedford VA Hospital-Alewife), Sat. only
- bus 76 (Hanscom AB-Alewife)
- Lexpress local bus 1 (Depot Sq.-E. Lexington)
- Lexpress local bus 2 (Depot Sq.-Lexington Ridge)

- Lexpress local bus 3 (Depot Sq.-Countryside & Emerson Garden Rd.)
- Lexpress local bus 4 (Depot Sq.-School & Lincoln Sts.)
- Lexpress local bus 5 (Depot Sq.-Malls)
- Lexpress local bus 6 (Depot Sq.-Diamond & Estabrook Schools)
- 128 Transportation Council shuttle from ALEWIFE (Red Line) to participating employers
🚲 Minuteman Commuter Bikeway

Lincoln
- CR Fitchburg/South Acton Line to LINCOLN

Littleton
- CR Fitchburg Line to LITTLETON/495

Lowell
🌐 p. 45
- CR Lowell Line to LOWELL
- Vermont Transit (Boston-White River Jct., VT; -Burlington, VT; and -Montréal, Québec) from SOUTH STA and Logan Airport to Gallagher Transportation Ctr. *(Thorndike St., N of Lowell Connector)*
- Flight Line from Logan Airport

See LRTA and MVRTA in Chapter 12

🚌 145 Thorndike St. (Route 3A)

Lynn
- CR Newburyport/Rockport Line to LYNN and RIVER WORKS
- x-bus 424 (Haymarket-Eastern & Essex Sts.), afternoon rush hour only
- x-bus 424W (Eastern & Essex Sts.-Wonderland), morning rush only
- bus 426 (Central Sq., Lynn-Haymarket)
- bus 426W (Central Sq., Lynn-Wonderland)
- bus 429 (Northgate-Central Sq., Lynn)
- bus 431 (Neptune Towers-Central Sq., Lynn)
- bus 435 (Liberty Tree Mall-Central Sq., Lynn) via Peabody Sq.
- bus 436 (Liberty Tree Mall-Central Sq., Lynn) via Goodwins Circle
- bus 439 (Central Sq., Lynn-Bass Point, Nahant), with rush hour express service to/from Haymarket
- x-bus 441 (Marblehead-Haymarket)
- x-bus 441W (Marblehead-Wonderland), weekends only
- x-bus 442 (Marblehead-Downtown Crossing)

Destinations

* x-bus 442W (Marblehead-Wonderland),
  weekends only
* x-bus 448 (Marblehead-Haymarket) via
  Logan Airport
* x-bus 449 (Marblehead-Downtown
  Crossing) via Logan Airport
* x-bus 450 (Salem Depot-Haymarket)
  via Highland & Western Aves.
* x-bus 450W (Salem Depot-
  Wonderland), weekends only
* x-bus 455 (Salem Depot-Haymarket)
  via Loring Ave.
* x-bus 455W (Salem Depot-Wonderland)
* x-bus 456 (Salem Depot-Central Sq.,
  Lynn)
* x-bus 459 (Salem Depot-Downtown) via
  Logan Airport

Central Sq.: all above buses and trains
except buses 424, 424W, 448, 449,
450, 450W

West Lynn: buses 424, 424W, 426, 426W,
434, 450, 450W, 455, 455W, 459

🚐 Broad St. (Rte. 1A) and Market St.
(downtown garage)

Lynnfield

* The Coach Company (Boston-
  Newburyport, Boston -Plaistow, NH)
  rush hour only, some trips serve Logan
  Airport
* x-bus 434 (Peabody-Haymarket), rush
  hour only
* bus 436 (Liberty Tree Mall-Central Sq.,
  Lynn) via Goodwins Circle
* Flight Line Seacoast Service from
  Logan Airport

Malden

* Orange Line to MALDEN CTR and OAK
  GROVE
* CR Reading/Haverhill Line to MALDEN
  CTR
* bus 97 (Malden Ctr.-Wellington)
* bus 99 (Boston Regional Medical Ctr.-
  Wellington)
* bus 101 (Malden Ctr.-Sullivan Sq.)
* bus 104 (Malden Ctr.-Sullivan Sq.)
* bus 105 (Malden Ctr.-Sullivan Sq.)
* bus 106 (Lebanon St./Malden-
  Wellington)
* bus 108 (Linden Sq.-Wellington)
* bus 109 (Linden Sq.-Sullivan Sq.)
* bus 119 (Northgate-Beachmont)
* bus 130 (Lebanon St./Melrose-Malden
  Ctr.)
* bus 131 (Melrose Highlands-Malden Ctr.)

* bus 132 (Redstone Plaza-Malden Ctr.)
* buses 136/137 (Reading Depot-Malden
  Ctr.)
* bus 411 (Revere/Jack Satter House-
  Malden Ctr.)
* bus 426 (Central Sq., Lynn-Haymarket)
* bus 426W (Central Sq., Lynn-
  Wonderland)
* bus 428 (Oaklandvale-Haymarket),
  rush hour only
* bus 429 (Northgate-Central Sq., Lynn)
* bus 430 (Appleton St., Saugus-Malden
  Ctr.)

Granada Highlands: buses 411, 428

Linden Sq.: buses 108, 109, 119, 411,
426, 426W, 428, 429

Main St.: buses 99, 106 (south of
Malden Sq.); buses 130, 131, 136, 137
(north of Malden Sq.)

Maplewood Sq./Salem St.: buses 106,
108, 411, 430

🚐 Entrance from Main St. at Malden/
Melrose line or from Winter St. E of
Washington St. (OAK GROVE)

Manchester, NH
See New Hampshire in Chapter 13

Manchester-by-the-Sea
* CR Rockport Line to MANCHESTER

Manomet (Plymouth)
See **Plymouth** for CR service
See PAL in Chapter 12

Mansfield
* CR Attleboro Line to MANSFIELD
* Mass Limousine from Logan Airport
See GATRA in Chapter 12

Marblehead
See **Swampscott** for CR service
* x-bus 441 (Marblehead-Haymarket)
* x-bus 442 (Marblehead-Downtown
  Crossing)
* x-bus 448 (Marblehead-Haymarket) via
  Logan Airport
* x-bus 449 (Marblehead-Downtown
  Crossing) via Logan Airport
🚲 Marblehead Bike Paths

Marlborough
* CR Framingham/Worcester Line to
  FRAMINGHAM; connect to Gulbankian
  Bus Lines (Marlborough/Solomon Pond
  Mall-Framingham), Sat. only

- Cavalier Coach (Boston-Northborough), 1 rush hour trip, serves Rte. 20
- Gulbankian Bus Lines (Boston-Hudson), rush hour only
- LIFT local bus 7 (Marlborough-Framingham)
- Mass Bay Limousine (Marlborough-Southborough CR station)
- Zebra Shuttle from Logan Airport

Marshfield
See **Pembroke** for service to Rte. 3/139 interchange
- Plymouth & Brockton (Boston-Duxbury) to Furnace Brook School., Marshfield Ctr., Brant Rock, and Green Harbor
- Plymouth & Brockton (Marshfield-Hanover-Braintree) from BRAINTREE (Red Line) to Furnace Brook School

Martha's Vineyard
See Cape Cod in Chapter 13

Mattapan (Boston)
- Red Line (Mattapan) to MATTAPAN
- CR Fairmount Line to MORTON ST
- bus 21 (Ashmont-Forest Hills)
- bus 24 (Wakefield Ave.-Mattapan)
- bus 26 (Ashmont-Norfolk & Morton Belt Line)
- bus 27 (Mattapan-Ashmont)
- **bus 28** (Mattapan-Ruggles)
- bus 29 (Mattapan-Jackson Sq.)
- bus 30 (Mattapan-Forest Hills or Roslindale Sq.)
- **bus 31** (Mattapan-Forest Hills)
- bus 33 (Mattapan-Dedham Line)
- bus 245 (Quincy Ctr.-Mattapan)
- JBL Bus Lines bus 716 (Mattapan-Canton)

Mattapan Sq.: Red Line, all above buses except 21 and 26

Mattapoisett
See SRTA in Chapter 12
🚌 I-95 Exit 19 (North St.)

Maynard
See **Acton** and **Concord** for CR service

Medfield
- Brush Hill (Boston-Milford), rush only

Medford
- Orange Line to WELLINGTON
- CR Lowell Line to WEST MEDFORD

- bus 80 (Arlington Ctr.-Lechmere)
- bus 90 (Davis Sq.-Wellington)
- bus 94 (Medford Sq.-Davis Sq.)
- bus 95 (W. Medford-Sullivan Sq.)
- bus 96 (Medford Sq.-Harvard Sta.)
- bus 99 (Boston Regional Medical Ctr.-Wellington)
- bus 100 (Elm St.-Wellington)
- bus 101 (Malden Ctr.-Sullivan Sq.)
- bus 108 (Linden Sq.-Wellington)
- bus 134 (N. Woburn-Wellington)
- x-bus 325 (Elm St., Medford-Haymarket), rush hour only
- x-bus 326 (W. Medford-Haymarket), rush hour only
- A&A Metro Trans. bus 710 (N. Medford-Medford Sq. or Meadow Glen Mall)

Fellsway: buses 100, 325
Medford Hillside: buses 80, 94, 96
Medford Sq.: buses 94, 95, 96, 101, 134, 326; and A&A Metro
W. Medford: CR; buses 80, 94, 95, 326
🚌 Revere Beach Pkwy. (Route 16) E. of Route 28 (WELLINGTON)

Medway
- Brush Hill (Boston-Milford), rush hour only, serves W. Medway

Melrose
- CR Reading/Haverhill Line to WYOMING HILL, MELROSE/CEDAR PARK, and MELROSE HIGHLANDS
- bus 106 (Lebanon St./Malden-Wellington), midday only
- bus 130 (Lebanon St./Melrose-Malden Ctr.)
- bus 131 (Melrose Highlands-Malden Ctr.)
- bus 132 (Redstone Plaza-Malden Ctr.)
- buses 136/137 (Reading Depot-Malden Ctr.)

Merrimac
- Flight Line Seacoast Service from Logan Airport
See MVRTA in Chapter 12

Methuen
See **Lawrence** for CR service
- Trombly Commuter Lines commuter bus (Boston-Methuen)
- Flight Line from Logan Airport
🚌 I-93 Exit 47 (Pelham St.)
See MVRTA in Chapter 12

Middleborough
See **Lakeville** for CR service
* Interstate Coach commuter bus (Boston-Middleboro/Bridgewater) to Town Hall, and Middleboro Rotary

Middleton
* Flight Line Seacoast Service from Logan Airport

Milford
* Brush Hill (Boston-Milford), rush only
* LIFT 6 (Framingham-Milford), connects with Boston buses and trains in Framingham
* Zebra Shuttle from Logan Airport

Millbury
* Peter Pan Bus Lines (Boston-Worcester, express)
See WRTA in Chapter 12
🚍 Mass Pike Exit 11

Millis
* Brush Hill (Boston-Milford), rush only

Milton
* Red Line (Mattapan) to MILTON, CENTRAL AVE, VALLEY RD, and CAPEN ST
* bus 215 (Quincy Ctr.-Ashmont)
* bus 217 (Wollaston-Ashmont)
* bus 240 (Avon Line or Holbrook/Randolph Sta.-Ashmont)
* bus 245 (Quincy Ctr.-Mattapan)
* BAT local bus 12 (Ashmont-Brockton)
* JBL bus 716 (Mattapan-Canton)
Blue Hill Ave.: JBL Bus Lines
E. Milton Sq.: buses 215, 217, 245
Milton Village: Red Line; buses 217, 240; BAT 12
Town Ctr.: buses 240, 245

Mission Hill (Boston)
* Green Line-E to BRIGHAM CIR, FENWOOD RD, MISSION PARK, and RIVERWAY
* Orange Line to ROXBURY CROSSING
* **bus 39** (Forest Hills-Back Bay Sta.)
* **bus 66** (Harvard Sta.-Dudley)
* Mission Hill Link Bus

Nahant
See **Lynn** for CR service
* bus 439 (Central Sq., Lynn-Bass Point, Nahant), with rush hour express service from Haymarket

Nantasket (Hull)
See **Hull**

Nantucket
See Cape Cod in Chapter 13

Nashua, NH
See New Hampshire in Chapter 13

Natick
* CR Framingham/Worcester Line to NATICK and WEST NATICK
* Natick Neighborhood Bus
* LIFT local buses 2 and 3 from Framingham to Rte. 9 malls

Needham
* CR Needham Line to HERSEY, NEEDHAM JCT, NEEDHAM CTR, and NEEDHAM HEIGHTS
* bus 59 (Needham Jct.-Watertown)
🚍 Chestnut St., 1/2 mile S of Route 135 (Needham Jct.); Great Plain Ave. (Rte. 135, 3/4 mile W of Route 128/I-95 Exit 18 (HERSEY)

New Bedford
🌐 p. 47
* American Eagle commuter bus (Boston-New Bedford) from SOUTH STA to SRTA Terminal *(Elm St.)*
* Bonanza Bus Lines (Albany, NY-Hyannis; New York-Hyannis via Providence, RI) from Fall River or Hyannis to SRTA Terminal
* Steamship Authority M/V *Schamonchi* ferry from Vineyard Haven, Martha's Vineyard to Billy Wood's Wharf (May-Oct.)
* Cuttyhunk Boat Lines M/V *Alert II* ferry from Cuttyhunk in the Elizabeth Islands to State Pier
See SRTA in Chapter 12
🚍 Elm & Pleasant Sts. (downtown); US 6 at Rte. 140 Exit 1; Kings Hwy at Rte. 140 Exit 4

Newbury
See **Newburyport** for CR service
* The Coach Co. (Boston-Newburyport) to Byfield, rush hour only
* Flight Line Seacoast Service from Logan Airport

Newburyport
* CR Newburyport Line to NEWBURYPORT
* C & J Trailways (Boston-Portsmouth,

*Frequent bus routes in **bold**; "x-bus" denotes express bus*

NH) from SOUTH STA (some trips via Logan Airport) to Trailways Transportation Center *(90 Storey Ave., I-95 & Rte. 113)*
• Vermont Transit (Boston-Portland, ME; Boston-Bangor, ME) from SOUTH STA (some trips from Logan Airport) to Trailways Transportation Center *(90 Storey Ave., I-95 & Rte. 113)*
• The Coach Co. (Boston-Amesbury, Boston-Newburyport) rush hours only
• Flight Line Seacoast Service from Logan Airport
See MVRTA in Chapter 12
Downtown: The Coach Co. (Boston-Newburyport), and MVRTA
🚌 Rte. 113, east of I-95 Exit 57

Newton
See the following neighborhoods:
Auburndale; Chestnut Hill; Newton Centre; Newton Corner; Newton Highlands; Newton Upper Falls; Newtonville; Nonantum; Riverside; West Newton
🚲 Dr. Paul Dudley White Bike Path, Charles River Bike Path

Newton Centre (Newton)
• Green Line-D to NEWTON CENTRE
• bus 52 (Dedham Mall-Watertown)
• Newton Nexus local bus

Newton Corner (Newton)
• bus 52 (Dedham Mall-Watertown)
• **bus 57** (Watertown Sq.-Kenmore)
• x-bus 501 (Brighton Ctr.-Downtown)
• x-bus 502 (Watertown-Copley Sq.)
• x-bus 504 (Watertown-Downtown)
• x-bus 553 (Roberts-Downtown)
• x-bus 554 (Waverley Sq.-Downtown)
• x-bus 556 (Waltham Highlands-Downtown)
• x-bus 558 (Auburndale-Downtown)
• Newton Nexus local bus

Newton Highlands (Newton)
• Green Line-D to NEWTON HIGHLANDS and ELIOT
• bus 52 (Dedham Mall-Watertown)
• bus 59 (Needham Jct.-Watertown)
• Newton Nexus local bus

Newton Upper Falls (Newton)
• bus 59 (Needham Jct.-Watertown)
• Newton Nexus local bus

Newtonville (Newton)
• CR Framingham/Worcester Line to NEWTONVILLE
• bus 59 (Needham Jct.-Watertown)
• x-bus 553 (Roberts-Downtown)
• x-bus 554 (Waverley Sq.-Downtown)
• x-bus 556 (Waltham Highlands-Downtown)
• Newton Nexus local bus

Nonantum (Newton)
• bus 59 (Needham Jct.-Watertown)
• x-bus 556 (Waltham Highlands-Downtown)
• x-bus 558 (Auburndale-Downtown)
• Newton Nexus local bus

Norfolk
• CR Franklin Line to NORFOLK

North Andover
See **Andover** and **Lawrence** for CR service
• Flight Line Seacoast Service from Logan Airport
See MVRTA in Chapter 12

North Attleborough
See GATRA in Chapter 12

North End (Boston)
🌐 p. 29
• Green and Orange Lines and north CR Lines to NORTH STA
• Green and Orange Lines to HAYMARKET
• bus 6 (Marine Indust. Pk.-Haymarket)
• bus 92 (Assembly Sq.-Downtown)
• **bus 93** (Sullivan Sq.-Downtown)
• **bus 111** (Woodlawn or Broadway & Park Ave.-Haymarket)
• x-bus 325 (Elm St., Medford-Haymarket), rush hour only
• x-bus 326 (W. Medford-Haymarket), rush hour only
• x-bus 424 (Haymarket-Eastern & Essex Sts.), afternoon rush only
• bus 426 (Central Sq., Lynn-Haymarket)
• bus 428 (Oaklandvale-Haymarket), rush hour only
• x-bus 434 (Peabody-Haymarket), one rush hour trip
• x-bus 441 (Marblehead-Haymarket)
• x-bus 442 (Marblehead-Haymarket) via Logan Airport
• x-bus 450 (Salem Depot-Haymarket)

via Highland & Western Aves.
- x-bus 455 (Salem Depot-Haymarket) via Loring Ave.
- MVRTA (Lawrence-Andover-Boston) to HAYMARKET
- Trombly Commuter Lines (Boston-Methuen) to HAYMARKET

Hanover St.: bus 6

North Reading
- Flight Line Seacoast Service from Logan Airport

Northampton
See Western Massachusetts, Chapter 13

Northborough
- Cavalier Coach (Boston-Northborough), 1 rush hour trip, serves Rte. 20

Norton
See **Attleboro** for CR service
See GATRA in Chapter 12

Norwood
- CR Franklin Line to NORWOOD DEPOT, NORWOOD CENTRAL, and WINDSOR GARDENS
- bus 34E (Walpole Ctr.-Forest Hills)

Peabody
- x-bus 434 (Peabody-Haymarket), rush hour only
- bus 435 (Liberty Tree Mall-Central Sq., Lynn) via Peabody Sq.
- bus 436 (Liberty Tree Mall-Central Sq., Lynn) via Goodwins Circle
- bus 465 (Liberty Tree Mall-Salem Depot)
- bus 468 (Danvers Sq.-Salem Depot)
- The Coach Co. (Boston-Newburyport)
- Logan Express from Logan Airport
- Peabody Transit

Pepperell
See LRTA in Chapter 12

Pittsfield
See Western Massachusetts, Chapter 13

Plainville
See GATRA in Chapter 12

Plymouth
- CR Plymouth/Kingston Line to PLYMOUTH; for rush hour service see **Kingston**
- Plymouth & Brockton (Boston-Cape Cod; Boston-Plymouth) from Logan

airport, SOUTH STA, and Park Sq. to park-and-ride lot *(Rte. 3 Exit 5)*
- Plymouth & Brockton (Braintree-Plymouth) from BRAINTREE (Red Line-Braintree) to park-and-ride lot, one weekday reverse commute only

See PAL in Chapter 12
🚗 Rte. 3 Exit 5
🚲 Seaside Trail

Portland, ME
See Maine in Chapter 13

Providence, RI
🌐 p. 48
- CR Attleboro Line to PROVIDENCE weekdays only
- Amtrak (Acela Express and Acela Regional, Boston-New York) from SOUTH STA and BACK BAY STA to PROVIDENCE
- Bonanza Bus Lines from SOUTH STA
- Greyhound bus from SOUTH STA

See RIPTA and GATRA in Chapter 12
🚗 Gaspee St. opposite State House; off Canal St. (downtown); 1 Bonanza Way, off Cemetery St., off North Main St.

Provincetown
See Cape Cod in Chapter 13

Quincy
- Red Line (Braintree) to NORTH QUINCY, WOLLASTON, QUINCY CTR, and QUINCY ADAMS
- CR Plymouth and Middleborough Lines to QUINCY CTR
- bus 210 (Quincy Ctr.-North Quincy or Fields Corner)
- bus 211 (Quincy Ctr.-Squantum)
- bus 212 (Quincy Ctr.-North Quincy)
- bus 214 (Quincy Ctr.-Germantown)
- bus 215 (Quincy Ctr.-Ashmont)
- bus 216 (Quincy Ctr.-Houghs Neck)
- bus 217 (Wollaston-Ashmont)
- bus 220 (Quincy Ctr.-Hingham)
- bus 221 (Quincy Ctr.-Fort Point)
- bus 222 (Quincy Ctr.-E. Weymouth)
- bus 225 (Quincy Ctr.-Weymouth Landing)
- bus 230 (Quincy Ctr.-Montello Sta.)
- bus 236 (Quincy Ctr.-South Shore Plaza)
- bus 238 (Quincy Ctr.-Holbrook/ Randolph Sta.)
- bus 245 (Quincy Ctr.-Mattapan)

*Frequent bus routes in **bold**; "x-bus" denotes express bus*

- Quincy Commuter Boat ferry from Quincy Shipyard to Long Wharf Marriott, Boston via Logan Airport
- Interstate Coach commuter bus (Boston-Canton Commerce Ctr.) to QUINCY ADAMS

Randolph
- CR Middleborough-Lakeville Line to HOLBROOK/RANDOLPH
- bus 238 (Quincy Ctr.-Holbrook/ Randolph Sta.)
- bus 240 (Holbrook/Randolph Sta.- Ashmont)
- BAT local bus 12 (Ashmont-Brockton)

Raynham
- Bloom Bus Lines (Boston-Taunton) from SOUTH STA to Raynham Dog Track

Reading
- CR Haverhill/Reading Line to READING
- buses 136/137 (Reading Depot- Malden Ctr.)
- Flight Line Seacoast Service from Logan Airport

Rehoboth
See GATRA in Chapter 12

Revere
- Blue Line to SUFFOLK DOWNS, BEACHMONT, REVERE BEACH and WONDERLAND
- bus 110 (Wonderland-Wellington)
- bus 116 (Wonderland-Maverick) via Revere St.
- bus 117 (Wonderland-Maverick) via Beach St.
- bus 119 (Northgate-Beachmont)
- bus 411 (Revere/Jack Satter House- Malden Ctr.)
- x-bus 424 (Haymarket-Eastern & Essex Sts.), afternoon rush hour only
- x-bus 424W (Eastern & Essex Sts.- Wonderland), morning rush only
- bus 426 (Central Sq., Lynn-Haymarket)
- bus 426W (Central Sq., Lynn- Wonderland)
- bus 428 (Oaklandvale-Haymarket), rush hour only
- bus 429 (Northgate-Central Sq., Lynn)
- x-bus 434 (Peabody Sq.-Haymarket)
- x-bus 441 (Marblehead-Haymarket)
- x-bus 441W (Marblehead- Wonderland), weekends only

- x-bus 442 (Marblehead-Downtown Crossing)
- x-bus 442W (Marblehead- Wonderland), weekends only
- x-bus 448 (Marblehead-Haymarket) via Logan Airport
- x-bus 449 (Marblehead-Downtown Crossing) via Logan Airport
- x-bus 450 (Salem Depot-Haymarket) via Highland & Western Aves.
- x-bus 450W (Salem Depot- Wonderland), weekends only
- x-bus 455 (Salem Depot-Haymarket) via Loring Ave.
- x-bus 455W (Salem Depot-Wonderland)
- x-bus 459 (Salem Depot-Downtown) via Logan Airport

Revere Ctr.: buses 110, 116, 117, 119, 411

🚗 Rte. 1A, N. of Bell Circle, Rte. 60 (Wonderland)

Riverside (Newton)
- Green Line-D to RIVERSIDE
- x-bus 500 (Riverside-Downtown)
- Greyhound (Boston-Albany NY) from SOUTH STA
- Peter Pan Bus Lines (Boston-New York, NY, -Albany, NY, -Springfield, -Amherst, and -Worcester) from SOUTH STA
- Vermont Transit (Boston-Keene, NH; Boston-Rutland, VT) from SOUTH STA
- Newton Nexus local bus
- Waltham CitiBus local buses 16 and 17

🚗 Grove St. at Rte. 128/I-95 exit 22

Rockland
- Plymouth & Brockton (Boston-Cape Cod; -Duxbury; -Plymouth; and -Scituate) from Logan Airport, SOUTH STA, and Park Sq. to park-and-ride lot *(Rte. 228)*
- Plymouth & Brockton (Braintree- Hanover-Marshfield) from BRAINTREE (Red Line-Braintree) to park-and-ride lot

🚗 Rte. 228 at Rte. 3 Exit 14, on Hingham/Norwell line

Rockport
⊕ p. 50
- CR Rockport Line to ROCKPORT
See CATA in Chapter 12

For buses to ⊤ stations see diagrams pp. 119-130

Roslindale (Boston)
- CR Needham Line to ROSLINDALE VILLAGE
- bus 14 (Roslindale Sq.-Heath St.)
- bus 30 (Mattapan-Forest Hills or Roslindale Sq.)
- **bus 32** (Wolcott Sq. or Cleary Sq.-Forest Hills)
- bus 34 (Dedham Line-Forest Hills)
- bus 34E (Walpole Ctr.-Forest Hills)
- bus 35 (Dedham Mall-Forest Hills)
- bus 36 (Charles River-Forest Hills)
- bus 37 (Baker & Vermont-Forest Hills)
- bus 37/38 (Baker & Vermont-Forest Hills), Sat. morning and Sunday only
- bus 38 (Wren St.-Forest Hills)
- bus 40 (Georgetowne-Forest Hills)
- bus 50 (Cleary Sq.-Forest Hills)
- bus 51 (Cleveland Cir.-Forest Hills)

Roslindale Sq.: CR; and all above buses except **32**, 37/38, 38

Rowley
- CR Newburyport Line to ROWLEY
- Flight Line Seacoast Service from Logan Airport

Roxbury (Boston)
See also **Mission Hill, Jamaica Plain,** and **West Roxbury**

⊕ p. 37

- Orange Line to RUGGLES and ROXBURY CROSSING
- Silver Line to LENOX ST, MELNEA CASS BLVD, and DUDLEY STA
- **bus 1** (Harvard-Dudley)
- bus 8 (Harbor Pt./UMass or Dudley Sta.-Kenmore)
- **bus 15** (Kane Sq. or Fields Corner-Ruggles)
- bus 19 (Fields Corner-Ruggles)
- **bus 22** (Ashmont-Ruggles) via Talbot Ave.
- **bus 23** (Ashmont-Ruggles) via Washington St.
- **bus 28** (Mattapan-Ruggles)
- bus 29 (Mattapan-Jackson Sq.)
- bus 41 (Centre & Eliot Sts.-JFK/UMass)
- bus 42 (Forest Hills-Ruggles)
- **bus 43** (Ruggles-Park & Tremont Sts.)
- bus 44 (Jackson Sq.-Ruggles)
- bus 45 (Franklin Park-Ruggles)
- bus 47 (Central Sq.-Broadway)

- bus 48 (Jamaica Plain Loop)
- **bus 66** (Harvard Sta.-Dudley)
- bus 170 (Oak Park-Dudley Sq.)
- bus 171 (Dudley Sta.-Logan Airport)
- bus CT2 (Sullivan Sq.-Ruggles)
- bus CT3 (Beth Israel Deaconess-Andrew)

Blue Hill Ave.: bus 45
Dudley Sq.: Silver Line (DUDLEY STA) and buses **1,** 8, 14, **15,** 19, **23, 28,** 41, 42, 44, 45, 47, **66,** 170, 171
Egleston Sq.: buses **22,** 29, 42, 44
Grove Hall: buses 14, 19, **23, 28,** 45
Warren St.: buses 19, **23, 28**
⊛ Southwest Corridor Bike Path

Salem
⊕ p. 51
- CR Newburyport/Rockport Line to SALEM
- x-bus 450 (Salem Depot-Haymarket) via Highland & Western Aves.
- x-bus 450W (Salem Depot-Wonderland), weekends only
- bus 451 (N. Beverly-Salem Depot)
- x-bus 455 (Salem Depot-Haymarket) via Loring Ave.
- x-bus 456 (Salem Depot-Cent. Sq., Lynn)
- x-bus 459 (Salem Depot-Downtown) via Logan Airport
- bus 465 (Liberty Tree Mall-Salem Depot)
- bus 468 (Danvers Sq.-Salem Depot)
- ⇔ Bridge St. at North St. (Rtes. 107 & 114)

Salisbury
- Flight Line Seacoast Service from Logan Airport

Saugus
- bus 426 (Central Sq., Lynn-Haymarket)
- bus 426W (Central Sq., Lynn-Wonderland)
- bus 428 (Oaklandvale-Haymarket), rush hour only
- bus 429 (Northgate-Central Sq., Lynn)
- bus 430 (Appleton St., Saugus-Malden Ctr.)

Scituate
- Plymouth & Brockton (Boston-Scituate) from SOUTH STA and Park Sq. to N. Scituate, Egypt Country Store, Fire Sta., Scituate Harbor, and Greenbush

*Frequent bus routes in **bold**; "x-bus" denotes express bus*

Seekonk
See GATRA in Chapter 12

Sharon
• CR Attleboro Line to SHARON

Sherborn
See **Framingham, Natick,** or **Wellesley** for CR service

Shirley
• CR Fitchburg Line to SHIRLEY

Shrewsbury
See WRTA in Chapter 12

Somerset
See SRTA in Chapter 12
🚗 I-95 Exit 4 (Rte. 103)

Somerville
🌐 p. 43 (Davis Square)
• Red Line to PORTER and DAVIS
• Orange Line to SULLIVAN SQ
• bus 80 (Arlington Ctr.-Lechmere)
• bus 83 (Rindge Ave.-Central Sq.)
• bus 85 (Spring Hill-Kendall/MIT)
• bus 86 (Sullivan Sq.-Reservoir/ Cleveland Cir.)
• bus 87 (Arlington Ctr. or Clarendon Hill-Lechmere)
• bus 88 (Clarendon Hill-Lechmere)
• bus 89 (Clarendon Hill-Sullivan Sq.)
• bus 90 (Davis Sq.-Wellington)
• bus 91 (Sullivan Sq.-Central Sq.)
• bus 92 (Assembly Sq.-Downtown)
• bus 94 (Medford Sq.-Davis Sq.)
• bus 95 (W. Medford-Sullivan Sq.)
• bus 96 (Medford Sq.-Harvard Sta.)
• bus 101 (Malden Ctr.-Sullivan Sq.)
• bus CT2 (Sullivan Sq.-Ruggles)
Ball Sq./Magoun Sq.: buses 80, 89
E. Somerville/Winter Hill: buses 89, 101
Highland Ave./City Hall: buses 88, 90
Powderhouse Sq.: buses 80, 89, 94, 96; or 10min walk from DAVIS
Union Sq.: buses 85, 86, 87, 91
W. Somerville/Teele Sq.: buses 87, 88, 89; or 10min walk from DAVIS

South Attleborough
See **Attleboro**

South Boston (Boston)
• Red Line to BROADWAY and ANDREW

• bus 3 (City Pt.-Bedford & Chauncy Sts.)
• bus 4 (North Sta.-World Trade Center)
• bus 5 (City Pt.-McCormack Housing)
• bus 6 (Marine Ind. Pk.-Haymarket)
• **bus 7** (City Point-Otis & Summer Sts.)
• **bus 9** (City Point-Copley Sq.)
• bus 10 (City Point-Copley Sq.)
• **bus 11** (City Point-Downtown)
• bus 16 (Forest Hills-Andrew or UMass)
• bus 17 (Fields Corner-Andrew)
• bus 18 (Ashmont-Andrew)
• bus 47 (Central Sq.-Broadway)
• bus CT3 (Beth Israel Deaconess-Andrew)
• Inner Harbor Ferry from Lovejoy Wharf, serves World Trade Center
• Boston Coach free shuttle from SOUTH STA to World Trade Center (6am-8pm, Mon-Fri)
Perkins Sq.: buses 5, **9,** 10

South End (Boston)
🌐 p. 27 (Back Bay)
• Orange Line to BACK BAY STA and MASSACHUSETTS AVE
• Silver Line to HERALD ST, EAST BERKELEY ST, UNION PARK ST, NEWTON ST, WORCESTER SQ, and MASSACHUSETTS AVE
• Green Line (all trains) to ARLINGTON and COPLEY, walk 3 blocks S
• Green Line-E to PRUDENTIAL and SYMPHONY, walk 2 blocks S
• **bus 1** (Harvard-Dudley)
• bus 8 (Harbor Pt./UMass or Dudley Sta.-Kenmore)
• **bus 9** (City Point-Copley Sq.)
• bus 10 (City Point-Copley Sq.)
• **bus 43** (Ruggles-Park & Tremont Sts.)
• bus 47 (Central Sq.-Broadway)
• x-bus 275/276 (Boston Medical Ctr.-Long Island Hospital)
• bus CT3 (Beth Israel Deaconess Andrew)
🚴 Southwest Corridor Bike Path

Southborough
• CR Worcester Line to SOUTHBOROUGH
• Gulbankian Bus Lines (Marlborough/ Solomon Pond Mall-Framingham), Saturday only
• Gulbankian Bus Lines (Boston-Hudson), rush hour only
• LIFT local bus 7 (Marlborough-Framingham)

- Mass Bay Limousine from Westborough or Marlborough to Southborough CR station
- Zebra Shuttle from Logan Airport

Springfield
See Western Massachusetts, Chapter 13

Stockbridge
See Western Massachusetts, Chapter 13

Stoneham
See **Malden, Medford, Melrose, Wakefield,** and **Winchester** for CR service
- bus 99 (Boston Regional Medical Ctr.-Wellington)
- bus 132 (Redstone Plaza-Malden Ctr.)

Stoughton
- CR Stoughton Line to STOUGHTON
See BAT in Chapter 12

Stow
See **Acton** for CR service

Sturbridge
- Peter Pan Bus Lines (Boston-Old Sturbridge Village) from SOUTH STA

Sudbury
See **Lincoln** and **Weston** for CR service
- Cavalier Coach (Boston-Northborough), 1 rush hour trip, serves Rte. 20

Swampscott
- CR Newburyport/Rockport Line to SWAMPSCOTT
- x-bus 441 (Marblehead-Haymarket)
- x-bus 441W (Marblehead-Wonderland), weekends only
- x-bus 442 (Marblehead-Downtown Crossing)
- x-bus 442W (Marblehead-Wonderland), weekends only
- x-bus 448 (Marblehead-Haymarket) via Logan Airport
- x-bus 449 (Marblehead-Downtown Crossing) via Logan Airport
- x-bus 455 (Salem Depot-Haymarket) via Loring Ave.
- x-bus 455W (Salem Depot-Wonderland)
- x-bus 459 (Salem Depot-Downtown) via Logan Airport

Swansea
See SRTA in Chapter 12

Taunton
- American Eagle (Boston-New Bedford) from SOUTH STA to Silver City Galleria
- Bloom Bus Lines (Boston-Taunton) from SOUTH STA to Bloom Terminal (*10 Oak St.*)
See GATRA in Chapter 12

Tewksbury
See **Lowell** for CR service
- Flight Line from Logan Airport
See LRTA in Chapter 12

Topsfield
- The Coach Co. (Boston-Haverhill), rush hour only, serves Rte. 1
- Flight Line Seacoast Service from Logan Airport

Townsend
See LRTA in Chapter 12

Tyngsboro
- Flight Line from Logan Airport
See LRTA in Chapter 12

Waban (Newton)
- Green Line-D to WABAN

Wakefield
- CR Reading/Haverhill Line to GREENWOOD and WAKEFIELD
- buses 136/137 (Reading Depot-Malden Ctr.)

Walpole
- CR Franklin Line to PLIMPTONVILLE (rush hour only) and WALPOLE
- bus 34E (Walpole Ctr.-Forest Hills)

Waltham
- CR Fitchburg/South Acton Line to WALTHAM and BRANDEIS/ROBERTS
- bus 70 (Cedarwood or Watertown Sq.-Univ. Park)
- bus 70A (North Waltham-Univ. Park)
- bus 170 (Oak Park-Dudley Sq.), rush hour "reverse commute" only
- x-bus 505 (Central Sq., Waltham-Downtown Boston), rush only
- x-bus 553 (Roberts-Downtown)
- x-bus 554 (Waverley Sq.-Downtown)
- x-bus 556 (Waltham Highlands-Downtown)
- x-bus 558 (Auburndale-Downtown)
- Waltham CitiBus local buses

- Waltham-Lexington Express from ALEWIFE to participating employers

Central Sq.: CR; buses 70, 70A, 505, 553, 554, 556, 558

Wareham
- Bonanza Bus Lines (Boston-Woods Hole) from Logan Airport and SOUTH STA to Main St. *(Deca's Variety Store)* and Rte. 28 *(Mill Pond Diner)*
See OWL in Chapter 12
🚌 US 6 at junction Rtes. 28 & 25

Watertown
- bus 52 (Dedham Mall-Watertown)
- **bus 57** (Watertown Sq.-Kenmore)
- bus 59 (Needham Jct.-Watertown)
- bus 70 (Cedarwood or Watertown Sq.-Univ. Park)
- bus 70A (North Waltham-Univ. Park)
- **bus 71** (Watertown Sq.-Harvard Sta.)
- **bus 73** (Waverley Sq.-Harvard Sta.)
- x-bus 502 (Watertown-Copley Sq.)
- x-bus 504 (Watertown-Downtown)
- x-bus 554 (Waverley Sq.-Downtown)
- x-bus 558 (Auburndale-Downtown)

Watertown Sq.: buses 52, **57,** 59, 70, 70A, **71,** 502, 504
🚲 Dr. Paul Dudley White Bike Path

Wayland
See **Lincoln** and **Weston** for CR service
- Cavalier Coach (Boston-Northborough), 1 rush hour trip, serves Rte. 20

Wellesley
- CR Framingham/Worcester Line to WELLESLEY FARMS, WELLESLEY HILLS, and WELLESLEY SQ
🚌 Washington St. at Jct. Routes 135 and 16, next to Post Office (Wellesley Sq.)

Wenham
- CR Newburyport Line to HAMILTON/WENHAM
- Flight Line Seacoast Service from Logan Airport

West Boylston
See WRTA in Chapter 12

West Bridgewater
See **Bridgewater** for CR service
- Interstate Coach commuter bus (Boston-Middleboro/Bridgewater),

serves Main & River Sts., Elm Sq., Hockomock, and Rte. 106 & 24 park-and-ride lot
See BAT in Chapter 12

West Newton (Newton)
- CR Framingham/Worcester Line to WEST NEWTON
- x-bus 505 (Waltham-Downtown), rush hour only
- x-bus 553 (Roberts-Downtown)
- x-bus 554 (Waverley Sq.-Downtown)

West Roxbury (Boston)
- CR Needham Line to BELLEVUE, HIGHLAND, and WEST ROXBURY
- bus 34 (Dedham Line-Forest Hills)
- bus 34E (Walpole Ctr.-Forest Hills)
- bus 35 (Dedham Mall-Forest Hills)
- bus 36 (Charles River-Forest Hills)
- bus 37 (Baker & Vermont-Forest Hills)
- bus 37/38 (Baker & Vermont-Forest Hills), Sat. morning and Sunday only
- bus 38 (Wren St.-Forest Hills)
- bus 40 (Georgetowne-Forest Hills)
- bus 51 (Cleveland Cir.-Forest Hills)
- bus 52 (Dedham Mall-Watertown)

Centre St.: CR; buses 35, 36, 37, 37/38, 38
Washington St.: buses 34, 34E, 40

Westborough
- CR Worcester Line to WESTBOROUGH
- Mass Bay Limousine (Westborough-Southborough CR station)
- Zebra Shuttle from Logan Airport

Westford
- Flight Line from Logan Airport
See LRTA in Chapter 12

Weston
- CR Fitchburg/South Acton Line to KENDAL GREEN, HASTINGS, and SILVER HILL (rush hour only)
- Cavalier Coach (Boston-Northborough), 1 rush hour trip, serves Rte. 20

Westwood
- CR Attleboro/Stoughton Line to ROUTE 128 STA
- CR Franklin Line to ISLINGTON
- bus 34E (Walpole Ctr.-Forest Hills)
- Amtrak (Acela Express and Acela Regional, Boston-New York) from

SOUTH STA and BACK BAY STA to ROUTE 128 STA
- Brush Hill (Boston-Milford), rush hour only, serves Rte. 109
- Vineyard Express bus between Rte. 128 park-and-ride lot and Martha's Vineyard via Woods Hole and Steamship Authority ferry

Washington St. (Rte. 1A): bus 34E
🚌🚌 University Ave. (ROUTE 128 STA)

Weymouth
- CR Plymouth/Kingston Line to SOUTH WEYMOUTH
- bus 220 (Quincy Ctr.-Hingham)
- bus 221 (Quincy Ctr.-Fort Point)
- bus 222 (Quincy Ctr.-E. Weymouth)
- bus 225 (Quincy Ctr.-Weymouth Landing)
- JBL Bus Lines commuter bus (Weymouth-Braintree) from BRAINTREE to Weymouth Commons, Mediterranean Woods, Gaslight Village, Columbian Sq., Tall Oaks Dr., Queen Anne's Gate, and Stone Run East
- JBL Bus Lines commuter bus (Boston-Whitman) from downtown Boston and SOUTH STA to Weymouth Landing, Rte. 18, and S. Weymouth *(Columbian Sq. and Gaslight Village)*

Whitman
- CR Plymouth/Kingston Line to WHITMAN
- JBL Bus Lines commuter bus (Boston-Whitman) from downtown Boston and SOUTH STA to Whitman Ctr.

Wilmington
- CR Lowell Line to WILMINGTON
- CR Haverhill Line to NORTH WILMINGTON

Winchester
- CR Lowell Line to WEDGEMERE and WINCHESTER CTR
- bus 134 (N. Woburn-Wellington)
- bus 350 (North Burlington-Alewife)

Winchester Ctr.: CR and bus 134

Winthrop
- Paul Revere Transportation Co. bus 712 (Point Shirley-Orient Hts.) via Winthrop Highlands
- Paul Revere Transportation Co. bus 713 (Point Shirley-Orient Hts.) via Winthrop Centre

Woburn
- CR Lowell Line to ANDERSON/WOBURN and MISHAWUM
- bus 134 (N. Woburn-Wellington)
- bus 350 (North Burlington-Alewife)
- x-bus 354 (Woburn-Haymarket), rush hour only
- x-bus 355 (Mishawum Sta.-Boston), rush hour only
- Amtrak (Boston-Portland, ME) from NORTH STA to Anderson Regional Transportation Center *(Atlantic Ave. at I-93 Exit 37C)*
- Logan Express from Logan Airport to Anderson Regional Transportation Center *(Atlantic Ave. at I-93 Exit 37C)*

Woburn Sq.: buses 134, 354

Woods Hole (Falmouth)
See Cape Cod in Chapter 13

Worcester
⊕ p. 52
- CR Framingham/Worcester Line to WORCESTER
- Greyhound (Boston-New York, NY; Boston-Albany, NY) from SOUTH STA and RIVERSIDE to Worcester Bus Terminal *(75 Madison St.)*
- Peter Pan Bus Lines (Boston-Worcester) from SOUTH STA and RIVERSIDE to Worcester Bus Terminal
- Amtrak from SOUTH STA, BACK BAY STA, and FRAMINGHAM to Union Sta.

See WRTA in Chapter 12

Wrentham
See **Franklin** or **Norfolk** for CR service

Route Details

Commuter and sightseeing boats at Long Wharf, Boston

SUSAN WILSON

This section's chapters will help you determine whether a given train, bus, or ferry will serve your needs. Every route of every branch of service is detailed: the stations or streets served, the frequency of service, how long trips will take, and where transit connections are possible. If you have a specific destination in mind, first consult either Chapter 6, "Place Listings – How to Get There" or Chapter 7, "Cities and Towns" to find routes serving your destination; then check this section for the route details. MTBA services appear in Chapters 8-11; other carrier services are detailed in Chapter 12. For destinations outside of Eastern Massachusetts, see Chapter 13. Airport information is in Chapter 14.

The information in these chapters is current as of early 2003, but routes and schedules do change, so it's always a good idea to obtain the most current schedule from the carrier. See page 185, "Transit Telephone Numbers and Websites" for company contact information.

Chapter 8:
MBTA Rapid Transit

Use the tables below to determine frequency of service and trip times in minutes for MBTA rapid transit lines. The diagrams following the tables show the bus connections available at each station, along with station addresses and fare zones, if any. For MBTA holiday schedule changes, see "Holiday Service" on page 6. In case you're out and about at odd hours, see "First and Last Rapid Transit Service" just before the diagrams. For general information about using MBTA rapid transit, see Chapter 1, "The T (MBTA Transit)."

Red Line	Trip Time	Rush	wk-day	wk-night	allSat	allSun
			Frequency in minutes			

Alewife—Ashmont   37   8   12   12   13   14

Stations: Alewife, Davis, Porter, Harvard, Central, Kendall/MIT, Charles/MGH, Park Street, Downtown Crossing, South Station, Broadway, Andrew, JFK/UMass, Savin Hill, Fields Corner, Shawmut, Ashmont.
• **Trip times from Park Street:** Kendall/MIT 4 min., Harvard 11 min., Alewife 20 min.; JFK/UMass 8 min., Fields Corner 13 min., Ashmont 17 min.

Alewife—Braintree   48   7   12   12   13   14

Stations: Alewife, Davis, Porter, Harvard, Central, Kendall/MIT, Charles/MGH, Park Street, Downtown Crossing, South Station, Broadway, Andrew, JFK/UMass, North Quincy, Wollaston, Quincy Center, Quincy Adams, Braintree.
• **Trip times from Park Street:** North Quincy 17 min., Quincy Center 22 min., Braintree 28 min.

Ashmont—Mattapan   10   5   10   12   8-13   12

Stations: Ashmont, Cedar Grove, Butler St., Milton, Central Ave., Valley Rd., Capen St., Mattapan. Connects w/Alewife-Ashmont trains at Ashmont.

Green Line

	Trip Time	Rush	wk-day	wk-night	allSat	allSun
		---- **Frequency in minutes** ----				

B Line

Boston College—Government Ctr. 45   5   8   10   6-8   5-10

Stations: 22 stops on Commonwealth Ave, Kenmore, Hynes Convention Ctr./ICA, Copley, Arlington, Boylston, Park Street, Government Ctr.
• **Trip times from Park Street:** Kenmore 12 min., Packards Cor. 26 min., Boston Coll. 43 min.

C Line

Cleveland Circle—Government Ctr. 34   6   6   10   5-10   7-10

Stations: 13 stops on Beacon St. in Brookline, Kenmore, Hynes Convention Ctr./ICA, Copley, Arlington, Boylston, Park Street, Government Ctr.
• **Trip times from Park Street:** Coolidge Corner 24 min., Cleveland Circle 32 min.

D Line

Riverside—Lechmere 57   5   10   10   6-10   7-10

Stations: Riverside, Woodland, Waban, Eliot, Newton Highlands, Newton Centre, Chestnut Hill, Reservoir, Beaconsfield, Brookline Hills, Brookline Village, Longwood, Fenway, Kenmore, Hynes Convention Ctr./ICA, Copley, Arlington, Boylston, Park Street, Government Ctr., Haymarket, North Station, Science Park, Lechmere
• **Trip times from Park Street:** Reservoir 27 min., Riverside 44 min., Lechmere 13 min.

E Line

Heath St.—Lechmere 36   7   9   10   7-10   5-10

Stations: 9 stops on Huntington and So. Huntington Aves., Symphony, Prudential, Copley, Arlington, Boylston, Park St., Government Ctr., Haymarket, North Sta., Science Park, Lechmere
• **Trip times from Park Street:** Lechmere 13 min.; Brigham Circle 16 min., Heath St. 22 min.

Orange Line

Oak Grove—Forest Hills 33   5   8   13   8-14   14

Stations: Oak Grove, Malden Ctr., Wellington, Sullivan Sq., Community College, North Station, Haymarket, State, Downtown Crossing, Chinatown, NE Medical Ctr., Back Bay Station, Massachusetts Ave., Ruggles, Roxbury Crossing, Jackson Sq., Stony Brook, Green St., Forest Hills.
• **Trip times from Downtown Crossing:** Community College 5 min., Oak Grove 15 min.; Back Bay Station 6 min., Forest Hills 18 min.

Blue Line

Wonderland—Bowdoin 23   4   9   11   9-12   14

Stations: Wonderland, Revere Beach, Beachmont, Suffolk Downs, Orient Heights, Wood Island, Airport, Maverick, Aquarium, State, Government Ctr., Bowdoin (closed nights and weekends).
• **Trip times from Government Ctr.:** Airport 9 min., Orient Hghts 13 min., Wonderland 21 min.

Silver Line Bus Rapid Transit (BRT)

Dudley Sta.—Downtown Crossing 16-21   5   9   11   6   8

Stations: Dudley Station, 8 stops on Washington St., NE Medical Ctr., Chinatown, Downtown Crossing, Boylston
• **Trip times from Dudley Station:** Washington and E. Berkeley Sts. 10-12 min., Downtown Crossing (Temple and Tremont Sts.) 16-21 min.

First and Last Rapid Transit Service

Use this table as a general guide. Remember that not all "last runs" can be used to connect to other lines. Call the MBTA at 617/222-3200 for details.

	First Train			Last Train	N-Owl[1]
	M-F.	Sat.	Sun.	Daily	Fri, Sat
Red Line					
Alewife-Ashmont	5:16	5:16	6:00	12:22	2:15
Alewife-Braintree	5:24	5:24	6:08	12:15[2]	2:15
Ashmont-Alewife	5:16	5:16	6:00	12:30	2:15
Braintree-Alewife	5:15	5:16	6:00	12:18	2:30
Mattapan-Ashmont	5:05	5:05	5:51	12:50	—
Ashmont-Mattapan	5:17	5:15	6:01	1:05	—
Green Line					
B–Boston College-Gov't Ctr.	5:01	4:45	5:20	12:10	2:20
B–Gov't Ctr.-Boston College	5:34	5:35	6:06	12:48	2:30
C–Cleveland Cir.-Gov't Ctr.	5:01	4:50	5:30	12:10	2:20
C–Gov't Ctr.-Cleveland Cir.	5:30	5:34	6:18	12:40	2:30
D–Riverside-Lechmere	4:56	4:55	5:40	12:00	2:30
D–Lechmere-Riverside	5:45	5:41	6:37	12:45[3]	2:30
E–Heath St.-Lechmere	5:30	5:30	6:15	12:45	2:20
E–Lechmere-Heath St.	5:01	5:01	5:35	12:30	2:30
Orange Line					
Oak Grove-Forest Hills	5:16	5:16	6:00	12:26	2:30
Forest Hills-Oak Grove	5:16	5:16	6:00	12:22	2:30
Blue Line					
Wonderland-Government Ctr.	5:13	5:25	5:58	12:26	2:20
Orient Heights-Gov't Ctr.	5:13	5:13	6:05	12:33	2:20
Government Ctr.-Wonderland	5:29	5:27	6:21	12:49	2:30
Silver Line BRT					
Dudley Sta.-Downtown Crossing	5:15	5:19	6:00	12:25	—
Downtown Crossing-Dudley Sta.	5:31	5:36	6:16	12:45	—

1 Night Owl bus service extends the hours of rapid transit (and select bus routes) on Friday and Saturday nights. **Note:** all Night Owl buses begin and end at Government Ctr.; Green E Line service runs to Forest Hills; for service to Lechmere take Orange Line northbound service and for Dudley Station take Orange Line southbound service.

2 If you miss the last Braintree train, take the last Ashmont train to Fields Corner. There, bus 210 awaits this train before making its final, special run to all Braintree-branch stations (Mon-Fri only).

3 This train departs from Government Ctr. The last train departs Lechmere at 12:32.

RAPID TRANSIT STATIONS

STATION ADDRESS & CONNECTING SERVICES

&. P Alewife

Alewife Brook Pkwy and Cambridge Park Dr, Cambridge
62-Bedford
67-Turkey Hill
76-Hanscom Field
79-Arlington Heights
84-Arlmont Village
350-Burlington
351-Oak Park (express)

&. Davis
Tufts University

1 College Ave and 1 Holland St, Somerville
Tufts shuttle (Joseph Trans)
87-Arlington Ctr-Lechmere
88-Clarendon Hill-Lechmere
90-Wellington via Sullivan
94-Medford Sq via W Medford
96-Medford Sq-Harvard

&. Porter

1900 Massachusetts Ave at 830 Somerville Ave, Cambridge
Commuter Rail—Fitchburg, South Acton
77-Arlington Heights-Harvard   83-Rindge Ave-Central
77A-North Cambridge-Harvard 96-Medford Sq-Harvard

&. Harvard

1400 Massachusetts Ave at 1 Brattle St, Cambridge
Bentley College shuttle
Wellesley Coll shuttle (G&W)
LMA Shuttle M2
1-Dudley via Massachusetts Av
66-Dudley via Brookline
68-Kendall/MIT
69-Lechmere
71-Watertown Sq
72-Huron Ave
72/75-Belmont Ctr
73 Waverley
74/75-Belmont Ctr
77-Arlington Heights
77A-North Cambridge
78-Arlmont
86-Sullivan-Reservoir
96-Medford Sq

&. Central

650 Massachusetts Ave at 1 Prospect St, Cambridge
LMA Shuttle M2
CT1-Central-Boston Med Ctr
1-Harvard-Dudley
47-Broadway
64-Oak Sq-Kendall, Univ Park
70-Cedarwood-Univ Park
70A-North Waltham-Univ Park
83-Rindge Ave
91-Sullivan

&. Kendall/MIT

Main St, Broadway, and Third St, Cambridge
CambridgeSide Galleria shuttle (The Wave)
EZ Ride to Cambridgeport
CT2-Ruggles-Sullivan
64-Oak Sq (rush hours)
68-Harvard Sq
85-Spring Hill

Charles/MGH

Charles Circle, 350 Cambridge St at 160 Charles St, Boston

&. Park Street

120 Tremont St at 1 Park St, Boston
Green Line
walkway to Downtown Crossing
Commuter buses
43-Ruggles
55-Queensberry St

&.Downtown Crossing
Washington

450 Washington St at 1 Summer St, Boston
*Gulbankian (Hudson-Boston)
Orange Line
Green Line via walkway
Silver Line Bus Rapid Transit
3-City Pt-Chinatown
7-City Pt via Fan Pier
11-City Pt via Bayview
92-Assembly Sq
93-Sullivan
448-Marblehead
449-Marblehead
459-Salem
500-Riverside (express)
501-Brighton Center (express)
504-Watertown (express)
505-Waltham (express)
553-Roberts via Waltham &
   Newton Corner
554-Waverley via Waltham &
   Newton Corner
556-Waltham Highlands or
   Cedarwood
558-Auburndale

&. South Station

Dewey Sq, 200 Summer St at 600 Atlantic Ave, Boston
Commuter Rail
Amtrak
Interstate buses
Commuter buses
World Trade Center shuttle
   (Boston Coach)
3-City Point via Marine Ind Park
6-Marine Ind Park-Haymarket
7-City Point via Summer St
448-Marblehead-Downtown
449-Marblehead-Downtown
459-Salem-Downtown

&. Broadway

100 Dorchester Ave at 1 West Broadway, South Boston
3-City Point via Marine Ind Park
9-City Point-Copley
11-City Point-Downtown
47-Central Sq

To Ashmont or Braintree

* Bus stop is near rapid transit stop.

Red Line

RAPID TRANSIT STATIONS   STATION ADDRESS & CONNECTING SERVICES

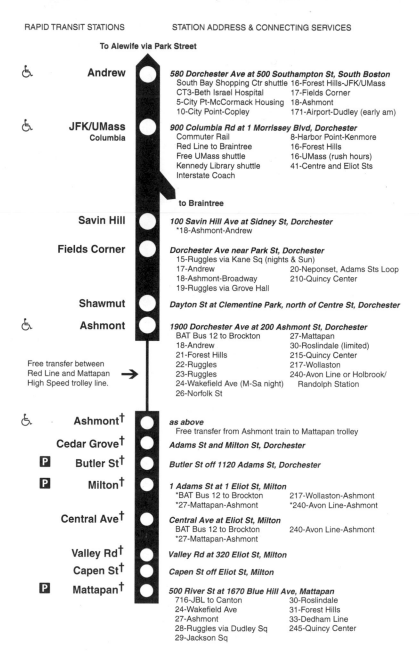

To Alewife via Park Street

♿ **Andrew**

580 Dorchester Ave at 500 Southampton St, South Boston
South Bay Shopping Ctr shuttle   16-Forest Hills-JFK/UMass
CT3-Beth Israel Hospital   17-Fields Corner
5-City Pt-McCormack Housing   18-Ashmont
10-City Point-Copley   171-Airport-Dudley (early am)

♿ **JFK/UMass**
Columbia

900 Columbia Rd at 1 Morrissey Blvd, Dorchester
Commuter Rail   8-Harbor Point-Kenmore
Red Line to Braintree   16-Forest Hills
Free UMass shuttle   16-UMass (rush hours)
Kennedy Library shuttle   41-Centre and Eliot Sts
Interstate Coach

to Braintree

Savin Hill

100 Savin Hill Ave at Sidney St, Dorchester
*18-Ashmont-Andrew

Fields Corner

Dorchester Ave near Park St, Dorchester
15-Ruggles via Kane Sq (nights & Sun)
17-Andrew   20-Neponset, Adams Sts Loop
18-Ashmont-Broadway   210-Quincy Center
19-Ruggles via Grove Hall

Shawmut

Dayton St at Clementine Park, north of Centre St, Dorchester

♿ **Ashmont**

1900 Dorchester Ave at 200 Ashmont St, Dorchester
BAT Bus 12 to Brockton   27-Mattapan
18-Andrew   30-Roslindale (limited)
21-Forest Hills   215-Quincy Center
22-Ruggles   217-Wollaston
23-Ruggles   240-Avon Line or Holbrook/
24-Wakefield Ave (M-Sa night)   Randolph Station
26-Norfolk St

Free transfer between
Red Line and Mattapan →
High Speed trolley line.

♿ **Ashmont†**

as above
Free transfer from Ashmont train to Mattapan trolley

Cedar Grove†

Adams St and Milton St, Dorchester

🅿 **Butler St†**

Butler St off 1120 Adams St, Dorchester

🅿 **Milton†**

1 Adams St at 1 Eliot St, Milton
*BAT Bus 12 to Brockton   217-Wollaston-Ashmont
*27-Mattapan-Ashmont   *240-Avon Line-Ashmont

Central Ave†

Central Ave at Eliot St, Milton
BAT Bus 12 to Brockton   240-Avon Line-Ashmont
*27-Mattapan-Ashmont

Valley Rd†

Valley Rd at 320 Eliot St, Milton

Capen St†

Capen St off Eliot St, Milton

🅿 **Mattapan†**

500 River St at 1670 Blue Hill Ave, Mattapan
716-JBL to Canton   30-Roslindale
24-Wakefield Ave   31-Forest Hills
27-Ashmont   33-Dedham Line
28-Ruggles via Dudley Sq   245-Quincy Center
29-Jackson Sq

* Bus stop is near rapid transit stop.

† Local Fare: 75¢ inbound between Mattapan and
   Ashmont (pay upon exit), except no fare collected
   inbound at Ashmont; No fare outbound.

RAPID TRANSIT STATIONS   STATION ADDRESS & CONNECTING SERVICES

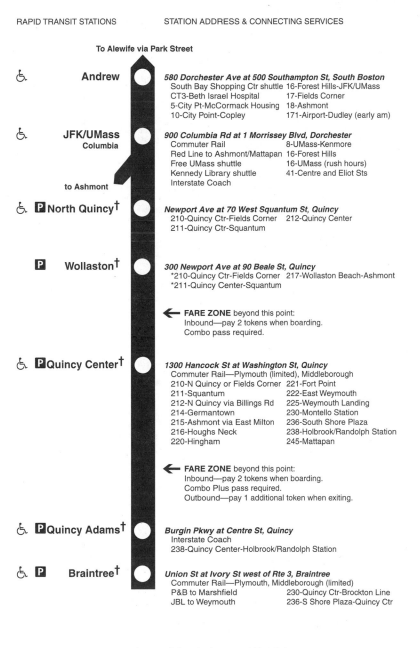

To Alewife via Park Street

    Andrew

580 Dorchester Ave at 500 Southampton St, South Boston
South Bay Shopping Ctr shuttle 16-Forest Hills-JFK/UMass
CT3-Beth Israel Hospital   17-Fields Corner
5-City Pt-McCormack Housing   18-Ashmont
10-City Point-Copley   171-Airport-Dudley (early am)

    JFK/UMass
      Columbia

900 Columbia Rd at 1 Morrissey Blvd, Dorchester
Commuter Rail   8-UMass-Kenmore
Red Line to Ashmont/Mattapan   16-Forest Hills
Free UMass shuttle   16-UMass (rush hours)
Kennedy Library shuttle   41-Centre and Eliot Sts
Interstate Coach

    to Ashmont

P North Quincy†

Newport Ave at 70 West Squantum St, Quincy
210-Quincy Ctr-Fields Corner   212-Quincy Center
211-Quincy Ctr-Squantum

P Wollaston†

300 Newport Ave at 90 Beale St, Quincy
*210-Quincy Ctr-Fields Corner   217-Wollaston Beach-Ashmont
*211-Quincy Center-Squantum

← **FARE ZONE** beyond this point:
Inbound—pay 2 tokens when boarding.
Combo pass required.

P Quincy Center†

1300 Hancock St at Washington St, Quincy
Commuter Rail—Plymouth (limited), Middleborough
210-N Quincy or Fields Corner   221-Fort Point
211-Squantum   222-East Weymouth
212-N Quincy via Billings Rd   225-Weymouth Landing
214-Germantown   230-Montello Station
215-Ashmont via East Milton   236-South Shore Plaza
216-Houghs Neck   238-Holbrook/Randolph Station
220-Hingham   245-Mattapan

← **FARE ZONE** beyond this point:
Inbound—pay 2 tokens when boarding.
Combo Plus pass required.
Outbound—pay 1 additional token when exiting.

P Quincy Adams†

Burgin Pkwy at Centre St, Quincy
Interstate Coach
238-Quincy Center-Holbrook/Randolph Station

P Braintree†

Union St at Ivory St west of Rte 3, Braintree
Commuter Rail—Plymouth, Middleborough (limited)
P&B to Marshfield   230-Quincy Ctr-Brockton Line
JBL to Weymouth   236-S Shore Plaza-Quincy Ctr

* Bus stop is near rapid transit stop.
† For local travel within Quincy and Braintree, spend
$2 to purchase 1 token and 1 "local fare warrant"
from collector, then redeem warrant for a $1 rebate
or a free exit at the collector's booth upon exiting.

121

Green Line

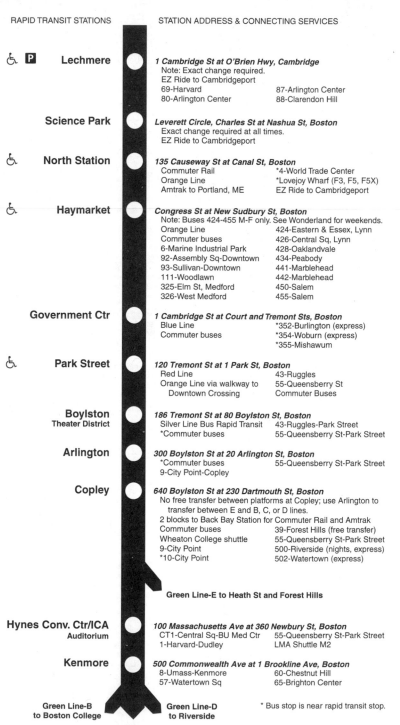

RAPID TRANSIT STATIONS — STATION ADDRESS & CONNECTING SERVICES

** Lechmere** ♿ 🅿️

1 Cambridge St at O'Brien Hwy, Cambridge
Note: Exact change required.
EZ Ride to Cambridgeport
69-Harvard
80-Arlington Center
87-Arlington Center
88-Clarendon Hill

Science Park

Leverett Circle, Charles St at Nashua St, Boston
Exact change required at all times.
EZ Ride to Cambridgeport

North Station ♿

135 Causeway St at Canal St, Boston
Commuter Rail
Orange Line
Amtrak to Portland, ME
*4-World Trade Center
*Lovejoy Wharf (F3, F5, F5X)
EZ Ride to Cambridgeport

Haymarket ♿

Congress St at New Sudbury St, Boston
Note: Buses 424-455 M-F only. See Wonderland for weekends.
Orange Line
Commuter buses
6-Marine Industrial Park
92-Assembly Sq-Downtown
93-Sullivan-Downtown
111-Woodlawn
325-Elm St, Medford
326-West Medford
424-Eastern & Essex, Lynn
426-Central Sq, Lynn
428-Oaklandvale
434-Peabody
441-Marblehead
442-Marblehead
450-Salem
455-Salem

Government Ctr

1 Cambridge St at Court and Tremont Sts, Boston
Blue Line
Commuter buses
*352-Burlington (express)
*354-Woburn (express)
*355-Mishawum

Park Street ♿

120 Tremont St at 1 Park St, Boston
Red Line
Orange Line via walkway to
  Downtown Crossing
43-Ruggles
55-Queensberry St
Commuter Buses

Boylston
Theater District

186 Tremont St at 80 Boylston St, Boston
Silver Line Bus Rapid Transit
*Commuter buses
43-Ruggles-Park Street
55-Queensberry St-Park Street

Arlington

300 Boylston St at 20 Arlington St, Boston
*Commuter buses
9-City Point-Copley
55-Queensberry St-Park Street

Copley

640 Boylston St at 230 Dartmouth St, Boston
No free transfer between platforms at Copley; use Arlington to
  transfer between E and B, C, or D lines.
2 blocks to Back Bay Station for Commuter Rail and Amtrak
Commuter buses
Wheaton College shuttle
9-City Point
*10-City Point
39-Forest Hills (free transfer)
55-Queensberry St-Park Street
500-Riverside (nights, express)
502-Watertown (express)

Green Line-E to Heath St and Forest Hills

Hynes Conv. Ctr/ICA
Auditorium

100 Massachusetts Ave at 360 Newbury St, Boston
CT1-Central Sq-BU Med Ctr
1-Harvard-Dudley
55-Queensberry St-Park Street
LMA Shuttle M2

Kenmore

500 Commonwealth Ave at 1 Brookline Ave, Boston
8-Umass-Kenmore
57-Watertown Sq
60-Chestnut Hill
65-Brighton Center

Green Line-B
to Boston College

Green Line-D
to Riverside

* Bus stop is near rapid transit stop.

Green Line-C to Cleveland Circle

Green Line-B

RAPID TRANSIT STATIONS   STATION ADDRESS & CONNECTING SERVICES

To Government Center via Park Street

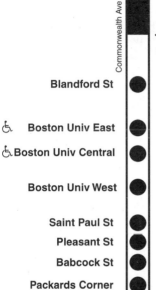

Kenmore — *500 Commonwealth Ave at 1 Brookline Ave, Boston*
Green Line-C (Cleveland Cir)   57-Watertown Sq
Green Line-D (Riverside)   60-Chestnut Hill
8-Harbor Point   65-Brighton Center

← **FARE ZONE** beyond this point:
Inbound—pay $1 exact change when boarding.
Local Bus or Subway pass accepted.
Outbound—no fare.

Blandford St — *Commonwealth Ave and Blandford St, Boston*
57-Watertown Sq-Kenmore (limited Blandford St to Babcock St:
inbound drop-off only; outbound pick-up only for passengers
traveling beyond Packards Corner)

🚹 **Boston Univ East** — *Commonwealth Ave near Granby St, Boston*
57-Watertown Sq-Kenmore (limited: see Blandford St above)

🚹 **Boston Univ Central** — *Commonwealth Ave and Saint Mary's St, B.U. Bridge, Boston*
*CT2-Sullivan-Ruggles   *47-Central-Broadway
57-Watertown Sq-Kenmore (limited: see Blandford St above)

Boston Univ West — *Commonwealth Ave and Amory St, Boston*
*CT2-Sullivan-Ruggles   *47-Central-Broadway
57-Watertown Sq-Kenmore (limited: see Blandford St above)

Saint Paul St — 57-Watertown Sq-Kenmore (limited: see Blandford St above)

Pleasant St — 57-Watertown Sq-Kenmore (limited: see Blandford St above)

Babcock St — 57-Watertown Sq-Kenmore (limited: see Blandford St above)

Packards Corner — 57-Watertown Sq-Kenmore

Fordham Rd

🚹 **Harvard Ave** — 66-Harvard-Dudley

Griggs St, Long Ave

Allston St

Warren St

Summit Ave

🚹 **Washington St** — 65-Brighton Center-Kenmore via Brookline Village

Mount Hood Rd

Sutherland Rd

Chiswick Rd

Chestnut Hill Ave — *Commonwealth Ave and Chestnut Hill Ave, Boston*
Green Line-C at Cleveland Circle (2 blocks south)
Green Line-D at Reservoir (3 blocks south)
86-Sullivan-Cleveland Circle

South St

Greycliff Rd

🚹 **Boston College** — *Commonwealth Ave and Lake St, Boston*

◯ Rapid Transit
● Surface Streetcar

123

Green Line-C

RAPID TRANSIT STATIONS | STATION ADDRESS & CONNECTING SERVICES

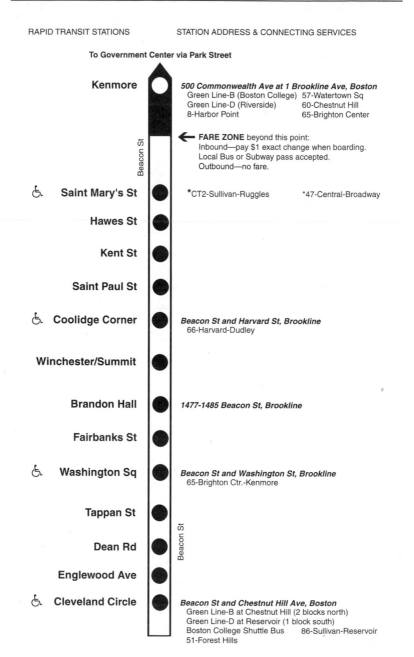

To Government Center via Park Street

Kenmore — *500 Commonwealth Ave at 1 Brookline Ave, Boston*
Green Line-B (Boston College)   57-Watertown Sq
Green Line-D (Riverside)   60-Chestnut Hill
8-Harbor Point   65-Brighton Center

◄ **FARE ZONE** beyond this point:
Inbound—pay $1 exact change when boarding.
Local Bus or Subway pass accepted.
Outbound—no fare.

Beacon St

♿ **Saint Mary's St** — *CT2-Sullivan-Ruggles   *47-Central-Broadway

Hawes St

Kent St

Saint Paul St

♿ **Coolidge Corner** — *Beacon St and Harvard St, Brookline*
66-Harvard-Dudley

Winchester/Summit

Brandon Hall — *1477-1485 Beacon St, Brookline*

Fairbanks St

♿ **Washington Sq** — *Beacon St and Washington St, Brookline*
65-Brighton Ctr.-Kenmore

Tappan St

Beacon St

Dean Rd

Englewood Ave

♿ **Cleveland Circle** — *Beacon St and Chestnut Hill Ave, Boston*
Green Line-B at Chestnut Hill (2 blocks north)
Green Line-D at Reservoir (1 block south)
Boston College Shuttle Bus   86-Sullivan-Reservoir
51-Forest Hills

◯ Rapid Transit
● Surface Streetcar

* Bus stop is near rapid transit stop.

RAPID TRANSIT STATIONS

STATION ADDRESS & CONNECTING SERVICES

To Lechmere via Park Street

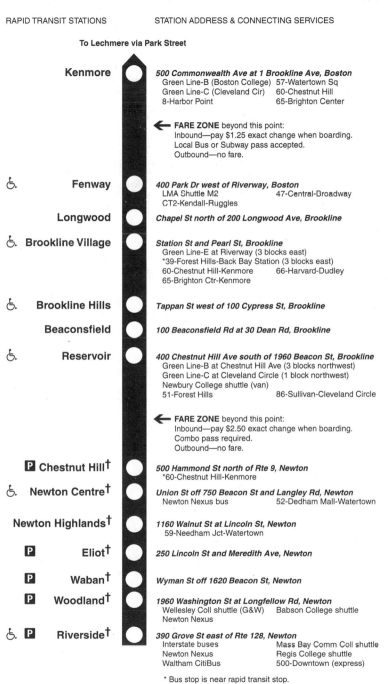

Kenmore

500 Commonwealth Ave at 1 Brookline Ave, Boston
Green Line-B (Boston College)   57-Watertown Sq
Green Line-C (Cleveland Cir)   60-Chestnut Hill
8-Harbor Point   65-Brighton Center

← **FARE ZONE** beyond this point:
Inbound—pay $1.25 exact change when boarding.
Local Bus or Subway pass accepted.
Outbound—no fare.

&. **Fenway**

400 Park Dr west of Riverway, Boston
LMA Shuttle M2   47-Central-Broadway
CT2-Kendall-Ruggles

Longwood

Chapel St north of 200 Longwood Ave, Brookline

&. **Brookline Village**

Station St and Pearl St, Brookline
Green Line-E at Riverway (3 blocks east)
*39-Forest Hills-Back Bay Station (3 blocks east)
60-Chestnut Hill-Kenmore   66-Harvard-Dudley
65-Brighton Ctr-Kenmore

&. **Brookline Hills**

Tappan St west of 100 Cypress St, Brookline

Beaconsfield

100 Beaconsfield Rd at 30 Dean Rd, Brookline

&. **Reservoir**

400 Chestnut Hill Ave south of 1960 Beacon St, Brookline
Green Line-B at Chestnut Hill Ave (3 blocks northwest)
Green Line-C at Cleveland Circle (1 block northwest)
Newbury College shuttle (van)
51-Forest Hills   86-Sullivan-Cleveland Circle

← **FARE ZONE** beyond this point:
Inbound—pay $2.50 exact change when boarding.
Combo pass required.
Outbound—no fare.

P **Chestnut Hill**†

500 Hammond St north of Rte 9, Newton
*60-Chestnut Hill-Kenmore

&. **Newton Centre**†

Union St off 750 Beacon St and Langley Rd, Newton
Newton Nexus bus   52-Dedham Mall-Watertown

Newton Highlands†

1160 Walnut St at Lincoln St, Newton
59-Needham Jct-Watertown

P **Eliot**†

250 Lincoln St and Meredith Ave, Newton

P **Waban**†

Wyman St off 1620 Beacon St, Newton

P **Woodland**†

1960 Washington St at Longfellow Rd, Newton
Wellesley Coll shuttle (G&W)   Babson College shuttle
Newton Nexus

&. **P** **Riverside**†

390 Grove St east of Rte 128, Newton
Interstate buses   Mass Bay Comm Coll shuttle
Newton Nexus   Regis College shuttle
Waltham CitiBus   500-Downtown (express)

* Bus stop is near rapid transit stop.

† Newton local coupons are issued when you get off any
inbound train between Woodland and Chestnut Hill. They
are good for $1.25 off next inbound trip.

Green Line-E

Copley – Forest Hills (Arborway)

RAPID TRANSIT STATIONS   STATION ADDRESS & CONNECTING SERVICES

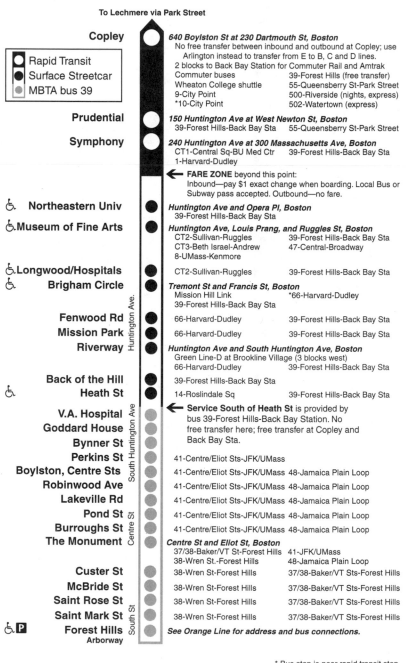

To Lechmere via Park Street

Copley

640 Boylston St at 230 Dartmouth St, Boston
No free transfer between inbound and outbound at Copley; use
Arlington instead to transfer from E to B, C and D lines.
2 blocks to Back Bay Station for Commuter Rail and Amtrak

○ Rapid Transit	Commuter buses	39-Forest Hills (free transfer)
● Surface Streetcar	Wheaton College shuttle	55-Queensberry St-Park Street
◍ MBTA bus 39	9-City Point	500-Riverside (nights, express)
	*10-City Point	502-Watertown (express)

Prudential
150 Huntington Ave at West Newton St, Boston
39-Forest Hills-Back Bay Sta   55-Queensberry St-Park Street

Symphony
240 Huntington Ave at 300 Massachusetts Ave, Boston
CT1-Central Sq-BU Med Ctr   39-Forest Hills-Back Bay Sta
1-Harvard-Dudley

← **FARE ZONE** beyond this point:
Inbound—pay $1 exact change when boarding. Local Bus or
Subway pass accepted. Outbound—no fare.

♿ **Northeastern Univ**
Huntington Ave and Opera Pl, Boston
39-Forest Hills-Back Bay Sta

♿**Museum of Fine Arts**
Huntington Ave, Louis Prang, and Ruggles St, Boston
CT2-Sullivan-Ruggles   39-Forest Hills-Back Bay Sta
CT3-Beth Israel-Andrew   47-Central-Broadway
8-UMass-Kenmore

♿**Longwood/Hospitals**
CT2-Sullivan-Ruggles   39-Forest Hills-Back Bay Sta

♿ **Brigham Circle**
Tremont St and Francis St, Boston
Mission Hill Link   *66-Harvard-Dudley
39-Forest Hills-Back Bay Sta

Fenwood Rd
66-Harvard-Dudley   39-Forest Hills-Back Bay Sta

Mission Park
66-Harvard-Dudley   39-Forest Hills-Back Bay Sta

Riverway
Huntington Ave and South Huntington Ave, Boston
Green Line-D at Brookline Village (3 blocks west)
66-Harvard-Dudley   39-Forest Hills-Back Bay Sta

(Huntington Ave.)

Back of the Hill
39-Forest Hills-Back Bay Sta

♿ **Heath St**
14-Roslindale Sq   39-Forest Hills-Back Bay Sta

← **Service South of Heath St** is provided by
bus 39-Forest Hills-Back Bay Station. No
free transfer here; free transfer at Copley and
Back Bay Sta.

V.A. Hospital
Goddard House
Bynner St

Perkins St
41-Centre/Eliot Sts-JFK/UMass

Boylston, Centre Sts
41-Centre/Eliot Sts-JFK/UMass 48-Jamaica Plain Loop

Robinwood Ave
41-Centre/Eliot Sts-JFK/UMass 48-Jamaica Plain Loop

Lakeville Rd
41-Centre/Eliot Sts-JFK/UMass 48-Jamaica Plain Loop

Pond St
41-Centre/Eliot Sts-JFK/UMass 48-Jamaica Plain Loop

Burroughs St
41-Centre/Eliot Sts-JFK/UMass 48-Jamaica Plain Loop

The Monument
Centre St and Eliot St, Boston
37/38-Baker/VT St-Forest Hills 41-JFK/UMass
38-Wren St.-Forest Hills 48-Jamaica Plain Loop

(South Huntington Ave) *(Centre St)*

Custer St
38-Wren St-Forest Hills 37/38-Baker/VT Sts-Forest Hills

McBride St
38-Wren St-Forest Hills 37/38-Baker/VT Sts-Forest Hills

Saint Rose St
38-Wren St-Forest Hills 37/38-Baker/VT Sts-Forest Hills

Saint Mark St
38-Wren St-Forest Hills 37/38-Baker/VT Sts-Forest Hills

♿**P** **Forest Hills**
Arborway
(South St)
See Orange Line for address and bus connections.

* Bus stop is near rapid transit stop.

Orange Line

Oak Grove – Downtown Crossing

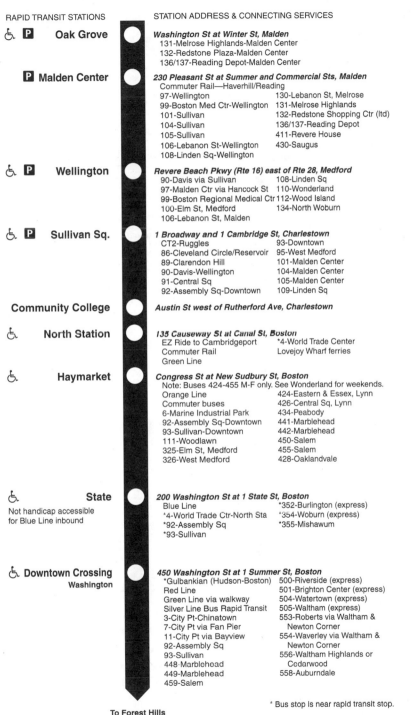

RAPID TRANSIT STATIONS	STATION ADDRESS & CONNECTING SERVICES
♿ 🅿 **Oak Grove**	**Washington St at Winter St, Malden** 131-Melrose Highlands-Malden Center 132-Redstone Plaza-Malden Center 136/137-Reading Depot-Malden Center
🅿 **Malden Center**	**230 Pleasant St at Summer and Commercial Sts, Malden** Commuter Rail—Haverhill/Reading 97-Wellington, 130-Lebanon St, Melrose 99-Boston Med Ctr-Wellington, 131-Melrose Highlands 101-Sullivan, 132-Redstone Shopping Ctr (ltd) 104-Sullivan, 136/137-Reading Depot 105-Sullivan, 411-Revere House 106-Lebanon St-Wellington, 430-Saugus 108-Linden Sq-Wellington
♿ 🅿 **Wellington**	**Revere Beach Pkwy (Rte 16) east of Rte 28, Medford** 90-Davis via Sullivan, 108-Linden Sq 97-Malden Ctr via Hancock St, 110-Wonderland 99-Boston Regional Medical Ctr, 112-Wood Island 100-Elm St, Medford, 134-North Woburn 106-Lebanon St, Malden
♿ 🅿 **Sullivan Sq.**	**1 Broadway and 1 Cambridge St, Charlestown** CT2-Ruggles, 93-Downtown 86-Cleveland Circle/Reservoir, 95-West Medford 89-Clarendon Hill, 101-Malden Center 90-Davis-Wellington, 104-Malden Center 91-Central Sq, 105-Malden Center 92-Assembly Sq-Downtown, 109-Linden Sq
Community College	**Austin St west of Rutherford Ave, Charlestown**
♿ **North Station**	**135 Causeway St at Canal St, Boston** EZ Ride to Cambridgeport, *4-World Trade Center Commuter Rail, Lovejoy Wharf ferries Green Line
♿ **Haymarket**	**Congress St at New Sudbury St, Boston** Note: Buses 424-455 M-F only. See Wonderland for weekends. Orange Line, 424-Eastern & Essex, Lynn Commuter buses, 426-Central Sq, Lynn 6-Marine Industrial Park, 434-Peabody 92-Assembly Sq-Downtown, 441-Marblehead 93-Sullivan-Downtown, 442-Marblehead 111-Woodlawn, 450-Salem 325-Elm St, Medford, 455-Salem 326-West Medford, 428-Oaklandvale
♿ **State** Not handicap accessible for Blue Line inbound	**200 Washington St at 1 State St, Boston** Blue Line, *352-Burlington (express) *4-World Trade Ctr-North Sta, *354-Woburn (express) *92-Assembly Sq, *355-Mishawum *93-Sullivan
♿ **Downtown Crossing** Washington	**450 Washington St at 1 Summer St, Boston** *Gulbankian (Hudson-Boston), 500-Riverside (express) Red Line, 501-Brighton Center (express) Green Line via walkway, 504-Watertown (express) Silver Line Bus Rapid Transit, 505-Waltham (express) 3-City Pt-Chinatown, 553-Roberts via Waltham & Newton Corner 7-City Pt via Fan Pier, 554-Waverley via Waltham & Newton Corner 11-City Pt via Bayview, 556-Waltham Highlands or Cedarwood 92-Assembly Sq, 558-Auburndale 93-Sullivan 448-Marblehead 449-Marblehead 459-Salem

To Forest Hills

* Bus stop is near rapid transit stop.

Orange Line

RAPID TRANSIT STATIONS STATION ADDRESS & CONNECTING SERVICES

To Oak Grove via Downtown Crossing

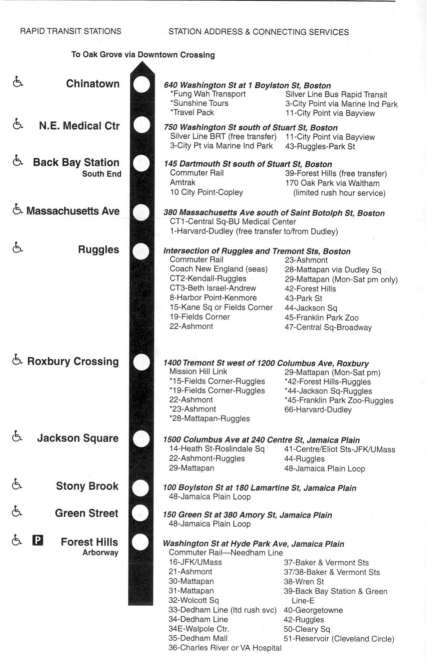

♿ **Chinatown**

640 Washington St at 1 Boylston St, Boston
*Fung Wah Transport	Silver Line Bus Rapid Transit
*Sunshine Tours	3-City Point via Marine Ind Park
*Travel Pack	11-City Point via Bayview

♿ **N.E. Medical Ctr**

750 Washington St south of Stuart St, Boston
Silver Line BRT (free transfer)	11-City Point via Bayview
3-City Pt via Marine Ind Park	43-Ruggles-Park St

♿ **Back Bay Station**
South End

145 Dartmouth St south of Stuart St, Boston
Commuter Rail	39-Forest Hills (free transfer)
Amtrak	170 Oak Park via Waltham
10 City Point-Copley	(limited rush hour service)

♿ **Massachusetts Ave**

380 Massachusetts Ave south of Saint Botolph St, Boston
CT1-Central Sq-BU Medical Center
1-Harvard-Dudley (free transfer to/from Dudley)

♿ **Ruggles**

Intersection of Ruggles and Tremont Sts, Boston
Commuter Rail	23-Ashmont
Coach New England (seas)	28-Mattapan via Dudley Sq
CT2-Kendall-Ruggles	29-Mattapan (Mon-Sat pm only)
CT3-Beth Israel-Andrew	42-Forest Hills
8-Harbor Point-Kenmore	43-Park St
15-Kane Sq or Fields Corner	44-Jackson Sq
19-Fields Corner	45-Franklin Park Zoo
22-Ashmont	47-Central Sq-Broadway

♿ **Roxbury Crossing**

1400 Tremont St west of 1200 Columbus Ave, Roxbury
Mission Hill Link	29-Mattapan (Mon-Sat pm)
*15-Fields Corner-Ruggles	*42-Forest Hills-Ruggles
*19-Fields Corner-Ruggles	*44-Jackson Sq-Ruggles
22-Ashmont	*45-Franklin Park Zoo-Ruggles
*23-Ashmont	66-Harvard-Dudley
*28-Mattapan-Ruggles	

♿ **Jackson Square**

1500 Columbus Ave at 240 Centre St, Jamaica Plain
14-Heath St-Roslindale Sq	41-Centre/Eliot Sts-JFK/UMass
22-Ashmont-Ruggles	44-Ruggles
29-Mattapan	48-Jamaica Plain Loop

♿ **Stony Brook**

100 Boylston St at 180 Lamartine St, Jamaica Plain
48-Jamaica Plain Loop

♿ **Green Street**

150 Green St at 380 Amory St, Jamaica Plain
48-Jamaica Plain Loop

♿ **■** **Forest Hills**
Arborway

Washington St at Hyde Park Ave, Jamaica Plain
Commuter Rail—Needham Line	
16-JFK/UMass	37-Baker & Vermont Sts
21-Ashmont	37/38-Baker & Vermont Sts
30-Mattapan	38-Wren St
31-Mattapan	39-Back Bay Station & Green
32-Wolcott Sq	Line-E
33-Dedham Line (ltd rush svc)	40-Georgetowne
34-Dedham Line	42-Ruggles
34E-Walpole Ctr.	50-Cleary Sq
35-Dedham Mall	51-Reservoir (Cleveland Circle)
36-Charles River or VA Hospital	

* Bus stop is near rapid transit stop.

RAPID TRANSIT STATIONS

STATION ADDRESS & CONNECTING SERVICES

♿ **P** **Wonderland** ⬤

1300 North Shore Rd (Rte 1A), opposite dog track, Revere
Note: "W" buses are weekends only. See Haymarket for M-F.
110-Wellington   441/441W-Marblehead
116-Maverick   442/442W-Marblehead
117-Maverick   448-Marblehead-Downtown
411-Satter House-Malden Ctr   449-Marblehead-Downtown
424W-Eastern & Essex, Lynn   450W-Salem
426W-Central Sq, Lynn   455W-Salem

♿ **Revere Beach** ⬤

220 Shirley Ave and 300 Ocean Ave, Revere
*110-Wonderland-Wellington   *411-Revere House-Malden Ctr
*117-Wonderland-Maverick

♿ **P** **Beachmont** ⬤

630 Winthrop Ave at 1 Bennington St, Revere
119-Northgate & Beachmont Loop

♿ **P** **Suffolk Downs** ⬤

1230 Bennington St and Walley St, East Boston

♿ **P** **Orient Heights** ⬤

1000 Bennington St, north of 990 Saratoga St, East Boston
Paul Revere buses: 120-Orient Heights-Maverick
—712-Winthrop Highlands
—713-Winthrop Center

♿ **Wood Island** ⬤

450 Bennington St, north of Rte 1A, East Boston
112-Wellington   121-Maverick (am rush)
120-Orient Heights-Maverick

Airport ⬤

Airport access road and Porter St, East Boston
Free Massport shuttle to airline terminals (details in Chapter 14)

Maverick ⬤

220 Sumner St at Chelsea and Meridian Sts, East Boston
114-Bellingham Sq   120-Orient Heights
116-Wonderland   120-Jeffries Point Loop
117-Wonderland   121-Wood Island

♿ **Aquarium** ⬤

Dockside Restaurant, 183 State St, Boston
6-Marine Ind Park-Haymarket   Long Wharf ferries

♿ **State** ⬤

Not handicap accessible
for Blue Line inbound

200 Washington St at 1 State St, Boston
Wheelchair access only for outbound platform (to Wonderland).
Wheelchair users heading inbound can go to Government Center,
then cross platform and come back to State.
Orange Line   *352-Burlington (express)
*4-World Trade Ctr-North Sta *354-Woburn (express)
*92-Assembly Sq   *355-Mishawum
*93-Sullivan

Government Ctr ⬤

1 Cambridge St at Court and Tremont Sts, Boston
Green Line   *352-Burlington (express)
Commuter buses   *354-Woburn (express)
                         *355-Mishawum

Bowdoin ⬤

Cambridge St at New Chardon and Bowdoin Sts, Boston
Open Mon-Fri 5:15am-6:30pm. Closed Sat and Sun.

* Bus stop is near
rapid transit stop.

*Blue Line train at
Aquarium station.*

129

BUS RAPID TRANSIT STATIONS   STATION ADDRESS & CONNECTING SERVICES

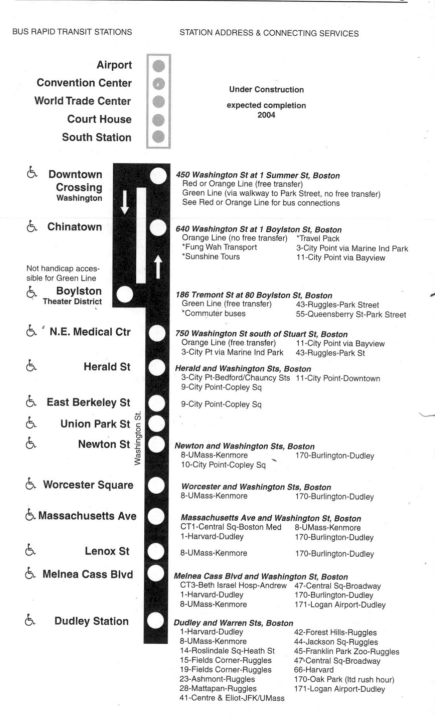

Airport
Convention Center
World Trade Center
Court House
South Station

Under Construction

expected completion
2004

♿ **Downtown Crossing**
Washington

450 Washington St at 1 Summer St, Boston
Red or Orange Line (free transfer)
Green Line (via walkway to Park Street, no free transfer)
See Red or Orange Line for bus connections

♿ **Chinatown**

640 Washington St at 1 Boylston St, Boston
Orange Line (no free transfer)   *Travel Pack
*Fung Wah Transport   3-City Point via Marine Ind Park
*Sunshine Tours   11-City Point via Bayview

Not handicap accessible for Green Line

♿ **Boylston**
Theater District

186 Tremont St at 80 Boylston St, Boston
Green Line (free transfer)   43-Ruggles-Park Street
*Commuter buses   55-Queensberry St-Park Street

♿ **N.E. Medical Ctr**

750 Washington St south of Stuart St, Boston
Orange Line (free transfer)   11-City Point via Bayview
3-City Pt via Marine Ind Park   43-Ruggles-Park St

♿ **Herald St**

Herald and Washington Sts, Boston
3-City Pt-Bedford/Chauncy Sts   11-City Point-Downtown
9-City Point-Copley Sq

♿ **East Berkeley St**

9-City Point-Copley Sq

♿ **Union Park St**

♿ **Newton St**

Newton and Washington Sts, Boston
8-UMass-Kenmore   170-Burlington-Dudley
10-City Point-Copley Sq

♿ **Worcester Square**

Worcester and Washington Sts, Boston
8-UMass-Kenmore   170-Burlington-Dudley

♿ **Massachusetts Ave**

Massachusetts Ave and Washington St, Boston
CT1-Central Sq-Boston Med   8-UMass-Kenmore
1-Harvard-Dudley   170-Burlington-Dudley

♿ **Lenox St**

8-UMass-Kenmore   170-Burlington-Dudley

♿ **Melnea Cass Blvd**

Melnea Cass Blvd and Washington St, Boston
CT3-Beth Israel Hosp-Andrew   47-Central Sq-Broadway
1-Harvard-Dudley   170-Burlington-Dudley
8-UMass-Kenmore   171-Logan Airport-Dudley

♿ **Dudley Station**

Dudley and Warren Sts, Boston
1-Harvard-Dudley   42-Forest Hills-Ruggles
8-UMass-Kenmore   44-Jackson Sq-Ruggles
14-Roslindale Sq-Heath St   45-Franklin Park Zoo-Ruggles
15-Fields Corner-Ruggles   47-Central Sq-Broadway
19-Fields Corner-Ruggles   66-Harvard
23-Ashmont-Ruggles   170-Oak Park (ltd rush hour)
28-Mattapan-Ruggles   171-Logan Airport-Dudley
41-Centre & Eliot-JFK/UMass

Washington St.

Chapter 9:
MBTA Commuter Rail

The table below shows the number of trips made during various time periods. A slash (/) separates morning and evening rush hour trips. Stations use numbers in parentheses (1A) to indicate fare zones, and an asterisk (*) denotes a station with very limited service. An alphabetical list of stations with zones, lines, and addresses follows. Rapid transit connections are given; for bus connections, see Chapter 10, "MBTA Buses." For holiday schedule changes, see "Holiday Service" on page 6, and for general information about using MBTA Commuter Rail, see Chapter 1, "The T (MBTA Transit)."

	Trip Time	Rush	Day	Night	Sat Trips	Sun Trips
		Weekday Trips				

Newburyport/Rockport Line (N/R)
• *Green and Orange lines:* North Station

North Station—Beverly Depot	:35	10/10	9	7	13	13

Stations: Chelsea (1B), River Works*(2), Lynn (2), Swampscott (3), Salem (3), Beverly Depot (4).

North Station—Rockport	1:10	3/4	4	4	7	7

Stations: Beverly Depot (4), Montserrat (4), Prides Crossing*(5), Beverly Farms (5), Manchester-by-the-Sea (6), W. Gloucester (7), Gloucester (7), Rockport (8).

North Station—Newburyport	1:05	5/4	4	3	6	6

Stations: Beverly Depot (4), N. Beverly (5), Hamilton/Wenham (5), Ipswich (6), Rowley (7), Newburyport (8).

Haverhill/Reading Line (H/R)
• *Green and Orange lines:* North Station; **Orange Line:** *Malden Center*

North Station—Reading	:28	7/6	6	5	6	6

Stations: Malden (1B), Wyoming Hill (1), Melrose/Cedar Park (1), Melrose Highlands (1), Greenwood (2), Wakefield (2), Reading (2).

North Station—Haverhill	1:05	6/4	3	4	6	6

Stations: Reading (2), N. Wilmington (3), Ballardvale (4), Andover (5), Lawrence (6), Bradford (7), Haverhill (7).

Lowell Line (LWL)
• *Green and Orange lines:* North Station

North Station—Lowell	:45	5/5	7	5	8	8

Stations: W. Medford*(1B), Wedgemere (1), Winchester Ctr. (1), Mishawum (2), Anderson/Woburn (2), Wilmington (3), N. Billerica (5), Lowell (6).

Fitchburg Line (FCH)
• *Green and Orange lines:* North Station; **Red Line:** *Porter*

North Station—South Acton	:55	5/5	5	4	8	7

Stations: Porter (1B), Belmont Ctr.* (1), Waverley*(1), Waltham (2), Brandeis/Roberts (2), Kendal Green (3), Hastings*(3), Silver Hill* (3), Lincoln (4), Concord (5), W. Concord (5), S. Acton (6).

North Station—Fitchburg	1:30	4/3	4	4	6	4

Stations: S. Acton (6), Littleton/495 (7), Ayer (8), Shirley (8), N. Leominster (9), Fitchburg (9).

	Trip Time	—— Weekday Trips ——			Sat Trips	Sun Trips
		Rush	Day	Night		

Framingham/Worcester Line (F/W)

• **Red Line:** *South Station;* **Orange Line:** *Back Bay Station*

South Station—Framingham :50 8/7 5 3 9 8

Stations: Back Bay Station (1A), Yawkey* (1A), Newtonville* (1), W. Newton* (2), Auburndale* (3), Wellesley Farms (3), Wellesley Hills (3), Wellesley Sq. (3), Natick (4), W. Natick (4), Framingham (5).

South Station—Worcester 1:15 4/4 2 3 5 5

Stations: Framingham (5), Ashland (6), Southborough (6), Westborough (6), Grafton (8), Worcester (9).

Needham Line (NDM)

• **Red Line:** *South Station;* **Orange Line:** *Back Bay Station, Ruggles, Forest Hills*

South Station—Needham Jct. :40 5/5 4 4 9 —

Stations: Back Bay Station (1A), Ruggles* (1A), Forest Hills (1B), Roslindale (1), Bellevue (1), Highland (1), W. Roxbury (1), Hersey (2), Needham Jct. (2), Needham Ctr. (2), Needham Hts. (2).

Franklin Line (FKL)

• **Red Line:** *South Station;* **Orange Line:** *Back Bay Station, Ruggles*

South Station—Forge Park/495 1:05 7/6 4 4 9 7

Stations: Back Bay Station (1A), Ruggles* (1A), Readville* (2), Endicott (2), Dedham Corp. Ctr. (2), Islington (3), Norwood Depot* (3), Norwood Central (3), Windsor Gardens* (4), Plimptonville* (4), Walpole (4), Norfolk (5), Franklin (6), Forge Park/495 (6).

Attleboro/Stoughton Line (A/S)

• **Red Line:** *South Station;* **Orange Line:** *Back Bay Station, Ruggles*

South Station—Stoughton :44 4/4 4 3 — —

Stations: Back Bay Station (1A), Ruggles* (1A), Hyde Park (1), Rte. 128 Station (2), Canton Jct. (3), Canton Ctr. (3), Stoughton (4)

South Station—Providence 1:10 5/5 3 3 9 7

Stations: Back Bay Station (1A), Ruggles* (1A), Hyde Park (1), Rte. 128 Sta. (2), Canton Jct. (3), Sharon (4), Mansfield (6), Attleboro (7), So. Attleboro (7), Providence, RI (9). No service to Providence on weekends.

Fairmount Line (FMT)

• **Red Line:** *South Station*

South Station—Readville :20 6/5 7 3 — —

Stations: Uphams Corner (1A), Morton St. (1B), Fairmount (1), Readville (2).

Middleborough/Lakeville Line (M/L)

• **Red Line:** *South Station, JFK/UMass, Quincy Center, Braintree*

South Sta.—Middleboro/Lakeville 1:00 4/4 3 2 7 7

Stations: JFK/UMass* (1A), Quincy Ctr. (1), Braintree* (2), Holbrook/Randdolph (3), Montello (4), Brockton (4), Campello (5), Bridgewater (6), Middleborough/Lakeville (8).

	Trip Time	— Weekday Trips —			Sat Trips	Sun Trips
		Rush	Day	Night		

Plymouth/Kingston Line (P/K)
• *Red Line: South Station, JFK/UMass, Quincy Center, Braintree*

South Station—Halifax	:50	5/4	6	3	8	8

Stations: JFK/UMass* (1A), Quincy Ctr.* (1), Braintree (2), So. Weymouth (3), Abington (4), Whitman (5), Hanson (6), Halifax (7).

South Station—Kingston	:56	5/4	3	3	5	5

Stations: Halifax (7), Kingston/Rte. 3 (8).

South Station—Plymouth	1:00	—	3	—	3	3

Stations: Halifax (7), Plymouth (8).

Commuter Rail Station Locations

Station Name (zone; line [abbreviations in chart above], Rapid Transit line [if any]) address

Abington &(4; P/K) Centre St., Abington
Anderson/Woburn &(2; LWL) 100 Atlantic Ave. off Commerce Way, Woburn
Andover &(5; H/R) 17 Railroad Ave. between Main St. and Essex St.
Ashland &(6; F/W) Pleasant St. and Rte. 135 west of Ashland High School
Attleboro &(7; A/S) South Main and Wall Sts.
Auburndale (3; F/W) Lexington St. at the Mass. Pike, Newton
Ayer (8; FCH) Depot Sq on south side of Main
Back Bay Station &(1A; F/W, NDM, FKL, A/S, Orange) Dartmouth St., Boston
Ballardvale &(4; H/R) Andover St. near River St., Andover
Bellevue &(1; NDM) Colbert St. and Centre St., West Roxbury
Belmont Center (1; FCH) Common and Concord Aves. behind the Lions Club
Beverly Depot &(4; N/R) Park St. across from the Post Office
Beverly Farms &(5; N/R) West St. at Oak St.
Bradford &(7; H/R) Railroad and Laurel Aves., Haverhill
Braintree &(2; M/L, P/K, Red) Ivory St. between Union and Pearl Sts., Braintree
Brandeis/Roberts &(2; FCH) South St. and Sawyer St., Waltham
Bridgewater &(6; M/L) Great Hill Parking Lot, Bridgewater State College
Brockton &(4; M/L) Brockton Police Station and Commercial St., Brockton
Campello &(5; M/L) Plain St. and Riverside Ave., Brockton
Canton Center &(3; A/S) Washington St. near bank
Canton Junction &(3, A/S) Beaumont St. and Sherman St.
Chelsea (1B; N/R) Arlington St. and Sixth St.
Concord (5; FCH) 90 Thoreau St.

Dedham Corporate Center &(2; FKL) East St. off Rte. 128 to Allied Drive
Endicott (2; FKL) Washington Ave. off East St., Dedham
Fairmount (1; FMT) Fairmount Ave. and Truman Highway, Hyde Park
Fitchburg &(9; FCH) Rte. 2A east of Rte. 12
Forest Hills &(1B; NDM, Orange) Washington St., Boston
Forge Park/495 &(6; FKL) Rte. 140 off Rte. 495, Franklin
Framingham (5; F/W) Rte. 126 and Rte. 135
Franklin (6; FKL) Depot St. off East Central St. and Main St.
Gloucester &(7; N/R) Washington St. at Railroad Ave.
Grafton &(8; F/W) Pine St. at Rte. 30, Grafton
Greenwood (2; H/R) 907 Main St., Wakefield
Halifax &(7; P/K) Garden Rd. off Rte. 36
Hamilton/Wenham &(5; N/R) Bay Rd. at Walnut
Hanson &(6; P/K) Main St. (Rte. 27), Hanson
Hastings (3; FCH) Viles St. south of North Ave., Weston
Haverhill &(7, H/R) Washington St. at Railroad Sq. 3 blocks west of bus depot
Hersey &(2; NDM) Great Plain Ave., Needham
Highland &(1; NDM) Corey St. and Hastings St., West Roxbury
Holbrook/Randolph (3; M/L) Union St., Randolph
Hyde Park &(1; A/S) Hyde Park Ave. and Cleary Square
Ipswich &(6; N/R) south of Topsfield Rd., Downtown Ipswich
Islington (3; FKL) Carrol St. off East St., Westwood
JFK/Umass &(1A; M/L, P/K, Red) Columbia Rd. near Old Colony Ave., Dorchester

Route Details

Kendal Green (3; FCH) Church St., 1 block south of North Ave. (Rte. 117), Weston

Kingston/Rte 3& (8; P/K) Marion Dr., Kingston

Lawrence& (6; H/R) Merrimack and Parker Sts.

Lincoln (4; FCH) Lincoln Rd. north of Rte. 117

Littleton/495 (7; FCH) Foster St. off Taylor St.

Lowell& (6; LWL) Thorndike St. north of the Lowell Connector

Lynn& (2; N/R) Monroe St. and Market St.

Malden Center (1B; H/R, Orange) Commercial and Pleasant Sts.

Manchester& (6; N/R) Beach St. south of Summer St.

Mansfield& (6; A/S) Crocker St. off Rte. 106

Melrose Highlands (1; H/R) Franklin St. near Greenwood St.

Melrose/Cedar Park (1; H/R) W. Emerson St., 2 blocks south of Lynn Fells Pkwy.

Middleborough/Lakeville& (8; M/L) Rte. 105

Mishawum& (2; LWL) Mishawum Rd., 1 block east of Rte. 128 Washington St. exit, Woburn

Montello& (4; M/L) Montello, Howard, Sparks, Fields St., Brockton

Montserrat& (4; N/R) btwn Essex and Spring Sts., Beverly

Morton St (1B; FMT) Morton St. near Star Market, Hyde Park

Natick (4; F/W) Walnut St. and Rte. 27

Needham Center& (2; NDM) Great Plain Ave. and Eaton Square

Needham Heights& (2; NDM) Corner of Highland Ave. and West St.

Needham Junction& (2; NDM) Junction St. off Chestnut St.

Newburyport& (8; N/R) Boston Way & Parker St. off Rte. 1, Newburyport

Newtonville (1; F/W) btwn Harvard and Walnut

Norfolk& (5; FKL) Rte. 115, Norfolk Center

North Beverly& (5; N/R) Enon St. at Dodge St.

North Billerica& (5; LWL) Ruggles St. and Carlton St. off Mount Pleasant St.

North Leominster (9; FCH) 568 Main St.

North Station& (n/a; N/R, H/R, LWL, FCH, Green, Orange) 135 Causeway St., Boston

North Wilmington (3; H/R) Middlesex Ave., west of Interstate 93 at the junction of Rte. 62

Norwood Central& (3; FKL) Broadway St. east of Washington St. near the hospital

Norwood Depot& (3; FKL) Railroad Ave., Hill St.

Plimptonville (4; FKL) Plimpton St. east of Rte. 1A, Walpole

Plymouth& (8; P/K) Cordage Park, Plymouth

Porter& (1B; FCH, Red) Mass. Ave., Cambridge

Prides Crossing (5; N/R) Hale St., Beverly

Providence, RI& (9; A/S) 100 Gaspee St.

Quincy Center& (1; M/L, P/K, Red) 1300 Hancock St. at Washington St., Quincy

Reading& (2; H/R) High St. and Lincoln St.

Readville& (2; FKL, FMT) Hyde Park Av., Boston

River Works (2; N/R) General Electric plant

Rockport (8; N/R) Railroad Ave. off Rte. 127

Roslindale& (1; NDM) Belgrade and South Sts.

Route 128 Station& (2; A/S) 100 University Ave. exit 13 off Rte. 128, Westwood

Rowley& (7; N/R) Railroad Ave. off 1A, Rowley

Ruggles& (1A; NDM, FKL, A/S, Orange) Ruggles St. and Columbus Ave., Boston

Salem& (3; N/R) Bridge St. and North St.

Sharon (4; A/S) Rte. 27 near Sharon Center

Shirley (8; FCH) Main St. and Phoenix St.

Silver Hill (3; FCH) Silver Hill Rd. off Merriam St., Weston

South Acton (6; FCH) Central St. near Main St.

South Attleboro& (7; A/S) Newport Ave. (Rte. 1A) and Colvin St. off Rte. 95

South Station& (n/a; F/W, NDM, FKL, A/S, FMT, M/L, P/K. Red) Atlantic Ave., Boston

South Weymouth& (3; P/K) Trotter Rd. off Rte. 18

Southborough& (6; F/W) Rte. 85 and Southville

Stoughton& (4; A/S) Wyman St. at RR Crossing

Swampscott& (3; N/R) Burrill St. and Railroad Av.

Uphams Corner (1A; FMT) Dudley St., Dorchester

Wakefield (2; H/R) Tuttle St. and North Ave.

Walpole (4; FKL) West St., near Walpole Center

Waltham (2; FCH) Elm St. and Moody St.

Waverley (1; FCH) Trapelo Rd. and Lexington St., Belmont

Wedgemere (1; LWL) Mystic Valley Parkway, Winchester

Wellesley Farms (3; F/W) 90 Glen Rd.

Wellesley Hills (3; F/W) 339 Washington St. west of Cliff Rd.

Wellesley Square (3; F/W) Washington St. and Crest Rd.

West Concord& (5; FCH) Comm. Ave. and Main

West Gloucester& (7; N/R) Essex Ave. (Rte. 138), south of Magnolia Ave.

West Medford (1B;) High St., near RR crossing

West Natick& (4; F/W) Rte. 135 and Mill St.

West Newton (2; F/W) Rte. 16, West Newton

West Roxbury& (1; NDM) LaGrange St. north of Centre St.

Westborough& (6; F/W) Smith Valve Pky & Fisher

Whitman& (5; P/K) South Ave.(Rte. 27)

Wilmington (3; LWL) Rte. 129/38 near Rte. 62

Winchester Center (1; LWL) btwn Waterfield Rd./Common St. and Church St./Main St.

Windsor Gardens (4; FKL) Windsor Gardens, Rte. 1A, Norwood

Worcester& (9; F/W) Washington Sq.

Wyoming Hill (1; H/R) West Wyoming Ave. just west of Main St., Melrose

Yawkey& (1A; F/W) Brookline Ave. behind the Red Sox Parking lot, Boston

Chapter 10:
MBTA Buses

Every MBTA bus route is detailed below. Trip length and service frequency (the interval between buses) are shown in minutes. A slash (/) separates different morning and evening rush hour frequencies. Additional details include major streets listed in the order traveled, rapid transit and Commuter Rail connections, and special fare notes or route deviations where necessary. For holiday schedules see "Holiday Service" on page 6. For general information about using MBTA buses see Chapter 1, "The T (MBTA Transit)."

Two rapid transit stations, one-half mile apart, have the same name: "Massachusetts Ave." These two stations are distinguished in the tables by "(OL)" for the Orange Line stop and "(SL)" for the Silver Line Bus Rapid Transit stop. The following abbreviations are also used:

BIKE: Bus is equipped with front-mounted bicycle rack.

EXPRSS: Connects outlying communities with downtown Boston via major highways with few or no intermediate stops.

FREQNT: Service near the frequency of rapid transit (every 10-15 minutes weekdays—9 minutes or less during rush hours—and 13-30 minutes on nights and weekends). Exception: bus 7 has no Sunday service.

LIFT &: Buses are equipped with wheelchair lifts. An asterisk (*) denotes partial service—at least half the trips have lift-equipped buses. Call 800/LIFT-BUS one day in advance to arrange LIFT service on other routes.

N-OWL: Night Owl service. Extends Fri.-Sat. night schedule until 2:30am.

X-TOWN: Crosstown service. Facilitates transfer from one rapid transit line to another without traveling to and from downtown.

		Trip Time	Rush	wk-day	wk-night	allSat	allSun
			----- **Frequency in minutes** -----				

Silver Line Bus Rapid Transit (BRT) – see Chapter 8, "MBTA Rapid Transit"

1	**Harvard—Dudley**	36-46	10	12	13	12	18-20

X-TOWN
FREQNT
N-OWL
LIFT &

CAMBRIDGE: Mass. Ave, Central Sq, MIT, Harvard Bridge; *BACK BAY:* Mass. Ave, Symphony Hall, *SOUTH END:* Boston City Hospital; *ROXBURY:* Melnea Cass Blvd, Washington St; *RAPID TRANSIT:* Harvard, Central, Hynes Convention Ctr/ICA, Symphony, Mass. Ave (OL), Mass. Ave (SL), Dudley Sta, Melnea Cass Blvd.

NOTE: Free transfer (with $1 fare) between Dudley Sta and Mass. Ave (OL).

3	**City Pt—Chinatown**	20-25	12/22	—	—	—	—

LIFT &

S. BOSTON: E. First St, Summer St, Marine Ind. Park, Northern Ave, Congress St, S. Boston Haul Rd, W. 4th St Bridge; *BOSTON:* Harrison Ave, Herald St, Washington St, Essex St; *RAPID TRANSIT:* New England Medical Ctr, Broadway, South Station, Chinatown, Herald St; *COMMUTER RAIL:* South Station.

4	**North Station—World Trade Ctr**	22	15	—	—	—	—

LIFT &

BOSTON: Causeway St, Congress St, Atlantic St, Pearl St; *S. BOSTON:* Seaport Blvd; *RAPID TRANSIT:* North Station.

		Trip Time	Rush	------------- Frequency in minutes ------------- wk-day	wk-night	allSat	allSun

5

City Pt—McCormack Housing 19-20 — 60 — 60 —

S. BOSTON: E. 4th St/E. Broadway, Perkins Sq, Dorchester St, Andrew Sq, Preble St, Old Colony Ave; *RAPID TRANSIT:* Andrew.

6

LIFT &

Marine Ind Pk—Haymarket 23-26 30 — — — —

S. BOSTON: Black Falcon Ave, Summer St, Congress St; *BOSTON:* South Station, Atlantic Ave, Commercial St, Hanover St; *RAPID TRANSIT:* South Station, Aquarium, Haymarket; *COMMUTER RAIL:* South Station.

7

FREQNT

City Pt—Downtown 22 10 18 30 25 —

S. BOSTON: E. 4th St/E. Broadway, L St, Summer St, Congress St; *BOSTON:* South Station, Federal St, Franklin St, Otis St; *RAPID TRANSIT:* South Station, Downtown Crossing; *COMMUTER RAIL:* South Station.

8

X-TOWN
LIFT &

UMass—Kenmore 48-61 12/20 45 35 35 35

DORCHESTER: UMass, Mt. Vernon St, Columbia Rd, Mass. Ave, South Bay Mall; *SOUTH END:* Boston City Hospital, Harrison Ave; *ROXBURY:* Washington St, Dudley Sq, Melnea Cass Blvd; *FENWAY:* Ruggles St, Ave. Louis Pasteur, Longwood Ave, Longwood Medical Area, Brookline Ave; *RAPID TRANSIT:* JFK/UMass, Ruggles, Museum of Fine Arts, Kenmore, Dudley Sta, Newton St, Mass. Ave (SL), Lenox St, Melnea Cass Blvd; *COMMUTER RAIL:* Ruggles.

NOTE: Rush hour: additional service from Dudley Sta to Kenmore every 13/20 min.

9

FREQNT
X-TOWN

City Pt—Copley Sq 24-33 8/11 12 30 20-30 30

S. BOSTON: E. 4th St/E. Broadway, Perkins Sq, W. Broadway; *SOUTH END:* Herald St, Berkeley/Arlington Sts; *BACK BAY:* St. James Ave/Boylston St; *RAPID TRANSIT:* Broadway, Copley, Arlington, Herald St, E. Berkeley St.

10

X-TOWN

City Pt—Copley Sq 30-45 20 35 35 25 40

S. BOSTON: E. 4th St/E. Broadway, Perkins Sq, Dorchester St, Andrew Sq, Southampton St, South Bay Mall; *SOUTH END:* Newmarket Sq, Mass. Ave, Albany St, Boston City Hospital, E. Newton St, W. Dedham St; *BACK BAY:* Dartmouth St; *RAPID TRANSIT:* Andrew, Back Bay Station, Copley, Newton St; *COMMUTER RAIL:* Back Bay Station.

11

FREQNT

City Pt—Downtown 17-25 6/11 15 30 20 30

S. BOSTON: E. 8th St, W. 7th St, Dorchester Ave; *BOSTON:* E. Berkeley, Washington/Surface Artery, Chauncy St, Bedford St; *RAPID TRANSIT:* Broadway, New England Medical Ctr, Chinatown (except night), Herald St, Downtown Crossing.

NOTE: Night: City Pt to Kneeland/Washington Sts only.

14

Roslindale—Heath St 28-38 30 45 — 30 —

ROSLINDALE: Cummins Hwy, American Legion Hwy; *DORCHESTER:* Blue Hill Ave, Franklin Park, Grove Hall; *ROXBURY:* Warren St, Dudley Sta, Dudley St, Centre St, Heath St; *RAPID TRANSIT:* Dudley Sta, Jackson Sq, Heath St.

15

FREQNT

Kane Sq—Ruggles 23-29 5/9 15 20 16 45

DORCHESTER: Hancock St, Uphams Corner, Dudley St; *ROXBURY:* Dudley Sq, Malcom X Blvd; *RAPID TRANSIT:* Ruggles, Fields Corner (night and Sunday), Roxbury Crossing, Dudley Sta; *COMMUTER RAIL:* Uphams Corner, Ruggles.

NOTE: Night and Sunday: Fields Corner to Ruggles on Geneva Ave, Bowdoin St, Kane Sq, then regular route. No fare inbound from Dudley Sta to Ruggles.

16

X-TOWN

Forest Hills—Andrew or UMass 28-34 15 30 40 30 30

JAMAICA PLAIN: Circuit Dr, Franklin Park; *DORCHESTER:* Columbia Rd, Uphams Corner, South Bay Mall (limited), Boston St; *SOUTH BOSTON:* Andrew Sq; *RAPID TRANSIT:* Forest Hills, JFK/UMass (rush hour), Andrew; *COMMUTER RAIL:* Forest Hills.

NOTE: Rush hour: regular route then Preble St, Old Colony Ave, Mt. Vernon St, UMass.

			Frequency in minutes			
	Trip Time	Rush	wk-day	wk-night	allSat	allSun

17   **Fields Corner—Andrew**   14-17   14   25   40   20   40

DORCHESTER: Geneva Ave, Bowdoin St, Kane Sq, Hancock St, Uphams Corner, Columbia Rd, Boston St; *RAPID TRANSIT:* Fields Corner, Andrew.

18   **Ashmont—Andrew**   19-21   30   60   —   60   60

DORCHESTER: Dorchester Ave, Fields Corner; *RAPID TRANSIT:* Ashmont, Fields Corner, Andrew, Savin Hill (one block).

19   **Fields Corner—Ruggles**   21-28   15/25   60   —   —   —

X-TOWN

DORCHESTER: Geneva Ave, Grove Hall; *ROXBURY:* Warren St, Dudley Sq, Malcolm X Blvd; *RAPID TRANSIT:* Fields Corner, Ruggles, Roxbury Crossing, Dudley Sta; *COMMUTER RAIL:* Ruggles.

NOTE: No fare inbound from Dudley Sta to Ruggles.

20   **Fields Corner—Neponset**   23   12   35   30   35   70

DORCHESTER: Adams St, Gallivan Blvd, Neponset Cir, Neponset Ave; *RAPID TRANSIT:* Fields Corner.

NOTE: Some trips serve Morrissey Blvd shops and Hallet Sq.

21   **Ashmont—Forest Hills**   11-18   10/12   20   40   45   60

X-TOWN

DORCHESTER: Gallivan Blvd; *MATTAPAN:* Morton St; *JAMAICA PLAIN:* Morton St, Shea Rotary; *RAPID TRANSIT:* Ashmont, Forest Hills; *COMMUTER RAIL:* Morton St, Forest Hills.

22   **Ashmont—Ruggles**   22-31   10   13   20   11-16   15-25

FREQNT
X-TOWN
LIFT &

DORCHESTER: Talbot Ave, Codman Sq, Blue Hill Ave, Franklin Park, Seaver St; *ROXBURY:* Egleston Sq, Columbus Ave, Jackson Sq; *RAPID TRANSIT:* Ashmont, Jackson Sq, Ruggles, Roxbury Crossing; *COMMUTER RAIL:* Ruggles.

NOTE: No fare inbound from Egleston Sq to Jackson Sq.

23   **Ashmont—Ruggles**   25-35   10   10   20   10-20   16-20

FREQNT
X-TOWN

DORCHESTER: Talbot Ave, Codman Sq, Washington St, Grove Hall; *ROXBURY:* Warren St, Dudley Sq, Malcolm X Blvd; *RAPID TRANSIT:* Ashmont, Ruggles, Roxbury Crossing, Dudley Sta; *COMMUTER RAIL:* Ruggles.

NOTE: No fare inbound from Dudley Sta to Ruggles.

24   **Wakefield Ave—Mattapan**   11-15   20/30   50   60   50   60

LIFT &

HYDE PARK: Metropolitan Ave, Highland St, Washington St, Truman Pkwy (loop), Fairmount Ave; *MATTAPAN:* River St; *RAPID TRANSIT:* Mattapan, Ashmont (night only); *COMMUTER RAIL:* Fairmount.

NOTE: Mon-Sat night: continues to Ashmont via River St and Dorchester Ave.

26   **Ashmont—Norfolk, Morton Belt**   22-26   15   30   30   30   60

DORCHESTER: Washington St, Gallivan Blvd, Morton St, Norfolk St, Codman Sq, Talbot Ave; *RAPID TRANSIT:* Ashmont; *COMMUTER RAIL:* Morton St.

27   **Mattapan—Ashmont**   11-12   35/30   30   60   30   60

LIFT &

MATTAPAN: River St, Mattapan Hospital; *DORCHESTER:* Lower Mills, Dorchester Ave; *RAPID TRANSIT:* Mattapan, Ashmont.

NOTE: Mon-Sat night: continues to Wakefield Ave via bus 24.

28   **Mattapan—Ruggles**   28-37   8/12   11   20   10-20   15

FREQNT
X-TOWN
N-OWL
LIFT & *

MATTAPAN: Blue Hill Ave; *DORCHESTER:* Franklin Park, Grove Hall; *ROXBURY:* Warren St, Dudley Sq, Malcolm X Blvd; *RAPID TRANSIT:* Mattapan, Ruggles, Roxbury Crossing, Dudley Sta; *COMMUTER RAIL:* Ruggles.

NOTE: No fare inbound from Dudley Sta to Ruggles.

Route Details

	Trip Time	Rush	wk-day	wk-night	allSat	allSun
		------------ Frequency in minutes ------------				

29   Mattapan—Jackson Sq   25-35   16/15   60   20   lim   —

MATTAPAN: Blue Hill Ave; *ROXBURY:* Franklin Park, Seaver St, Egleston Sq, Columbus Ave; *RAPID TRANSIT:* Jackson Sq, Ruggles (Mon-Sat night), Roxbury Crossing (Mon-Sat night), Mattapan; *COMMUTER RAIL:* Ruggles (Mon-Sat night).

NOTE: Mon-Sat night: continues to Ruggles. Some midday trips serve Franklin Field Housing Project. No fare inbound from Egleston Sq to Jackson Sq.

30   LIFT &   Mattapan—Forest Hills   29   30/20   30   40   50   60

DORCHESTER: Ashmont, Dorchester Ave, River St; *MATTAPAN:* Cummings Hwy; *ROSLINDALE:* Roslindale Sq, Washington St; *RAPID TRANSIT:* Mattapan, Forest Hills, Ashmont (Mon-Fri midday); *COMMUTER RAIL:* Forest Hills, Roslindale Village.

NOTE: Mon-Fri midday: Ashmont to Roslindale. Sunday: Mattapan to Roslindale.

31   FREQNT   X-TOWN   Mattapan—Forest Hills   11-17   10   12   20   13-20   20

MATTAPAN: Blue Hill Ave; *JAMAICA PLAIN:* Morton St; *RAPID TRANSIT:* Mattapan, Forest Hills; *COMMUTER RAIL:* Forest Hills.

32   FREQNT   LIFT &   Wolcott Sq—Forest Hills   14-20   10/5   12   12   12   30

HYDE PARK, ROSLINDALE, JAMAICA PLAIN: Hyde Park Ave, Cleary Sq; *RAPID TRANSIT:* Forest Hills; *COMMUTER RAIL:* Forest Hills, Readville, Hyde Park.

NOTE: Rush hour: additional service from Cleary Sq to Forest Hills every 5 min.

33   LIFT &   Dedham Line—Mattapan   22-28   30   60   —   60   —

HYDE PARK: River St, Turtle Pond Pkwy, Alwin St, River St, Cleary Sq; *MATTAPAN:* River St; *RAPID TRANSIT:* Mattapan.

34   LIFT &   Dedham Line—Forest Hills   14-19   9/8   30   60   30   60

W. ROXBURY: Washington St; *ROSLINDALE:* Roslindale Sq; *RAPID TRANSIT:* Forest Hills; *COMMUTER RAIL:* Forest Hills, Roslindale Village.

NOTE: For additional service see bus 34E.

34E   LIFT &   Walpole Ctr—Forest Hills   52-62   20   30   60   30   60

WALPOLE: East St, High Plain Ave, E. Walpole; *NORWOOD, WESTWOOD:* Washington St; *DEDHAM:* Dedham Sq, Dedham Mall; *W. ROXBURY:* Washington St; *ROSLINDALE:* Roslindale Sq; *RAPID TRANSIT:* Forest Hills; *COMMUTER RAIL:* Forest Hills, East Walpole, Walpole, Roslindale Village.

NOTE: Night and Sunday: E. Walpole to Forest Hills only. Fare: 75¢-$1.25.

35   Dedham Mall—Forest Hills   23-31   20/15   30   lim   30   60

DEDHAM: Washington St; *W. ROXBURY:* Stimson St, Centre St; *ROSLINDALE:* Belgrade Ave, Roslindale Sq, Washington St; *RAPID TRANSIT:* Forest Hills; *COMMUTER RAIL:* Forest Hills, Roslindale Village.

NOTE: Morning rush hour: Stimson St to Forest Hills only.

36   LIFT &   Charles River—Forest Hills   18-24   11/15   30   30   30   30

W. ROXBURY: Spring St, Centre St; *ROSLINDALE:* Belgrade Ave, Roslindale Sq, Washington St; *RAPID TRANSIT, COMMUTER RAIL:* Forest Hills.

NOTE: Some trips also serve VA Hospital or Rivermoor Industrial Area.

37   Baker and Vermont—Forest Hills   15-23   20/15   30   —   30   —

W. ROXBURY: Vermont St, Baker St, Lasell St, LaGrange St, Centre St; *ROSLINDALE:* Belgrade Ave, Roslindale Sq, Washington St; *RAPID TRANSIT:* Forest Hills; *COMMUTER RAIL:* Forest Hills, Roslindale Village.

37/38   LIFT &   Baker and Vermont—Forest Hills   15-24   —   —   —   lim   60

W. ROXBURY: Vermont St, Baker St, Lasell St, LaGrange St, Centre St; *ROSLINDALE:* Centre St; *JAMAICA PLAIN:* Faulkner Hospital, Arnold Arboretum, The Monument, South St; *RAPID TRANSIT, COMMUTER RAIL:* Forest Hills.

NOTE: Saturday: early morning only.

	Trip Time	----------- Frequency in minutes -----------				
		Rush	wk-day	wk-night	allSat	allSun

38
LIFT &

Wren St—Forest Hills — 12-19 — 22 — 40 — 2 trips — 40 — —

W. ROXBURY: Park St, Anawan Ave; *ROSLINDALE:* Centre St; *JAMAICA PLAIN:* Faulkner Hospital, Arnold Arboretum, The Monument, South St; *RAPID TRANSIT, COMMUTER RAIL:* Forest Hills.

39
FREQNT
N-OWL
LIFT &

Forest Hills—Back Bay Station — 30-38 — 3/4 — 7 — 9 — 7 — 7

JAMAICA PLAIN: South St, The Monument, Centre St, VA Hospital, S. Huntington Ave; *MISSION HILL, FENWAY:* Huntington Ave; *BACK BAY:* Boylston St/St. James Ave; *RAPID TRANSIT:* Forest Hills, Green Line-E stops from Heath St through Prudential, Copley, Back Bay Station; *COMMUTER RAIL:* Forest Hills, Back Bay Station.

NOTE: Free transfer with $1 fare at Copley and Back Bay Station. Substitutes for Green Line-E streetcar from Heath St to Forest Hills.

40
LIFT &

Georgetowne—Forest Hills — 18-25 — 30 — 50 — — — 50 — —

HYDE PARK: Alwin St, Georgetowne Dr, W. Boundary Rd; *W. ROXBURY:* Washington St; *ROSLINDALE:* Roslindale Sq; *RAPID TRANSIT:* Forest Hills; *COMMUTER RAIL:* Forest Hills, Roslindale Village.

41
X-TOWN

Centre and Eliot Sts—JFK/UMass — 19-31 — 20 — 30 — 30 — 40 — 35

JAMAICA PLAIN: Centre St, Hyde Sq; *ROXBURY:* Jackson Sq, Centre St, Dudley St, Dudley Sq; *DORCHESTER:* Dudley St, Uphams Corner, Columbia Rd; *RAPID TRANSIT:* Jackson Sq, JFK/UMass, Dudley Sta; *COMMUTER RAIL:* Uphams Corner.

42
LIFT &

Forest Hills—Ruggles — 18-22 — 20 — 20 — 50 — 18 — 50

JAMAICA PLAIN: Washington St; *ROXBURY:* Egleston Sq, Dudley Sq, Malcolm X Blvd; *RAPID TRANSIT:* Forest Hills, Ruggles, Roxbury Crossing, Dudley Sta; *COMMUTER RAIL:* Forest Hills, Ruggles.

NOTE: Morning rush hour: additional service from Forest Hills to Dudley Sta every 10 min. No fare inbound from Dudley Sta to Ruggles.

43
FREQNT
LIFT &

Ruggles—Park Street — 14-21 — 10 — 15 — 20 — 15 — 20

SOUTH END: Tremont St; *BOSTON:* Park Plaza, circles Boston Common; *RAPID TRANSIT:* Ruggles, New England Medical Ctr, Boylston, Park Street; *COMMUTER RAIL:* Ruggles.

44

Jackson Sq—Ruggles — 17-25 — 11 — 20 — 30 — 16 — 45

JAMAICA PLAIN: Columbus Ave, Egleston Sq; *ROXBURY:* Seaver St, Humboldt Ave, Walnut Ave, Warren St, Dudley Sq, Malcolm X Blvd, Tremont St; *RAPID TRANSIT:* Jackson Sq, Ruggles, Roxbury Crossing, Dudley Sta; *COMMUTER RAIL:* Ruggles.

NOTE: No fare inbound from Dudley Sta to Ruggles or from Egleston Sq to Jackson Sq.

45

Franklin Park Zoo—Ruggles — 16-23 — 7/8 — 20 — 30 — 16 — 45

ROXBURY: Blue Hill Ave, Grove Hall, Dudley St, Dudley Sq, Malcolm X Blvd; *RAPID TRANSIT:* Ruggles, Roxbury Crossing, Dudley Sta; *COMMUTER RAIL:* Ruggles.

NOTE: No fare inbound from Dudley Sta to Ruggles.

47
X-TOWN
LIFT &

Central—Broadway — 39-45 — 20 — 20 — 45 — 20-40 — 40

CAMBRIDGE: Pearl/Brookline Sts; *FENWAY:* Park Dr, Brookline Ave, Longwood Medical Area, Longwood Ave, Ave. Louis Pasteur, Ruggles St; *ROXBURY:* Melnea Cass Blvd, Dudley Sq, Albany St; *SOUTH END:* Boston City Hospital; *S. BOSTON:* W. 4th St; *RAPID TRANSIT:* Central Sq, Broadway, B.U. Central (1 block), St. Mary's St (1 block), Fenway, Museum of Fine Arts, Ruggles, Dudley Sta, Melnea Cass Blvd; *COMMUTER RAIL:* Ruggles.

48
LIFT &

Jamaica Plain Loop — 26-30 — — — 30 — — — 35 — —

JAMAICA PLAIN: Centre St, Paul Gore St, Chestnut Ave; *ROXBURY:* Jackson Sq, Columbus Ave, Egleston Sq; *JAMAICA PLAIN:* Washington St, Green St, Amory St, Lamartine St, Green St; *RAPID TRANSIT:* Jackson Sq, Stony Brook, Green Street.

Route Details

		Trip Time	Rush	wk-day	wk-night	allSat	allSun
			------------ Frequency in minutes ------------				

50 **Cleary Sq—Forest Hills** 15-18 20 60 — 60 —

HYDE PARK: Austin/Summer Sts, West St; ROSLINDALE: Metropolitan Ave, Roslindale Sq, Washington St; RAPID TRANSIT: Forest Hills; COMMUTER RAIL: Roslindale Village, Hyde Park, Forest Hills.

51 **Cleveland Circle—Forest Hills** 24-30 20 60 60 60 —

X-TOWN
LIFT &

BROOKLINE: Chestnut Hill Ave, Lee St, Newton St, Grove St, Putterham Cir, Hancock Village; W. ROXBURY: Weld St; ROSLINDALE: Walter St, Roslindale Sq, Washington St; RAPID TRANSIT: Cleveland Circle (1 block), Reservoir, Chestnut Hill Ave (3 blocks), Forest Hills; COMMUTER RAIL: Roslindale Village, Forest Hills.

52 **Dedham Mall—Watertown** 41 30 45 — 90 —

DEDHAM: VFW Pkwy; W. ROXBURY: Charles River Loop, Spring St, Baker St; NEWTON: Oak Hill, Wiswall Rd, Dedham St, [Parker St, Newton Centre] or [Jewish Community Ctr, Winchester St], Centre St, Newton Corner; WATERTOWN: Galen St; RAPID TRANSIT: Newton Centre.

NOTE: Early morning and night: no mall service. Fare: 75¢-$1.25.

55 **Queensberry St—Park St** 14-19 17/30 60 30 30 30

LIFT &

FENWAY: Ipswich St; BACK BAY: Boylston St/Huntington & St. James, Copley Sq; BOSTON: circles Boston Common; RAPID TRANSIT: Hynes Convention Ctr/ICA, Copley, Arlington*, Boylston*, Park Street*.

NOTE: Night and weekend: Queensberry to Copley and does not serve * stations.

57 **Watertown—Kenmore** 23-29 6/8 9 15 9 15-30

FREQNT
N-OWL
LIFT &

WATERTOWN: Galen St; NEWTON: Newton Corner, Tremont St; BRIGHTON: Oak Sq, Washington St, Brighton Ctr, Cambridge St; ALLSTON: Union Sq, Brighton Ave, Commonwealth Ave; RAPID TRANSIT: Packard's Corner, Kenmore.

59 **Needham Jct—Watertown** 38 30 45 — 45 —

LIFT &

NEEDHAM: Chestnut St, Needham Ctr, Highland Ave, Needham Heights, Hillside Ave, Webster St, Central Ave; NEWTON: Newton Upper Falls, Chestnut St, Oak St, Elliott St or Needham St, Newton Highlands, Walnut St, Newtonville, Nonantum, Watertown St; RAPID TRANSIT: Newton Highlands; COMMUTER RAIL: Needham Jct, Needham Ctr, Needham Heights, Newtonville.

60 **Chestnut Hill—Kenmore** 20-30 22/24 30 30-60 30 60

LIFT &

BROOKLINE: Boylston St (Rte 9), Cypress St, High St, Brookline Village; FENWAY: Brookline Ave, Longwood Medical Area; RAPID TRANSIT: Brookline Village, Kenmore.

62 **Bedford VA Hospital—Alewife** 38-42 30/45 60 1 trip — —

LIFT &

BEDFORD: Springs Rd, Bedford Ctr, South Rd, Loomis St, Great Rd; LEXINGTON: Bedford St, Lexington Ctr, Mass. Ave; ARLINGTON: Arlington Heights, Park Ave, Rte 2; RAPID TRANSIT: Alewife.

NOTE: Night: Bedford Ctr to Alewife only. Saturday: see bus 62/76. Fare: 75¢-$1.25.

62/76 **Bedford VA Hospital—Alewife** 47-50 — — 60-70 —

LIFT &

BEDFORD: Springs Rd, South Rd, Loomis St, Great Rd; LEXINGTON: Hartwell Ave, Hanscom Air Base, Wood St, Marrett Rd (Rte 2A), Waltham St, Worthen Rd, Mass. Ave, Park Ave, Rte 2; RAPID TRANSIT: Alewife.

NOTE: Fare: 75¢-$1.25.

64 **Oak Sq—Univ. Park/Kendall** 27-35 20 30 60 60 60

BRIGHTON: Faneuil St, Hobart St, Brooks St, Birmingham Pkwy, N. Beacon St; ALLSTON: Union Sq, Cambridge St; CAMBRIDGE: Magazine St/Western Ave, Central Sq; REGULAR ROUTE: continues to University Park; RUSH HOUR: continues to Kendall/MIT; RAPID TRANSIT: Central, Kendall/MIT (rush hour only).

	Trip Time	Rush	wk-day	wk-night	allSat	allSun
		------------	Frequency in minutes	------------		

65
X-TOWN
LIFT &

Brighton Ctr—Kenmore   20-27   15/24   30   —   30   —

BRIGHTON: Washington St; *BROOKLINE:* Washington St, Brookline Village; *FENWAY:* Brookline Ave, Longwood Medical Area; *RAPID TRANSIT:* Washington St, Washington Sq, Brookline Village, Kenmore.

66
FREQNT
X-TOWN
N-OWL
LIFT &

Harvard Sta—Dudley   31-41   8/9   15   25   15   20-40

CAMBRIDGE: JFK St; *ALLSTON:* N. Harvard St, Cambridge St, Union Sq, Brighton Ave; *BROOKLINE:* Harvard St, Coolidge Corner, Brookline Village; *MISSION HILL:* Huntington Ave, Brigham Cir, Tremont St; *ROXBURY:* Roxbury Crossing, Malcolm X Blvd; *RAPID TRANSIT:* Harvard, Harvard Ave, Coolidge Corner, Brookline Village, Mission Park, Fenwood Rd, Brigham Circle, Roxbury Crossing, Dudley Sta.

67

Turkey Hill—Alewife   17-22   25   45   —   —   —

ARLINGTON: Washington St/Forest St & Summer St, Mill St, Mass. Ave, Arlington Ctr, Pleasant St, Rte 2; *RAPID TRANSIT:* Alewife.

68

Harvard—Kendall   15   30   30   —   —   —

CAMBRIDGE: Broadway; *RAPID TRANSIT:* Harvard, Kendall/MIT.

69
X-TOWN
LIFT &

Harvard—Lechmere   13-17   14/20   23   30   20   35

CAMBRIDGE: Cambridge St, Inman Sq, E. Cambridge; *RAPID TRANSIT:* Harvard, Lechmere.

70
LIFT &

Cedarwood—Univ. Park   32-55   17/20   30   30   40   15-20

WALTHAM: Stow St, Main St, Central Sq; *WATERTOWN:* Watertown Sq, Arsenal St; *BRIGHTON, ALLSTON:* Western Ave; *CAMBRIDGE:* River St/Western Ave; *RAPID TRANSIT:* Central; *COMMUTER RAIL:* Waltham.

NOTE: Saturday: additional service from Central Sq, Waltham to Central Sq, Cambridge via Watertown Sq.

70A
LIFT &

North Waltham—Univ. Park   43-57   30   lim   —   40   —

WALTHAM: Trapelo Rd, Smith St, Lincoln St, Lake St, Lexington St, Totten Pond Rd, Wyman St, Central Sq, Main St, then same route as bus 70; *RAPID TRANSIT:* Central; *COMMUTER RAIL:* Waltham.

71
FREQNT

Watertown—Harvard Sta   13-16   7/9   13   30   12-15   35

WATERTOWN, CAMBRIDGE: Mt. Auburn St, E. Watertown, Mt. Auburn Hospital; *RAPID TRANSIT:* Harvard.

NOTE: Saturday: additional limited service to North Cambridge.

72

Huron Ave—Harvard Sta   11-12   15   30   30   30   —

CAMBRIDGE: Aberdeen Ave, Huron Ave, Concord Ave, Garden St; *RAPID TRANSIT:* Harvard.

NOTE: Saturday night and Sunday: see bus 72/75.

72/75

Belmont Ctr—Harvard Sta   16-24   —   —   —   lim   40

BELMONT: Concord Ave, Bright Rd, Grove St; *CAMBRIDGE:* Huron Ave, Concord Ave, Garden St; *RAPID TRANSIT:* Harvard; *COMMUTER RAIL:* Belmont Ctr.

73
FREQNT

Waverley—Harvard Sta   13-16   5   10   30   15   35

BELMONT: Trapelo Rd, Cushing Sq; *WATERTOWN:* Belmont St; *CAMBRIDGE:* Mt. Auburn St, Mt. Auburn Hospital; *RAPID TRANSIT:* Harvard; *COMMUTER RAIL:* Waverley.

NOTE: Saturday: additional limited service to North Cambridge.

74/75

Belmont Ctr—Harvard Sta   16-24   17/19   30   40   30   —

BELMONT: Leonard St, Concord Ave, Bright Rd; *CAMBRIDGE:* [bus 74 – Blanchard Rd, Sancta Maria Hospital] or [bus 75 – Grove St, Huron Ave], Fresh Pond Pkwy, Concord Ave; *RAPID TRANSIT:* Harvard; *COMMUTER RAIL:* Belmont.

NOTE: Saturday night and Sunday: see bus 72/75.

Route Details

		Trip Time	Rush	------------ Frequency in minutes ------------ wk-day	wk-night	allSat	allSun

76 **Hanscom Air Base—Alewife** 39-43 30 60 60 * —

LEXINGTON: Wood St, Mass. Ave, Marrett Rd, Five Forks, Waltham St, Worthen Rd, Lexington Ctr, Mass. Ave, Pleasant St; *ARLINGTON:* Rte 2; *RAPID TRANSIT:* Alewife.

NOTE: *Saturday: see bus 62/76. Night: Five Forks to Alewife only. Fare: 75¢-$1.25.

77 **Arlington Heights—Harvard Sta** 22-31 8 11 12 8 15-20

FREQNT
LIFT & * *ARLINGTON:* Mass. Ave, Arlington Ctr; *CAMBRIDGE:* Mass. Ave, N. Cambridge, Porter Sq; *RAPID TRANSIT:* Porter, Harvard; *COMMUTER RAIL:* Porter.

NOTE: Morning rush hour inbound: buses marked "limited" will not pick up passengers between Cameron Ave and Harvard; use bus 77A instead. Saturday: see buses 71 and 73 for additional service.

77A **North Cambridge—Harvard Sta** 8-13 5-10/lim lim lim — —

LIFT & *CAMBRIDGE:* Mass. Ave, Porter Sq; *RAPID TRANSIT:* Porter, Harvard; *COMMUTER RAIL:* Porter.

NOTE: Night and weekend: see bus 77. See buses 71 and 73 for continuing service to Watertown Sq and Waverley Sq, and for additional Saturday service.

78 **Arlmont Village—Harvard Sta** 26-35 17/19 30 60 60 60

ARLINGTON: Appleton St, Wachusett Ave, Park Cir, Rte 2; *BELMONT:* Brighton St; *CAMBRIDGE:* Blanchard Rd, Sancta Maria Hospital, Concord Ave, Fresh Pond; *RAPID TRANSIT:* Harvard.

NOTE: Rush hour trips leave from Arlington Heights.

79 **Arlington Heights—Alewife** 16-20 12/11 25 45 — —

ARLINGTON: Mass. Ave, Arlington Ctr; *CAMBRIDGE:* Alewife Brook Pkwy; *RAPID TRANSIT:* Alewife.

80 **Arlington Ctr—Lechmere** 25-32 15/20 35 60 35 60

ARLINGTON: Medford St; *MEDFORD:* High St, Boston Ave, Medford Hillside, Tufts Univ; *SOMERVILLE:* College Ave, Powderhouse Sq, Broadway, Ball Sq, Magoun Sq, Medford St, McGrath Hwy; *RAPID TRANSIT:* Lechmere.

83 **Rindge Ave—Central** 19-26 10/20 30 60 25 40-60

LIFT & * *CAMBRIDGE:* Rindge Ave, Mass Ave, Porter Sq; *SOMERVILLE:* Somerville Ave, Park St, Beacon St; *CAMBRIDGE:* Inman Sq, Prospect St; *RAPID TRANSIT:* Porter, Central; *COMMUTER RAIL:* Porter.

84 **Arlmont Village—Alewife** 16 30 — — — —

ARLINGTON: Appleton St, Wachusett Ave, Park Ave, Rte 2; *RAPID TRANSIT:* Alewife.

85 **Spring Hill—Kendall/MIT** 10-14 30/40 40 — — —

SOMERVILLE: Summer St, Union Sq, Webster Ave; *CAMBRIDGE:* Windsor/Columbia Sts, Hampshire St, Broadway; *RAPID TRANSIT:* Kendall/MIT.

86 **Sullivan Sq—Cleveland Circle** 34-46 15/18 15-30 60 30 30

X-TOWN
LIFT & *SOMERVILLE:* Cambridge St, Washington St, Union Sq; *CAMBRIDGE:* Kirkland St, Harvard Sq, JFK St; *ALLSTON:* N. Harvard St, Western Ave; *BRIGHTON:* Market St, Brighton Ctr, Chestnut Hill Ave; *RAPID TRANSIT:* Sullivan Sq, Harvard, Chestnut Hill Ave (3 blocks), Cleveland Circle (1 block), Reservoir.

87 **Arlington Ctr—Lechmere** 23-30 16/15 30 30 24 35

X-TOWN *ARLINGTON:* Broadway; *SOMERVILLE:* Clarendon Hill, Broadway, Teele Sq, Holland St, Davis Sq, Elm St, Somerville Ave, Union Sq, McGrath Hwy; *RAPID TRANSIT:* Davis, Porter (1 block), Lechmere; *COMMUTER RAIL:* Porter (1 block).

NOTE: Night and weekend: Clarendon Hill to Lechmere only.

88 **Clarendon Hill—Lechmere** 18-22 10/15 30 30 24 35

X-TOWN *SOMERVILLE:* Broadway, Teele Sq, Holland St, Davis Sq, Highland Ave, Somerville Hospital, Medford St, McGrath Hwy; *RAPID TRANSIT:* Davis, Lechmere.

	Trip Time	Frequency in minutes				
		Rush	wk-day	wk-night	allSat	allSun

89 Clarendon Hill—Sullivan Sq

| 14-21 | 9/12 | 30 | 60 | 30 | 60 |

SOMERVILLE: Broadway, Teele Sq, Powderhouse Sq, Ball Sq, Magoun Sq, Winter Hill, E. Somerville; *RAPID TRANSIT:* Sullivan Sq.

90 Davis—Wellington
X-TOWN

| 28 | 30/35 | 35-70 | 60 | 60 | — |

SOMERVILLE: Highland Ave, Somerville Hospital, City Hall, Cross St, Broadway; *CHARLESTOWN:* Sullivan Sq; *SOMERVILLE:* Middlesex Ave, Assembly Sq; *MEDFORD:* Fellsway; *RAPID TRANSIT:* Davis, Sullivan Sq, Wellington.

91 Sullivan Sq—Central
X-TOWN

| 12-17 | 30 | 25 | 60 | 20 | 40 |

SOMERVILLE: Cambridge St, Washington St, Union Sq, Newton St, Springfield St; *CAMBRIDGE:* Inman Sq, Prospect St; *RAPID TRANSIT:* Sullivan Sq, Central.

92 Assembly Sq—Downtown

| 14-22 | 12/13 | 30 | 60 | 30 | — |

SOMERVILLE: Middlesex Ave; *CHARLESTOWN:* Sullivan Sq, Main St, City Sq; *BOSTON:* N. Washington St, Haymarket, Congress St, Franklin St, Washington St; *RAPID TRANSIT:* Sullivan Sq, Haymarket, State (except night) Downtown Crossing (except night).

NOTE: Rush hour: Sullivan Sq to Downtown only. Night: Sullivan Sq to Haymarket only.

93 Sullivan Sq—Downtown
FREQNT
LIFT &

| 14-22 | 5/7 | 20 | 30-60 | 20 | 40-60 |

CHARLESTOWN: Bunker Hill St, Charlestown Navy Yard, Chelsea St, City Sq; *BOSTON:* N. Washington St, Haymarket, Congress St, Franklin St, Washington St; *RAPID TRANSIT:* Sullivan Sq, Haymarket, State (except night), Downtown Crossing (except night).

NOTE: Night: Sullivan Sq to Haymarket only. Some trips serve Charlestown Navy Yard via Vine St.

94 Medford Sq—Davis

| 18-22 | 22/20 | 40 | 45 | 40 | 40 |

MEDFORD: High St, W. Medford, Boston Ave, Tufts Univ.; *SOMERVILLE:* College Ave, Powderhouse Sq; *RAPID TRANSIT:* Davis; *COMMUTER RAIL:* W. Medford.

95 West Medford—Sullivan Sq
LIFT & *

| 18-24 | 20 | 30 | 60 | 30 | 60 |

MEDFORD: Playstead Rd, High St, Medford Sq, Mystic Ave; *RAPID TRANSIT:* Sullivan Sq; *COMMUTER RAIL:* W. Medford.

96 Medford Sq—Harvard Sta

| 21-29 | 15/20 | 40 | 45 | 30 | 60 |

MEDFORD: Main St, George St, Winthrop St, Boston Ave, Tufts Univ; *SOMERVILLE:* College Ave, Powderhouse Sq, Davis Sq, Elm St; *CAMBRIDGE:* Beech St, Porter Sq, Mass. Ave; *RAPID TRANSIT:* Davis, Porter, Harvard; *COMMUTER RAIL:* Porter.

97 Malden Ctr—Wellington

| 16-20 | 30 | 60 | — | 60 | 60 |

MALDEN: Commercial St, Medford St, Main St; *EVERETT:* Belmont St, Hancock St, Everett Sq, Sweetser Cir, Broadway, Gateway Ctr, Revere Beach Pkwy; *RAPID TRANSIT:* Malden Ctr, Wellington, *COMMUTER RAIL:* Malden Ctr.

99 Boston Reg. Medical—Wellington

| 22-26 | 20 | 20 | 60 | 30 | 60 |

STONEHAM: Woodland Rd; *MEDFORD:* Highland Ave; *MALDEN:* Malden Hospital, Clifton St, Summer St, Malden Ctr, Malden Sq; *EVERETT:* Main St; *RAPID TRANSIT:* Malden Ctr, Wellington; *COMMUTER RAIL:* Malden Ctr.

100 Elm St—Wellington

| 12-18 | 20 | 35 | 60 | 30 | 60 |

MEDFORD: Fellsway, Roosevelt Cir, Fellsway West, Fellsway, Revere Beach Pkwy; *RAPID TRANSIT:* Wellington.

NOTE: Weekend night: Roosevelt Cir to Wellington only.

101 Malden Ctr—Sullivan Sq

| 23-32 | 12 | 30 | 60 | 30 | 60 |

MALDEN: Malden Sq, Malden Sq shopping area (except rush hour), Pleasant St; *MEDFORD:* Salem St, Medford Sq, Main St; *SOMERVILLE:* Broadway, Winter Hill, E. Somerville; *RAPID TRANSIT:* Malden Ctr, Sullivan Sq; *COMMUTER RAIL:* Malden Ctr.

NOTE: Morning rush hour: additional service Medford Sq to Sullivan Sq every 12 min.

Route Details

	Trip Time	Rush	wk-day	wk-night	allSat	allSun
			------------- Frequency in minutes -------------			

104 **Malden Ctr—Sullivan Sq**   16-23   15   30   60   30   60

MALDEN: Malden Sq, Ferry St; *EVERETT:* Glendale Sq, Broadway, Everett Sq; *RAPID TRANSIT:* Malden Ctr, Sullivan Sq; *COMMUTER RAIL:* Malden Ctr.

105 **Malden Ctr—Sullivan Sq**   25-28   30   70   —   60   60

MALDEN: Malden Sq, Eastern Ave, Bowdoin St, Newland St, Bryant St, Cross St; *EVERETT:* Main St, Sweetser Cir, Broadway; *RAPID TRANSIT:* Malden Ctr, Sullivan Sq; *COMMUTER RAIL:* Malden Ctr.

106 **Lebanon St, Malden—Wellington**   21-24   20   30   60   30   60

MALDEN: Lebanon St, Salem St, Malden Sq, Malden Ctr; *EVERETT:* Main St, Sweetser Cir, Revere Beach Pkwy; *RAPID TRANSIT:* Malden Ctr, Wellington; *COMMUTER RAIL:* Malden Ctr.

NOTE: Midday: some trips serve Lebanon St and/or Franklin Sq. Weekend night: Lebanon St to Malden Ctr only.

108
&. LIFT
Linden Sq—Wellington   29-34   30/20   30   60   30   60

MALDEN: Lynn St, Beach St, Salem St, Malden Sq, Malden Ctr, Pleasant St, Highland Ave; *MEDFORD:* Middlesex Ave, Riverside Ave, Fellsway; *RAPID TRANSIT:* Malden Ctr, Wellington; *COMMUTER RAIL:* Malden Ctr.

NOTE: Morning rush hour: additional service from Linden Sq to Malden Ctr.

109 **Linden Sq—Sullivan Sq**   16-23   12/15   20-30   60   30   60

MALDEN: Eastern Ave; *EVERETT:* Glendale Sq, Broadway, Everett Sq; *RAPID TRANSIT:* Sullivan Sq.

110
X-TOWN
Wonderland—Wellington   23-28   20   30   60   30   60

REVERE: Beach St, Revere Ctr, Park Ave; *EVERETT:* Woodlawn, Elm St, Ferry St, Chelsea St, Everett Sq, Broadway; *RAPID TRANSIT:* Wonderland & Revere Beach (except weekend night), Wellington.

NOTE: Rush hour: additional service from Revere Ctr to Wellington every 10 minutes. Weekend night: Revere Ctr to Wellington only.

111
FREQNT
N-OWL
Revere Ctr—Haymarket   22-33   5/6   15   11   12-15   16-25

REVERE: Park Ave; *CHELSEA:* Woodlawn, Washington Ave, Bellingham Sq, Chelsea Sq, Tobin Bridge; *CHARLESTOWN:* City Sq, Rutherford Ave; *BOSTON:* N. Washington St; *RAPID TRANSIT:* Haymarket; *COMMUTER RAIL:* Chelsea.

NOTE: Mon-Fri midday and weekend: Woodlawn to Haymarket only.

112
X-TOWN
LIFT &.
Wellington—Wood Island   42-47   30   35   —   35-50   45

EVERETT: Revere Beach Pkwy, Broadway, Everett Sq, Chelsea St; *CHELSEA:* Everett Ave, Spruce St, Admiral's Hill, Bellingham Sq, Chelsea Sq, Central Ave; *E. BOSTON:* Chelsea St; *RAPID TRANSIT:* Wellington, Wood Island; *COMMUTER RAIL:* Chelsea.

114 **Bellingham Sq—Maverick**   10-11   10/—   40   —   —   —

CHELSEA: Mystic Mall (midday), Hawthorne St, Chelsea Sq; *E. BOSTON:* Meridian St; *RAPID TRANSIT:* Maverick; *COMMUTER RAIL:* Chelsea.

NOTE: See buses 116 and 117 for additional service.

116 **Wonderland—Maverick**   28-30   18/20   30   40   30   50

REVERE: Ocean Ave, Revere St, Broadway, Revere Ctr; *CHELSEA:* Bellingham Sq, Chelsea Sq; *E. BOSTON:* Meridian St; *RAPID TRANSIT:* Wonderland, Maverick; *COMMUTER RAIL:* Chelsea.

NOTE: See buses 117 and 114 for additional service.

117 **Wonderland—Maverick**   25-31   17-20   23   40   30   50

REVERE: Beach St, Central St, Broadway, then as bus 116; *RAPID TRANSIT:* Wonderland, Revere Beach, Maverick; *COMMUTER RAIL:* Chelsea.

NOTE: See buses 114 and 116 for additional service.

	Trip Time	Rush	wk-day	wk-night	allSat	allSun
		----------- Frequency in minutes -----------				

119 LIFT ♿
Northgate—Beachmont
| 27 | 30 | 60 | 60 | 60 | 60 |

REVERE: Squire Rd, Beach St; *MALDEN:* Linden Sq, Washington Ave; *REVERE:* Malden St, Broadway, Revere Ctr, Winthrop Ave, Endicott Ave; *RAPID TRANSIT:* Beachmont.

120
Orient Heights—Maverick
| 20-21 | 15/20 | 20 | 60 | 30 | 50 |

E. BOSTON: Boardman St, Waldemar Ave, Orient Ave, Orient Heights, Bennington St, Meridian St, Maverick Sq, Sumner St, Jeffries Pt, Maverick St; *RAPID TRANSIT:* Orient Heights, Wood Island, Maverick.

121
Wood Island—Maverick
| 11 | 30/25 | — | — | — | — |

E. BOSTON: Chelsea St, Eagle Sq, Lexington St, Meridian St; *RAPID TRANSIT:* Wood Island (morning rush hour only), Maverick.

NOTE: Evening rush hour: Eagle Sq to Maverick only.

130
Lebanon St, Melrose—Malden
| 14 | 30/45 | 90 | — | 90 | — |

MELROSE: Linwood Ave, Lebanon St; *MALDEN:* Sylvan St, Forest St, Main St, Malden Sq; *RAPID TRANSIT, COMMUTER RAIL:* Malden Ctr.

131
Melrose Highlands—Oak Grove
| 19 | 20 | 60 | — | — | — |

MELROSE: Franklin St, Main St, Porter St, Upham St, Laurel St, Grove St; *MALDEN:* Main St, Malden Sq; *RAPID TRANSIT:* Oak Grove (rush hour), Malden Ctr (except rush hour); *COMMUTER RAIL:* Melrose Highlands, Wyoming Hill, Malden Ctr (except rush hour).

NOTE: Some trips serve Melrose East Side via a different route.

132
Redstone Plaza—Malden
| 25 | 30/45 | 90 | — | 90 | — |

STONEHAM: Main St, South St, Pond St; *MELROSE:* Wyoming Ave, Pleasant St, Washington St; *MALDEN:* Summer St; *RAPID TRANSIT:* Oak Grove, Malden Ctr, *COMMUTER RAIL:* Wyoming Hill, Malden Ctr.

134 LIFT ♿
North Woburn—Wellington
| 44-48 | 60 | 60 | * | 60 | * |

WOBURN: Main St, Elm St, Main St, Woburn Sq; *WINCHESTER:* Main St, Winchester Ctr; *MEDFORD:* Winthrop St, High St, Medford Sq, Riverside Ave; *RAPID TRANSIT:* Wellington; *COMMUTER RAIL:* Winchester Ctr.

NOTE: *Mon-Sat night and Sunday: Medford Sq to Wellington. Additional Mon-Sat day service from W. Medford to Wellington. Fare: 75¢-$1.25.

136/ 137 LIFT ♿
Reading Depot—Malden
| 36-40 | 15/20 | 35 | 2 trips | 30 | — |

READING, WAKEFIELD: Reading Sq, [bus 136 – Salem St, Laurel St, Pleasant St] or [bus 137 – Main St, John St, North Ave]; *MELROSE:* Main St, Melrose Ctr; *MALDEN:* Main St, Malden Sq; *RAPID TRANSIT:* Oak Grove, Malden Ctr; *COMMUTER RAIL:* Reading, Wakefield, Greenwood, Malden Ctr.

NOTE: Trips alternate between 136 and 137. Additional trips from Wakefield Sq to Malden as bus 135. Fare: 75¢-$1.25.

170 EXPRSS
Burlington—Dudley
| 45-60 | 2/1 trips | — | — | — | — |

BEDFORD: Crosby Dr; *BURLINGTON:* Middlesex Tpk, 2nd Ave, Rte 128; *EXPRESS TO WALTHAM:* Wyman St, Bear Hill Rd, Main St, Central Sq, Moody St; *NEWTON:* River St, Mass. Pike; *EXPRESS TO BOSTON:* Mass. Ave, Washington St; *RAPID TRANSIT:* Back Bay Station, Silver Line BRT stops from Dudley Sta through Newton St; *COMMUTER RAIL:* Waltham, Back Bay Station.

NOTE: Morning: outbound only; evening: inbound only. Fare: $1.75.

171
Dudley—Logan Airport
| 30 | 2/0 trips | — | — | — | — |

Leaves Dudley Sta at 3:50am and 4:20am; serves Dudley Sta, Melnea Cass Blvd, Andrew and all Logan Airport Terminals.

USING TRANSIT

DESTINATIONS

ROUTE DETAILS

INDEX

	Trip Time	Rush	wk-day	wk-night	allSat	allSun
		------------- Frequency in minutes -------------				

210
X-TOWN

Quincy Ctr—Fields Corner — 23-25 / 30 / 60 / — / 30

QUINCY: Hancock St; *DORCHESTER:* Neponset Ave, Adams St, Gibson St, Geneva Ave; *RAPID TRANSIT:* Quincy Ctr, N. Quincy, Fields Corner (except Saturday); *COMMUTER RAIL:* Quincy Ctr.

NOTE: Some weekday and all Saturday trips: Quincy Ctr to N. Quincy only. Mon-Fri night: special trip meets last Ashmont train at Fields Corner and serves all Red Line Braintree-branch stations.

211

Quincy Ctr—Squantum — 24 / 30 / 60 / — / 60

QUINCY: Newport Ave, Beale St, Highland Ave, Wilson St, Harvard St, W. Squantum St, N. Quincy, E. Squantum St; *RAPID TRANSIT:* Quincy Ctr, Wollaston, N. Quincy; *COMMUTER RAIL:* Quincy Ctr.

212

Quincy Ctr—N. Quincy — 8 / 30/60 / lim / — / 60

QUINCY: Hancock St, Elm Ave, Billings Rd, Hancock St; *RAPID TRANSIT:* Quincy Ctr, N. Quincy; *COMMUTER RAIL:* Quincy Ctr.

214

Quincy Ctr—Germantown — 12 / 11/20 / 30 / * / 20 / *

QUINCY: Coddington St or McGrath Hwy, Sea St, Palmer St, Oceanview; *RAPID TRANSIT, COMMUTER RAIL:* Quincy Ctr.

NOTE: *Night and Sunday: see bus 216.

215
X-TOWN
LIFT ♿

Quincy Ctr—Ashmont — 25-30 / 20/30 / 30 / 60 / 35 / 60

QUINCY: Hancock St, School St, Water St, Copeland St; *W. QUINCY:* Willard St, Robertson St; *MILTON:* Adams St, E. Milton Sq, Granite Ave; *DORCHESTER:* Gallivan Blvd, Dorchester Ave; *RAPID TRANSIT:* Quincy Ctr, Ashmont, Milton (alt. trips on Sunday), Fields Corner (Sunday morning and night); *COMMUTER RAIL:* Quincy Ctr.

NOTE: Sunday: every other trip runs on Whitwell St and Adams St, and morning and night trips serve Fields Corner.

216

Quincy Ctr—Houghs Neck — 14 / 9/20 / 30 / 60 / 20 / 40

QUINCY: Coddington St, Sea St; *RAPID TRANSIT, COMMUTER RAIL:* Quincy Ctr.

NOTE: Night and Sunday: also serves Germantown via Palmer St.

217
X-TOWN

Wollaston Beach—Ashmont — 32 / 30/60 / 2 trips / — / * / —

QUINCY: Beach St, Wollaston, Beale St; *MILTON:* Adams St, E. Milton Sq; *DORCHESTER:* Lower Mills, Dorchester Ave; *RAPID TRANSIT:* Wollaston, Milton, Ashmont.

NOTE: *Saturday: see bus 245.

220
LIFT ♿

Quincy Ctr—Hingham — 26-31 / 10/25 / 30 / 60 / 30 / 60

QUINCY: Washington St; *WEYMOUTH:* Bridge St, N. Weymouth; *HINGHAM:* Lincoln St, Downer Ave, Otis St, Old Hingham Ctr, North St, Main St-Central St loop; *RAPID TRANSIT, COMMUTER RAIL:* Quincy Ctr.

NOTE: Some trips do not serve Old Hingham Ctr. For connecting service to Hull see JBL Hull-Hingham route in Chapter 12, "More Rail, Bus, and Ferry."

221
LIFT ♿

Quincy Ctr—Fort Point — 16-18 / 3/1 trips / — / — / — / —

QUINCY: Washington St; *WEYMOUTH:* Bridge St, N. Weymouth, Neck St, River St; *RAPID TRANSIT, COMMUTER RAIL:* Quincy Ctr.

222

Quincy Ctr—E. Weymouth — 21-23 / 12/20 / 30 / 60 / 30-60 / 60

QUINCY: Washington St; *WEYMOUTH:* Bridge St, N. Weymouth, Sea St, North St, Commercial St, [Middle St] or [Essex St, Broad St]; *RAPID TRANSIT, COMMUTER RAIL:* Quincy Ctr.

225

Quincy—Weymouth Landing — 18-20 / 10 / 30 / 60 / 30 / 60

QUINCY: Hancock St, [Quincy Ave, Scammell St, South St, Des Moines Rd] or [Quincy Ave, Shaw St], Fore River Shipyard; *BRAINTREE:* Quincy Ave; *WEYMOUTH:* Front Rd, Summer St, Federal St, Washington St; *RAPID TRANSIT, COMMUTER RAIL:* Quincy Ctr.

		Trip Time	------------ Frequency in minutes ------------				
			Rush	wk-day	wk-night	allSat	allSun
230	**Quincy Ctr—Montello**	42-52	25	60	60	60	60

QUINCY: Hancock St, Franklin St, Independence Ave; *BRAINTREE:* Washington St, Braintree Sta, S. Braintree Sq, Hancock St, Washington St; *HOLBROOK:* [Franklin St] or [Center St, Union St], Holbrook Sq, Brookville Sq to Brockton line; *RAPID TRANSIT:* Quincy Ctr, Braintree; *COMMUTER RAIL:* Quincy Ctr, Braintree, Montello, Holbrook/Randolph (limited).

NOTE: Fare: 75¢-$1.25.

236	**Quincy Ctr—South Shore Plaza**	31	20-60	60	—	60	60

LIFT &

QUINCY: Hancock St, Franklin St; *BRAINTREE:* Commercial St, Elm St, Middle St, Union St, Braintree Sta, S. Braintree Sq, Franklin St, Five Corners, Granite St; *RAPID TRANSIT, COMMUTER RAIL:* Quincy Ctr, Braintree.

NOTE: Some morning rush hour trips: Quincy Ctr to Braintree only.

238	**Quincy—Holbrook/Randolph**	25-30	20	55	60	15-60	70

LIFT &

QUINCY: Hancock St, Franklin St, Water St, Liberty St, Centre St, West St, Willard St; *BRAINTREE:* Granite St, South Shore Plaza, Five Corners, Pond St; *RANDOLPH:* North St, Crawford Sq, Union St; *RAPID TRANSIT:* Quincy Ctr, Quincy Adams (except Sunday); *COMMUTER RAIL:* Quincy Ctr, Holbrook/Randolph (Mon-Fri days only).

NOTE: Night and weekend: Quincy Ctr to Crawford Sq only. See bus 240 for connecting service to Ashmont. Fare: 75¢-$1.25.

240	**Avon Line—Ashmont**	23-24	20	30	60	30	70

LIFT &

RANDOLPH: Main St, Crawford Sq; *MILTON:* Randolph Ave, Reedsdale Rd, Milton Hospital, Central Ave; *DORCHESTER:* Lower Mills, Dorchester Ave; *RAPID TRANSIT:* Central Ave, Ashmont; *COMMUTER RAIL:* Holbrook/Randolph (alt. weekday trips).

NOTE: Every other weekday trip: Holbrook/Randolph station to Ashmont. Some weekend trips: Crawford Sq to Ashmont only. See bus 238 for related services. Fare: 75¢-$1.25.

245	**Quincy Ctr—Mattapan**	24-26	60/30	60	—	60	—

X-TOWN

QUINCY: Whitwell St, Adams St; *MILTON:* E. Milton Sq, [Edge Hill Rd, Pleasant St, Reedsdale Rd, Milton Hospital, Brook Rd] or [Brook Rd]; *RAPID TRANSIT:* Quincy Ctr, Mattapan; *COMMUTER RAIL:* Quincy Ctr.

325	**Elm St, Medford—Haymarket**	20	12/15	—	—	—	—

EXPRSS

MEDFORD: Fellsway West, Salem St; *EXPRESS TO BOSTON:* I-93; *RAPID TRANSIT:* Haymarket.

NOTE: Fare: $1.75 or 10-ride pass: $16.00.

326	**West Medford—Haymarket**	16	12/15	—	—	—	—

EXPRSS

MEDFORD: Playstead Rd, High St, Medford Sq; *EXPRESS TO BOSTON:* I-93; *RAPID TRANSIT:* Haymarket; *COMMUTER RAIL:* West Medford.

NOTE: Fare: $1.75 or 10-ride pass: $16.00.

350	**N. Burlington—Alewife**	30-50	20	60	60	60	50-60

LIFT &

BURLINGTON: Chestnut Ave, Cambridge St, Mall Rd, Burlington Mall (some trips); *WOBURN, WINCHESTER:* Cambridge St; *ARLINGTON:* Mystic St, Arlington Ctr, Mass. Ave, Alewife Brook Pkwy; *RAPID TRANSIT:* Alewife.

NOTE: Fare: 75¢-$1.25.

351	**Bedford Woods—Alewife**	45	30	—	—	—	—

EXPRSS
LIFT &

BEDFORD: Middlesex Tpk, Crosby Dr, Bedford St, Middlesex Tpk, 4th Ave, 3rd Ave, 2nd Ave; *EXPRESS TO CAMBRIDGE:* Rte 128, Rte 2; *RAPID TRANSIT:* Alewife.

NOTE: Morning trips: outbound only; evening trips: inbound only. Fare: $1.75.

352	**Burlington—State**	45	16/15	—	—	—	—

EXPRSS

BURLINGTON: Chestnut Ave, Cambridge St; *EXPRESS TO BOSTON:* Rte 128, I-93; *RAPID TRANSIT:* Haymarket, Government Ctr, State, Bowdoin.

NOTE: Fare: $2.75 or 10-ride pass: $25.

Route Details

		Trip Time	------------ Frequency in minutes ------------			
			Rush	wk-day	wk-night	allSat	allSun

354
EXPRSS
LIFT &

Woburn—State   40-45   15   90   1 trip   —   —

WOBURN: Cambridge Rd, Lexington St, Woburn Sq, Montvale Ave, Bow St, Salem St, Pine St; *EXPRESS TO BOSTON:* I-93; *RAPID TRANSIT:* Haymarket, Government Ctr, State, Bowdoin.

NOTE: Evening: continues to Chestnut Ave in Burlington. Fare: 75¢ local, $2.75 to Haymarket or 10-ride pass: $25.

355
EXPRSS
LIFT &

Mishawum—State   40   2/2 trips   —   —   —   —

WOBURN: Mishawum Rd, Washington St; *EXPRESS TO BOSTON:* I-93; *RAPID TRANSIT:* Haymarket, Government Ctr, State, Bowdoin.

NOTE: Morning: outbound only; evening: inbound only. Fare: $2.75 or 10-ride pass: $25.

411
X-TOWN

J. Satter House—Malden Ctr   41-43   35/50   60   —   60   —

REVERE: Ocean Ave, Wonderland, Revere/Beach Sts, Malden St, Northgate Mall; *MALDEN:* Linden Sq, Lynn St, Granada Highlands, Kennedy Dr, Broadway, Salem St, Malden Sq; *RAPID TRANSIT:* Wonderland (except morning rush hour), Revere Beach (except morning rush hour), Malden Ctr; *COMMUTER RAIL:* Malden Ctr.

NOTE: Morning rush hour: Granada Highlands to Malden Ctr only.

424
EXPRSS
LIFT & *

Haymarket—Eastern & Essex, Lynn   35   —/30   —   —   —   —

EXPRESS FROM BOSTON: Rte 1; *REVERE:* Broadway; *MALDEN:* Linden Sq; *SAUGUS:* Salem Tpk; *LYNN:* Western Ave, Eastern Ave; *RAPID TRANSIT:* Haymarket.

NOTE: Fare: 75¢-$1.25 or 10-ride pass: $16.

424W
LIFT & *

Eastern & Essex, Lynn—Wonderland   37   30/—   —   —   —   —

LYNN: Eastern Ave, Western Ave; *SAUGUS:* Salem Tpk; *REVERE:* Broadway; *RAPID TRANSIT:* Wonderland.

NOTE: All trips are inbound only.

426
EXPRSS

Central Sq, Lynn—Haymarket   46   40/15   60   60   —   —

LYNN: Market St, Western Ave, Summer St, Boston St; *SAUGUS:* Lincoln Ave; *MALDEN:* Linden Sq; *EXPRESS TO BOSTON:* Rte 1; *RAPID TRANSIT:* Haymarket; *COMMUTER RAIL:* Lynn, Salem Depot (night only).

NOTE: All morning and alternate evening rush hour: Haymarket to W. Lynn Garage only. Night: continues to Salem Depot. Weekend: see bus 426W. See bus 439 for connecting service to Nahant. Fare: 75¢-$1.75 or 10-ride pass: $16.

426W

Central Sq, Lynn—Wonderland   37-41   20/—   —   1 trip   60   60

LYNN: Market St, Western Ave, Summer St, Boston St; *SAUGUS:* Lincoln Ave; *REVERE:* Salem St, Squire Rd, Northgate Shopping Ctr, American Legion Hwy, Beach St, Ocean Ave; *RAPID TRANSIT:* Wonderland; *COMMUTER RAIL:* Lynn.

NOTE: All rush hour trips are inbound only.

428
EXPRSS

Oaklandvale—Haymarket   50-63   40   —   —   —   —

SAUGUS: Main St, Central St, Winter St, Lincoln Ave; *REVERE:* Salem St; *MALDEN:* Granada Highlands, Linden Sq; *EXPRESS TO BOSTON:* Rte 1; *RAPID TRANSIT:* Haymarket.

NOTE: Fare: 75¢-$2.75 or 10-ride pass: $25.

429

Northgate—Central Sq, Lynn   49-52   30   60   60   60   60

LYNN: Franklin St, Boston St, Myrtle St, Holyoke St, O'Callaghan Way/Garfield Ave; *SAUGUS:* Walnut St, Rte 1, Square One Mall (some trips), Essex St, Cliftondale Sq, Lincoln Ave; *REVERE:* Salem St; *MALDEN:* Linden Sq; *COMMUTER RAIL:* Lynn.

430

Saugus—Malden Ctr   33   30/45   60   2 trips   60   —

SAUGUS: Appleton St, Summer St, Main St, Saugus Ctr, Central St, Cliftondale, Essex St, Vine St, Rte 1, Square One Mall (some trips); *MALDEN:* Broadway, Salem St, Maplewood Sq, Malden Sq; *RAPID TRANSIT, COMMUTER RAIL:* Malden Ctr.

		Trip Time	Rush	------------- Frequency in minutes ------------- wk-day	wk-night	allSat	allSun

431

LIFT &

Neptune Tower—Cent. Sq, Lynn   5   1/2 trips   60   —   60   60

Connects with buses 435 and 436 to/from Liberty Tree Mall; *COMMUTER RAIL:* Lynn.

434

EXPRSS

LIFT &

Haymarket—Main St, Peabody   53   1/1   —   —   —   —

Leaves Peabody at 6:55am; leaves Haymarket at 5:20pm; also serves Goodwin Cir; *RAPID TRANSIT:* Haymarket.

435

LIFT &

Liberty Tree Mall—Cent. Sq, Lynn   45   1 trip/60   60   60   60   120

PEABODY: Central St, Main St, S. Peabody, Washington St, Lynn St; *LYNN:* Broadway, Chestnut St; *COMMUTER RAIL:* Lynn.

NOTE: Weeknight outbound: continues to Danvers Sq. See bus 431 for connecting service to Neptune Tower.

436

Liberty Tree Mall—Cent. Sq, Lynn   46-57   30/35   60   —   60   120

DANVERS: Endicott St; *PEABODY:* North Shore Mall, Essex Ctr Dr, Prospect St, Lowell St, Forest St, Centennial Dr, Lynnfield St; *LYNNFIELD:* Goodwin Cir; *LYNN:* Lynnfield St, Wyoma Sq, Chestnut St, Union St; *COMMUTER RAIL:* Lynn.

NOTE: Morning: North Shore Mall to Central Sq, Lynn only.

439

Central Sq, Lynn—Nahant   17   30   1 trip   —   —   —

LYNN: Nahant St; *NAHANT:* Nahant Rd, Castle Rd, Spring Rd, Willow Rd, Wharf St; *COMMUTER RAIL:* Lynn.

NOTE: Morning rush hour: see bus 426 for connecting service to Haymarket.

441/ 442

EXPRSS

LIFT & *

Marblehead—Haymarket   57-68   30/15   30   60   —   —

SWAMPSCOTT: [bus 441 – Salem St, Paradise St] or [bus 442 – Humphrey St]; *LYNN:* Lewis St, Central Sq, Lynnway, North Shore Rd; *EXPRESS TO BOSTON:* Haymarket; *RAPID TRANSIT:* Wonderland, Haymarket; *COMMUTER RAIL:* Lynn.

NOTE: Fare: 75¢-$2.75.

441/ 442W

LIFT & *

Marblehead—Wonderland   41-43   15/—   —   —   30   30

SWAMPSCOTT: [bus 441W – Salem St, Paradise St] or [bus 442W – Humphrey St]; *LYNN:* Lewis St, Central Sq, Lynnway, North Shore Rd; *RAPID TRANSIT:* Wonderland; *COMMUTER RAIL:* Lynn.

NOTE: All rush hour trips are inbound only. Fare: 75¢-$1.25.

448/ 449

EXPRSS

LIFT & *

Marblehead—Downtown   69-75   30   —   —   —   —

SWAMPSCOTT: [bus 448 – Salem St, Paradise St] or [bus 449 – Humphrey St]; *LYNN:* Lewis St, Central Sq, Lynnway, North Shore Rd; *EXPRESS TO BOSTON:* Logan Airport, South Station, Downtown Crossing; *RAPID TRANSIT:* Wonderland, South Station, Downtown Crossing; *COMMUTER RAIL:* Lynn, South Station.

NOTE: Fare: 75¢-$2.75.

450

EXPRSS

LIFT & *

Salem Depot—Haymarket   35-45   30   60   60   —   —

SALEM: Highland Ave; *LYNN:* Western Ave; *SAUGUS:* Salem Tpk; *REVERE:* Broadway; *EXPRESS TO BOSTON:* Rte 1; *RAPID TRANSIT:* Haymarket; *COMMUTER RAIL:* Salem Depot.

NOTE: Weekend: see bus 450W. Fare: 75¢-$1.25 or 10-ride pass: $16.

450W

LIFT & *

Salem Depot—Wonderland   38   —   —   —   60   60

SALEM: Highland Ave; *LYNN:* Western Ave; *SAUGUS:* Salem Tpk; *REVERE:* Broadway; *RAPID TRANSIT:* Wonderland; *COMMUTER RAIL:* Salem Depot.

451

N. Beverly—Salem Depot   33-37   60   60   —   60   —

BEVERLY: Enon St, Tozer/Dodge St, Cabot St, Beverly Ctr; *SALEM:* Bridge St; *COMMUTER RAIL:* Salem Depot.

NOTE: Saturday: Ellis Sq to Salem Depot only.

Route Details

		Trip Time	Rush	---- Frequency in minutes ---- wk-day	wk-night	allSat	allSun

455
EXPRSS
LIFT &

Salem Depot—Haymarket   69-71   60   60   60   —   —

SALEM: Lafayette St, Loring Ave; *SWAMPSCOTT:* Vinnin Sq, Essex St; *LYNN:* Union St, Central Sq, Common St, Western Ave, W. Lynn; *SAUGUS:* Marsh Rd (Salem Tpk); *REVERE:* American Legion Hwy, Bell Cir; *EXPRESS TO BOSTON:* Haymarket; *RAPID TRANSIT:* Haymarket; *COMMUTER RAIL:* Salem Depot, Lynn.

NOTE: Night: see bus 426. Weekend: see bus 455W. Fare: 75¢-$2.75.

455W
LIFT &

Salem Depot—Wonderland   53-60   30/—   —   —   30   60

SALEM: Lafayette St, Loring Ave; *SWAMPSCOTT:* Vinnin Sq, Essex St; *LYNN:* Union St, Central Sq, Common St, Western Ave, W. Lynn; *SAUGUS:* Salem Tpk; *REVERE:* American Legion Hwy, Bell Cir, Revere St; *RAPID TRANSIT:* Wonderland; *COMMUTER RAIL:* Salem Depot, Lynn.

NOTE: All rush hour trips are inbound only.

456
LIFT & *

Salem Depot—Central Sq, Lynn   25   —   60   —   —   —

SALEM: Highland Ave; *LYNN:* Western Ave, Eastern Ave, Union St; *COMMUTER RAIL:* Salem Depot, Lynn.

NOTE: Morning rush hour trips are outbound only.

459
EXPRSS
LIFT &

Salem—Logan, Downtown   75   4 trips   3 trips   —   —   —

Follows same route as bus 455 through Bell Cir; then *EXPRESS TO BOSTON:* Logan Terminal C, South Station, Downtown Crossing; *RAPID TRANSIT:* South Station, Downtown Crossing; *COMMUTER RAIL:* Salem Depot, Lynn, South Station.

NOTE: Fare: 75¢-$2.75.

465

Liberty Tree Mall—Salem Depot   32-37   1 trip/60   60   —   60   —

PEABODY: Prospect St, North Shore Mall, Andover St, Central St, Main St; *SALEM:* Boston St, Bridge St; *COMMUTER RAIL:* Salem Depot.

NOTE: Some trips continue to Danvers Sq.

468

Danvers Sq—Salem Depot   15   2/2 trips   —   —   —   —

DANVERS: High St, Liberty St, Water St; *PEABODY:* Margin St; *SALEM:* North St; *COMMUTER RAIL:* Salem Depot.

500
EXPRSS

Riverside—Downtown   20-24   15/25   —   4 trips   —   —

NEWTON: Riverside; *EXPRESS TO BOSTON:* Mass. Pike, Federal St, Franklin St, Otis St; *RAPID TRANSIT:* Riverside, Downtown Crossing, Copley (night).

NOTE: Night: via Copley Sq and Newton Corner. Fare: $2.75 or 10-ride pass: $25.

501
EXPRSS

Brighton Ctr—Downtown   23-25   4/5   —   —   —   —

BRIGHTON: Washington St, Oak Sq, Park St, Newton Corner; *EXPRESS TO BOSTON:* Mass. Pike, Federal St, Franklin St, Otis St; *RAPID TRANSIT:* Downtown Crossing.

NOTE: Inbound: no drop-off from Brighton to Newton Corner. Fare: $1.75 or 10-ride pass: $16.

502
EXPRSS

Watertown—Copley Sq   15-17   7/10   —   —   —   —

WATERTOWN: Galen St; *NEWTON:* Newton Corner; *EXPRESS TO BOSTON:* Mass. Pike, Stuart St, St. James Ave; *RAPID TRANSIT:* Copley.

NOTE: Midday and Saturday: see bus 504. Night: see bus 500. Fare: $1.75 or 10-ride pass: $16.

504
EXPRSS

Watertown—Downtown   25-29   7/10   30   —   35   —

WATERTOWN: Galen St; *NEWTON:* Newton Corner; *EXPRESS TO BOSTON:* Mass. Pike, Federal St, Franklin St, Otis St; *RAPID TRANSIT:* Downtown Crossing, Copley (midday and Saturday only).

NOTE: Mon-Fri midday and Saturday: serves Copley Sq. Night: see bus 500. Fare: $1.75 or 10-ride pass: $16.

		Trip	------------- **Frequency in minutes** -------------			
		Time	Rush	wk-day	wk-night	allSat	allSun

505
EXPRSS

Waltham—Downtown	29-36	7/12	lim	—	—	—

WALTHAM: Central Sq, Moody St; *NEWTON:* Lexington St, Auburndale, Commonwealth Ave, Washington St, W. Newton; *EXPRESS TO BOSTON:* Mass. Pike, Federal St, Franklin St, Otis St; *RAPID TRANSIT:* Downtown Crossing; *COMMUTER RAIL:* Waltham, Auburndale.

NOTE: Fare: $2.75 or 10-ride pass: $25.

553
EXPRSS

Roberts—Downtown	50	60	60	—	60	—

WALTHAM: South St, Brandeis Univ, Waltham Hospital, Main St, Central Sq, Moody St; *NEWTON:* River St, W. Newton, Austin St, Washington St, Newtonville, Newton Corner; *EXPRESS TO BOSTON:* Mass. Pike, Federal St, Franklin St, Otis St; *RAPID TRANSIT:* Downtown Crossing; *COMMUTER RAIL:* Brandeis/Roberts, Waltham, W. Newton, Newtonville.

NOTE: Saturday: Roberts to Newton Corner only. Fare: 75¢-$1.75.

554
EXPRSS

Waverley—Downtown	55	40/60	60	—	60	—

BELMONT: Lexington St; *WATERTOWN:* Belmont St; *WALTHAM:* Beaver St, Bentley College, Lexington St, Central Sq, Moody St; *NEWTON:* River St, W. Newton, Washington St, Newtonville, Newton Corner; *EXPRESS TO BOSTON:* Mass. Pike, Federal St, Franklin St, Otis St; *RAPID TRANSIT:* Downtown Crossing; *COMMUTER RAIL:* Waverley, Waltham, W. Newton, Newtonville.

NOTE: Saturday: Waverley to Newton Corner only. Fare: 75¢-$1.75.

556
EXPRSS

Waltham Highlands—Downtown	45	30	60	—	—	—

WALTHAM: Bacon St, Dale St, Hammond St, Main St, Central Sq, Moody St, High St; *NEWTON:* Crafts St, Walnut St, Newtonville, Washington St, Newton Corner; *EXPRESS TO BOSTON:* Mass. Pike, Federal St, Franklin St, Otis St; *RAPID TRANSIT:* Downtown Crossing; *COMMUTER RAIL:* Waltham, Newtonville.

NOTE: Midday: Waltham Highlands to Newton Corner only. Fare: 75¢-$1.75.

558
EXPRSS

Auburndale—Downtown	45	3 trips	3 trips	—	—	—

NEWTON: Commonwealth Ave, Lexington St, Rumford Ave; *WALTHAM:* Woerd Ave, Crescent St, Moody St, Central Sq, River St; *WATERTOWN:* Pleasant St; *NEWTON:* Chapel St, Adams St, Washington St, Newton St; *EXPRESS TO BOSTON:* Mass. Pike, Federal St, Franklin St, Otis St; *RAPID TRANSIT:* Downtown Crossing; *COMMUTER RAIL:* Auburndale, Waltham, Newtonville.

NOTE: Some midday trips: Auburndale to Newton Corner only. Fare: 75¢-$1.75.

CT1
X-TOWN
BIKE
LIFT &

Central—Boston Medical	20-27	15	30	—	—	—

ONLY AT THE FOLLOWING STOPS: CAMBRIDGE: Central Sq, University Park, MIT; *BOSTON:* Hynes Convention Ctr/ICA, Symphony, Mass. Ave (OL), Mass. Ave (SL), Boston Medical Ctr (3 stops); *RAPID TRANSIT:* Central, Hynes Convention Ctr/ICA, Symphony, Mass. Ave (OL), Mass. Ave (SL).

CT2
X-TOWN
BIKE
LIFT &

Sullivan Sq—Ruggles	47-50	20/25	35	—	—	—

ONLY AT THE FOLLOWING STOPS: CHARLESTOWN: Sullivan Sq; *SOMERVILLE:* Cobble Hill, McGrath Hwy, Union Sq (2 stops); *CAMBRIDGE:* Cambridge St, Portland St, Kendall/MIT, MIT, Hyatt Regency; *BOSTON:* Comm. Ave, Fenway, Beth Israel Hospital, Children's Hospital, Longwood Medical Area, Museum of Fine Arts, Ruggles; *RAPID TRANSIT:* Kendall/MIT, Fenway, Longwood/Hospitals, BU Central (1 block), Museum of Fine Arts, Ruggles, Sullivan Sq; *COMMUTER RAIL:* Ruggles.

CT3
X-TOWN
BIKE
LIFT &

Beth Israel—Andrew	24-29	15/20	30	—	—	—

ONLY AT THE FOLLOWING STOPS: BOSTON: Beth Israel Hospital, Children's Hospital, Avenue Louis Pasteur, Museum of Fine Arts, Ruggles, Melnea Cass Blvd, Boston Medical Ctr (3 stops), Andrew; *RAPID TRANSIT:* Museum of Fine Arts, Ruggles, Andrew, Melnea Cass Blvd; *COMMUTER RAIL:* Ruggles.

Chapter 11:
MBTA Ferries & Commuter Boats

MBTA Ferries are divided into two groups: Inner Harbor Ferries for short trips and Commuter Boats for longer trips to the South Shore. The tables below show boat frequency as the number of trips. Also shown are stops, fare information, and rapid transit connections. A slash (/) indicates different morning and evening frequencies. Bicycles are permitted on all MBTA ferries.

For seasonal, non-MBTA service to Provincetown, Salem, Gloucester, and Boston Harbor Islands plus on-demand water taxi service, see Chapter 12, "More Rail, Bus, and Ferry (Not the T)." For the fastest route from downtown Boston to Logan Airport see the Airport Water Shuttle in Chapter 14, "Regional Airports." For general information about using MBTA ferries, see Chapter 1, "The T (MBTA Transit)."

Inner Harbor Ferries

	Trip Time	Rush	Midday	Night	Sat Trips	Sun Trips
		—— Weekday Trips ——				

F3 North Station—Charlestown :05 7/8 7 — — —
Lovejoy Wharf near North Station to Charlestown Navy Yard. See bus 93 for additional service. *FARE:* $1.25 or 60 rides for $57. *RAPID TRANSIT:* North Station.

F4 Boston—Charlestown :10 10/12 12 2 17 17
Long Wharf, Boston to Charlestown Navy Yard. *FARE:* same as F3. *RAPID TRANSIT:* Aquarium.

F5/F5X North Station—So. Boston :20 10/10 7 — — —
Lovejoy Wharf near North Station to Federal Courthouse (Fan Pier) and World Trade Center, South Boston. Some F5 trips primarily debark at Courthouse and may depart early. F5X trips do not stop at Courthouse. Midday and last trip stop at Charlestown on request. *FARE:* same as F3. *RAPID TRANSIT:* North Station.

Commuter Boats

F1 Hingham—Boston :35 6/8 3 1 — —
Hingham Shipyard to Rowes Wharf, Boston. See bus 220 for connecting service from Hingham Shipyard to Quincy Center MBTA station. *FARE:* $5.00 or 10-ride pass $45. *RAPID TRANSIT:* Aquarium (3 blocks), South Station (4 blocks).

F2/F2H Quincy—Boston—Logan :45 4/5 6 4 10 9
Fore River Shipyard, Quincy to Long Wharf and Logan Airport, Boston. Six of the weekday trips operate as F2H and make an additional stop at Pemberton Point, Hull. *FARE:* Quincy-Boston $5; Hull-Boston $4; Quincy or Hull to Logan $12. *RAPID TRANSIT:* Aquarium.

COURTESY MBTA

ANDREW RUBEL

Chapter 12:
More Rail, Bus, and Ferry (Not the T)

The tables below show frequency in number of trips; stations or cities served; and other information for non-MBTA services which include Amtrak trains, Regional Transit Authority services, local buses, commuter buses, interstate buses, and ferries. A slash (/) indicates different morning and evening frequencies. For general information and a word about Boston's intermodal transit hub, South Station, see Chapter 2, "Not the T (Non-MBTA Transit)."

An Amtrak high-speed Acela train arriving at South Station in Boston.

ANDREW RUBEL

🚆 More Rail

	Trip Time	Rush	Day	Night	Sat Trips	Sun Trips
			Weekday Trips			

Amtrak   800/USA-RAIL; www.amtrak.com

In addition to the Boston routes below, Amtrak also runs the Vermonter from Washington, DC to St. Albans, VT via Springfield and Amherst, MA but not Boston.

Boston—New York—Washington   6-9:00   18 trips weekdays; Sat 13; Sun 16
South Station to Washington, DC via Back Bay Station and Route 128 Station, MA; Providence, Kingston, and Westerly, RI; Mystic, New London, Old Saybrook, New Haven, Bridgeport, and Stamford, CT; New York; Philadelphia; and many other points with some service continuing to Richmond, VA. One trip, the Twilight Shoreliner, departs daily at 9:10pm and arrives at 5:50am the next morning.

Springfield—New York—Washington   6-9:00   6 trips weekdays; Sat 5; Sun 6

South Station (one trip) or Springfield, MA to Washington, DC via Windsor Locks, Windsor, Hartford, Berlin, Meriden, Wallingford, and New Haven, CT, then continues as Boston route above. The trip that originates at South Station in Boston also serves Back Bay Station, Framingham, and Worcester, MA.

The Downeaster   2:45   4 trips each way daily
North Station to Portland, ME via Woburn and Haverhill, MA; Exeter, Durham (seasonal), and Dover, NH; and Wells, Saco-Biddeford, and Old Orchard Beach (seasonal), ME.

Lake Shore Limited   21:00   1 trip each way daily
Boston to Chicago, IL via New York State, Pennsylvania, Ohio, and Indiana. Massachusetts stops include South Station, Back Bay Station, Framingham, Worcester, Springfield, and Pittsfield.

🚌 More Buses

	Trip Time	Rush	Day	Night	Sat Trips	Sun Trips
		— Weekday Trips —				

A&A Metro — 508/697-0017; 800/437-3844; www.aametro.com

N. Medford—Medford Sq (T-bus 710) :30 4/4 7 — — —

Serves points in Medford including Meadow Glen Mall, Lawrence Hospital and others with connections to T-buses 94, 96, 99, 101, 134, and 326. This route is subsidized by the MBTA.

Alewife Shuttles—see Waltham CitiBus

American Eagle Motor Coach, Inc. — 508/993-5040

New Bedford—Boston 1:25 6/6 3 1 7 4

SRTA Terminal in New Bedford to South Station via Taunton. Bikes permitted for a small fee when space is available.

The B Line (Burlington Bus) — 781/270-1965; www.burlington.org

B Line routes 1-6 :30 9-11 trips hourly Mon-Fri 6am-6pm

Six loop routes serving Burlington schools, malls, Lahey Clinic (by request), and other locations. Connects with T-buses 350, 352, 354, Lexpress bus 5, and LRTA's Bl route. Service is run by Joseph's Limousine.

BAT—Brockton Area Transit — 508/580-1170

BAT runs 17 routes Mon-Sat most within Brockton, but also serving Avon, Bridgewater, Easton, Stoughton, and West Bridgewater. Points served include Westgate Mall, Massasoit Community College, Stonehill College, plus Brockton, Campello, and Montello Commuter Rail stations, and many other points in Brockton. BAT bus 12 (detailed below) offers frequent service to the Red Line at Ashmont. All routes begin at the BAT Center on Commercial St in Brockton Center.

BAT 12 Brockton—Ashmont :40 Mon-Sat every 15-30 min 5am-11pm

BAT Center in Brockton to Ashmont (Red Line) via Avon, Randolph, and Milton.

Bedford Local Transit — 781/275-2255; www.town.beford.ma.us

Bedford Common—Burlington Mall :30 2 trips Mon-Fri at 12noon and 3pm

Starting from the Old Town Hall, serves Bedford grocery stores and Burlington Mall.

Beverly Shoppers Shuttle — 978/232-9559

Run by the Beverly Chamber of Commerce, this around-town loop serves Beverly Depot Commuter Rail station (two morning loops are timed to meet trains), Beverly Hospital, the center of town, and many other points. Loops run Mon-Sat 8-11 times from around 7am-5:30pm.

Bloom's Bus Lines — 508/822-1991; www.bloombus.com

Bikes permitted for small fee when space is available. The Bloom Terminal is at 10 Oak St in Taunton.

Taunton—Boston 1:15 4/5 3 1 5 5

Bloom Terminal to South Station via Raynham, Easton, and Brockton (limited).

Taunton—Fall River :40 1/1 — — — —

Bloom Terminal to SRTA Terminal in Fall River.

Bonanza Bus Lines — 401/751-8800; www.bonanzabus.com

Bikes permitted on space-available basis, sometimes for a small fee. In addition to the Boston routes below, Bonanza serves (not via Boston) Pittsfield, Williamstown, and Hyannis, MA; Albany, NY; Hartford, CT; and Bennington, VT.

Boston—Providence, RI 1:30 17 trips daily each way approx. hourly

South Station to T.F. Green Airport in Providence via Foxborough (limited), Bonanza Bus Terminal in Providence, and Kennedy Plaza (RIPTA bus terminal) in downtown Providence.

Logan Airport—Falmouth 2:20 11 trips weekdays, Sat: 9, Sun: 8

Logan Airport to Woods Hole via Wareham (limited), Buzzard's Bay (limited), Bourne, Otis Air Base, and Falmouth.

	Trip Time	—— Weekday Trips —— Rush Day Night			Sat Trips	Sun Trips

Logan Airport—Providence, RI 1:15 12 trips daily every 1-2 hours
Logan Airport to Bonanza Terminal in Providence via Foxborough and South Station (limited).

Boston—New York, NY 5:00 7 trips each way daily every 2 hours
South Station express to Port Authority Terminal, New York, NY with one stop in Providence, RI. Four trips offer connecting service in Providence for local stops in RI, CT, and NY en route to Port Authority Terminal.

Boston—Newport, RI 1:40 8 trips weekdays, Sat and Sun: 6
South Station to Newport via Fall River, MA; Portsmouth, RI; and Middletown, RI.

BRTA—Berkshire RTA   413/499-2782; 800/292-BRTA

BRTA runs 18 routes serving Adams, Cheshire, Dalton, Great Barrington, Hinsdale, Lanesborough, Lee, Lenox, North Adams, Pittsfield, Stockbridge, and Williamstown. BRTA's hub is at Park Sq in Pittsfield—3 blocks E of the Amtrak station and 4 blocks NE of Pittsfield Bus Terminal where Peter Pan, Greyhound, and Bonanza buses stop. All BRTA buses have bike racks.

Brush Hill Tours   781/986-6100

Milford—Boston 1:17 1/1 — — — —
Milford to Copley Sq, Park Sq, and South Station in Boston via Medway, Millis, Medfield, Dover, and Westwood.

C&J Trailways   603/430-1100; www.cjtrailways.com

Boston—Durham, NH 2:00 18 trips each way, Sat and Sun: 16
South Station and/or Logan Airport to Portsmouth, NH via Newburyport, MA; 3 inbound and 7 outbound trips also serve Durham, NH. Some AM trips also stop at Haymarket. Bikes permitted on space-available basis.

CATA—Cape Ann Transit Authority   978/283-7278; www.canntran.com

CATA operates eight color-coded routes in Gloucester and Rockport radiating out from Downtown Gloucester, just 1/2 mile from Gloucester Commuter Rail station. Most routes run every 1-2 hours from 6:30am-5:30pm Mon-Fri and 9:30am-5:30pm on Sat with extra weekday rush service coordinated with Commuter Rail schedules. The Green and Yellow are downtown loops with Green running more frequently and providing a connection between downtown and the Commuter Rail station. Red, Blue, and Red/Blue go to Rockport and stop within 1/2 mile of Rockport Commuter Rail station (Blue actually stops at the station). Orange goes to Magnolia via Hammond Castle. Purple goes to West Gloucester via West Gloucester Commuter Rail station. A Saturday-only shuttle serves Liberty Tree Mall in Danvers and North Shore Mall in Peabody. By request, the Red line will stop at Rocky Neck where A.C. Cruise Line ferries from Boston dock (see "More Ferries" at the end of this chapter).

Cavalier Coach   617/330-1234

Northborough—Boston 1:00 1/1 — — — —
Government Center, South Station, and Park Sq in Boston to Northborough via Rte 20 through Weston, Wayland, Sudbury, and Marlborough.

CCRTA—Cape Cod RTA   508/775-8504; www.capecodtransit.org

CCRTA's service, called "The Breeze," consists of several bus routes—SeaLine, Villager, Bearses Way, Hyannis to Orleans (H2O), and North Truro/Provincetown Shuttle—plus trolley routes in Falmouth and Yarmouth. Altogether, towns served include Barnstable, Bourne, Chatham, Dennis, Falmouth, Harwich, Hyannis, Mashpee, Orleans, Provincetown, Sandwich, Truro, and Yarmouth. Buses make connections with Plymouth & Brockton in Hyannis, Orleans, Truro, and Provincetown; with Bonanza in Falmouth and Hyannis; and with ferry service in Woods Hole (Falmouth), Hyannis, and Provincetown. The Breeze runs Mon-Sat until 7pm with varying frequencies, and in season the North Truro/Provincetown Shuttle also runs Sunday. Fares range from $1 to $3.50. All buses are wheelchair accessible and all have bike racks. The

Route Details

two Islands, Martha's Vineyard and Nantucket, each have their own regional transit authority. Martha's Vineyard RTA can be reached at 508/627-9663 or www.vineyardtransit.com and Nantucket RTA is at 508/228-7025.

The Coach Company   800/874-3377; www.coachco.com

Boston—Newburyport or Plaistow, NH	1:35	7/7	—	—	—	—

Haymarket, Government Ctr (inbound), Park Street, Park Sq, and Copley Sq (inbound) to Newburyport with limited service to Logan Airport, Byfield (Newbury), Peabody, Amesbury, and Plaistow, NH.

Boston or Logan—Haverhill	2:00	2/2	—	—	—	—

Boston stops as above to Haverhill via Lynnfield, Topsfield, Boxford, Groveland, and Georgetown. Inbound trips serve Logan Airport.

Coach New England   800/310-9900; www.coachne.com

Boston—New York, NY	4:30	7 trips Mon-Fri, more on weekends

South Station express to Penn Station.

B.U. and Northeastern—New York, NY	4:50	2 Thur, 3 Fri, 1 Sat; 3 Sun

Northeastern Univ. (Ruggles MBTA station) and Boston Univ. (700 Commonwealth Ave) express to Penn Station when school is in session. Saturday trip is outbound, Sunday trips are inbound.

Concord Free Bus   978/318-3035

Runs Mon, Wed, and Fri mornings making stops at post offices, supermarkets, etc.

Concord Trailways   603/228-3300; www.concordtrailways.com

Bikes permitted in boxes when space available.

Boston—Concord or Manchester, NH	1:50	18 trips each way, 13 on weekends

Logan Airport and South Station express to Concord, NH and/or Manchester, NH.

Boston—Londonderry, NH	1:10	7/7	1	—	—	—

South Station express to Londonderry, NH.

Boston—Laconia or Tilton Jct, NH	3:00	2 trips each way daily

Logan Airport and South Station to Tilton Jct and Laconia, NH (1 trip each way) via Manchester and Concord, NH.

Boston—Conway or Berlin, NH	4:50	2 trips each way daily

Logan Airport and South Station to Conway or Berlin (1 trip each way) via Manchester, Concord, Meredith, and other points in NH. Berlin trips also serve Jackson, Pinkham Notch, and Gorham.

Boston—Littleton, NH	4:25	1 trip each way daily

Logan Airport and South Station to Littleton, NH via Manchester, Concord, Tilton Jct, Plymouth, Lincoln, and Franconia. One extra trip on Friday, Saturday, and Sunday serves Plymouth, NH during the school year.

Boston—Portland or Bangor, ME	2:15	12 trips daily hourly or bi-hourly

Logan Airport and South Station to Portland, ME. Some trips serve Bangor (5 hrs) and, during the school year, Univ. of Maine at Orono and Bowdoin College.

Maine Coastal Route	7:00	2 trips except Fri and Sun: 3/2

Logan Airport and South Station to Bangor, ME via Portland, Brunswick, Bath, Camden/Rockport, Belfast, and other coastal points with additional service to Univ. of Maine at Orono and Bowdoin College when school is in session. This schedule coordinates with Maine State Ferry service in Rockland to Vinalhaven and North Haven.

Chapter 12 • *More Rail, Bus, and Ferry (Not the T)*

	Trip Time	— Weekday Trips —			Sat Trips	Sun Trips
		Rush	Day	Night		

Dartmouth Coach
603/448-2800; www.concordtrailways.com
Boxed bikes permitted for small fee when space available.

Boston—Hanover, NH   2:50   7 bi-hourly trips each way; 6 on Sun
Logan Airport and South Station to Hanover, NH via New London and Lebanon.

Dedham Local Bus—see JBL Bus Lines

EZ Ride
617/8-EZ-INFO (839-4636); www.ezride.info

North Station—Cambridgeport   :30   weekday rush only, every 12 min
Serves North Station, Science Park, and Lechmere on the Green Line and Kendall/MIT on the Red Line plus University Park and points near Central Sq. The shuttle is run by Charles River TMA. Fare is $1.

FRTA—Franklin RTA
413/774-2262; http://users.rcn.com/frta
FRTA runs four routes Mon-Fri from Court Sq in Greenfield to surrounding towns including Athol, Bernardston, Charlemont, Deerfield, Erving, Gill, Hatfield, Northampton, Northfield, Orange, Shelburne Falls, and Whately. Fares range from $1 to $1.50 and there is no weekend or holiday service. The north and west routes serve Greenfield Community College and other schools and run only during the school year. The "Valley Route" runs four times per day to Northampton where connections can be made to Peter Pan and PVTA routes. Together FRTA and MART offer "Link" buses which meet Fitchburg Commuter Rail trains seven times daily and serve Athol, Gardner, Greenfield, Orange, Phillipston, Templeton, and Winchendon. Also see GMTA for connecting service.

Fung Wah Transport Vans, Inc.
617/338-0007; www.fungwahbus.com
Boston—New York, NY   4:30   15 trips each way mostly hourly
68 Beach St in Chinatown, Boston express to 139 Canal St in Chinatown, New York City.

GATRA—Greater Attleboro-Taunton RTA
508/823-8828; 508/222-6106; www.gatra.org
GATRA serves Attleboro, Berkley, Carver, Dighton, Kingston, Lakeville, Mansfield, Middleborough, North Attleborough, Norton, Plainville, Plymouth, Raynham, Rehoboth, Seekonk, Taunton, and Wareham. They offer six fixed routes each within Attleboro and Taunton as well as the three inter-town routes detailed below. Most routes run hourly approximately 12 times Mon-Fri and 8 times on Saturday. There is no Sunday or evening service. Fares range from 75¢ to $2.25. Taunton buses begin at the Bloom Bus Terminal in Taunton and Attleboro routes start at the Attleboro Bus Shelter just steps away from the Attleboro Commuter Rail station.

Route 18 Taunton—Attleboro   :32   3/3   3   —   3   —
Bloom Bus Terminal to Attleboro Bus Shelter via Norton Ctr. The schedule is fairly well coordinated with the Commuter Rail trains.

Route 19 Taunton—Providence, RI   :35   3/3   2   —   4   —
Bloom Bus Terminal to Kennedy Plaza in Providence via Seekonk Ctr. Kennedy Plaza is RIPTA's main terminal and is less than 1/2 mile from Union Station where connections can be made with Commuter Rail and Amtrak.

Route 140 Norton—Mansfield   :30   4/5   —   —   —   —
Norton Ctr to Mansfield Commuter Rail station. Bus schedule coordinates with Commuter Rail schedule for peak hour trains.

GMTA—Greenfield Montague TA
413/773-9478; www.gmta-transit.org
GMTA operates several routes serving points in Greenfield including Greenfield Community College and nearby Turners Falls. One trip each way Mon-Fri serves UMass at Amherst and another goes to Montague Ctr via Millers Falls four times Mon-Fri and twice on Sat. All GMTA routes begin at Court Sq in Greenfield where connections can be made with FRTA routes. There is no Sunday service and limited Saturday service. Fares range from $2-$2.50.

157

Route Details

	Trip Time	Rush	Weekday Trips — Day	Night	Sat Trips	Sun Trips

Greyhound—see Peter Pan and Greyhound

Gulbankian Bus Lines   508/460-0225

Hudson or Marlborough—Boston   1:20   2/2   —   —   —   —
Hudson to Boston including Copley Sq, Park Sq, State House, Park Street station, Downtown Crossing station (outbound only), South Station, and Financial District via Marlborough, Southborough, and Framingham.

Marlborough—Framingham   :40   4 trips each way on Sat only
Solomon Pond Mall in Marlborough to Framingham Commuter Rail station via Southborough.

Interstate Coach   508/583-2225; 781/344-2231

Middleboro/Bridgewater—Boston   1:00   5/5   —   —   —   —
Bridgewater to Park Sq and South Station with one stop in W. Bridgewater. One trip each way serves the town centers of Middleborough, Bridgewater and W. Bridgewater.

Canton—Boston   :40   3/4   —   —   —   —
All trips are reverse commute—mornings outbound, evenings inbound. Serves South Station, Park Sq (evenings only), JFK/UMass station, Quincy Adams station, and Canton Commerce Ctr.

JBL Bus Lines   781/843-4505

Canton—Mattapan (T-bus 716)   :30   3/3   3   —   9   —
Canton Ctr to Mattapan via Washington St, Rte 138, and Blue Hill Ave. This route is subsidized by the MBTA.

Hull—Hingham (T-bus 714)   :25   3/3   5   —   8   8
Pemberton Pt, Hull to Hingham Ctr. Coordinated with T-buses 220 and 221 for continuing service to Hingham Shipyard and Quincy Ctr. This route is subsidized by the MBTA. Limited ferry service to Quincy and Boston departs from Pemberton Pt (see Chapter 11, "MBTA Ferries & Commuter Boats").

South Weymouth—Braintree   :40   3/4   —   —   —   —
Weymouth to Braintree station (Red Line and Commuter Rail).

Whitman—Boston   1:30   2/2   —   —   —   —
Whitman to South Station, Government Ctr, and Financial District via Abington, Weymouth, and Braintree.

Dedham Local Bus   1:10   11 loops hourly Mon-Fri
Serves various points in Dedham and the V.A. Hospital in West Roxbury.

Lexpress   781/861-1210

Routes 1-6   :30   11-12 hourly trips Mon-Fri, 8 on Sat*
Loops begin in Lexington Ctr and connect with T-buses 62 and 76. Route 5 connects with T-bus 350, "the B Line" routes 1, 5, and 6, and LRTA Bl route at Burlington Mall. Route 2 connects with Waltham CitiBuses 14 and 23 at Waltham/Lexington town line. Lexpress has offered continuous service for 23 years—possibly the longest running suburban transit service in Greater Boston.
*No Saturday service in July or August.

LIFT (Local Intra-Framingham Transit)   508/620-4823

LIFT 2 and 3 Downtown Loop   1:00   12 hourly trips Mon-Fri, 8 on Sat
Begins in Framingham Ctr near the Commuter Rail station and serves Nobscot, Saxonville, and area malls. LIFT 2 runs clockwise; LIFT 3 runs counter-clockwise.

LIFT 4 Milford—Southborough   1:00   5/5   —   —   —   —
Milford park-and-ride to Southborough Commuter Rail station via Hopkinton.

	Trip Time	Rush	Weekday Trips Day	Night	Sat Trips	Sun Trips
LIFT 5 Hopkinton—Framingham	1:00	3/4	3	—	—	—

Hopkinton to Framingham via Ashland serving Ashland and Framingham Commuter Rail stations, schools, and shops.

LIFT 6 Milford—Framingham	1-2:00	3/3	3	—	—	—

Milford to Downtown Framingham via Hopkinton, Holliston, and Ashland serving Framingham Commuter Rail station and shopping centers.

LIFT 7 Marlborough—Framingham	2:00	14 hourly trips Mon-Fri				

Marlborough to Framingham via Southborough serving Framingham Commuter Rail station, schools, shops, and more.

Longwood Medical Area Shuttle
617/632-2800; www.masco.org

Seven shuttles are run by MASCO Transportation Management Association primarily for employees of their member institutions. The only route open to the public is listed below. Tickets must be purchased in advance at designated locations. Contact MASCO for details.

M2 Harvard—LMA	:25	18/18	12	3	15	—

Harvard Sq to Longwood Medical Area via Central Sq, MIT, and other points on Massachusetts Ave and in the Fenway/Longwood Area.

LRTA—Lowell RTA
978/452-6161; 978/459-7101; www.lrta.com

LRTA serves Acton, Billerica, Chelmsford, Dracut, Groton, Lowell, Pepperell, Tewksbury, Townsend, and Westford with several fixed routes within Lowell plus fixed routes from Lowell to Billerica, Tewksbury, Chelmsford, Tyngsborough, and Dracut. All buses originate at the Downtown Transit Ctr at Paige, Merrimack, and John Sts, which is 3/4 mile from Gallagher Transportation Terminal where Commuter Rail trains and intercity buses stop. The excellent "Downtown Shuttle" connects the two transit centers plus the Visitor Center and runs every 15 minutes Mon-Fri from 6am-6pm and Saturday from 10am-4pm. Most other service runs similar hours but less frequently. There is no Sunday service.

MART—Montachusett RTA
978/345-7711; 800/922-5636; www.montachusettrta.org

MART offers 13 routes in the cities of Fitchburg, Gardner, and Leominster, plus paratransit service for surrounding towns. Most routes run hourly Mon-Sat daytimes. There is no evening or Sunday service. Points served include Fitchburg and North Leominster Commuter Rail stations, Mt. Wachusett Community College and Fitchburg State College. Fares are 75¢. Together FRTA and MART offer "Link" buses which meet Fitchburg Commuter Rail trains seven times daily and serve Athol, Gardner, Greenfield, Orange, Phillipston, Templeton, and Winchendon.

Mass Bay Limousine
781/895-1100; www.massbaylimousine.com

Rail Link 1 (Westborough)	:30	3/4	—	—	—	—

Meets trains at Southborough Commuter Rail station and serves points in Westborough.

Rail Link 2 (Marlborough)	:30	3/4	—	—	—	—

Meets trains at Southborough Commuter Rail station and serves points in Marlborough.

Mission Hill Link
617/566-5509

Green, Red, and Blue Routes   :30   every 20-30 min Mon-Sat

Loops start at Brigham Cir (Green E Line) and serve Roxbury Crossing (Orange Line), NE Baptist Hospital, and other points in Roxbury. Green runs morning and evening, Red runs midday, and Blue runs afternoon. Mon-Fri routes run 6:30am-8:30pm; Saturday routes run from 9am-2pm.

MVRTA—Merrimack Valley RTA
978/469-MVRTA; www.mvrta.com

MVRTA serves Amesbury, Andover, Haverhill, Lawrence, Merrimac, Methuen, Newburyport, and North Andover. Buses generally run Mon-Fri 5am-6:30pm every 45 min and Sat from 8am-6pm every 40-80 min. Fares are $1 and various money-saving passes are available. All Haverhill buses depart from Washington Transit Station 3 blocks east of the Haverhill Commuter

Route Details

Trip	— Weekday Trips —			Sat	Sun
Time	Rush	Day	Night	Trips	Trips

Rail station. All Lawrence buses depart from Buckley Transportation Ctr which is 1/2 mile from Lawrence Commuter Rail station across the river. There are 25 routes in all—the longer-distance routes are detailed below.

01 Lawrence—Haverhill :45 4/4 7 — 14 —
Buckley Transportation Ctr to Washington Transit Station via Methuen. One trip serves Northern Essex Community College when school is in session. Continues east to Newburyport as bus 51 and west to Lowell as bus 41.

32 Lawrence—Andover :17 every 45 min Mon-Fri, 80 min Sat
Buckley Transportation Ctr to Andover Ctr and Andover Commuter Rail station.

41 Lawrence—Lowell :35 5/5 7 — 7 —
Buckley Transportation Ctr to Downtown Transportation Ctr in Lowell. Connects with LRTA buses.

51 Haverhill—Newburyport 1:20 5/5 6 — 8 —
Washington Transit Station to Newburyport via Northern Essex Community College, Merrimac, and Amesbury. Stops in Newburyport include the Commuter Rail station and the park-and-ride lot where C&J Trailways buses stop.

83 Lawrence—Hampton Beach 1:25 2 trips each way Mon-Fri summer
Buckley Transportation Ctr to Hampton Beach via Washington Sq Transit Ctr in Haverhill, plus Merrimac, Amesbury and Salisbury Beach.

Lawrence—Andover—Boston 1:25 2/2 — — — —
Buckley Transportation Ctr to Boston with three stops each in Lawrence and Andover. Boston stops are Haymarket (inbound), Government Ctr, Park Street (inbound), Essex & Tremont Sts (inbound), Essex & Lincoln Sts, Park Sq, and Copley Sq (inbound).

Natick Neighborhood Bus   508/647-6446 (7-11am)
NE, SW, and Saturday Bus   1:00 runs hourly Mon-Sat*
All loops start at Natick Common near the Natick Commuter Rail station and serve various points in town. Northeast runs 9:45am-5:45pm, Southwest runs 7:15am-5:15pm. Door-to-door service is available for the disabled.
*Saturday runs from 8am-5pm with a midday lunch break.

Newton Nexus   617/796-1288; www.ci.newton.ma.us/nexus/default.htm
Route 1   1:00 1/2 hourly Mon-Fri 12:30-5:30pm
Serves points in Newton including Newton Centre, Newton Highlands, Woodland, and Riverside on the Green D Line, Auburndale and Newtonville Commuter Rail stations. Connects with Waltham CitiBus 16.

Route 2   :30 1/2 hourly Mon-Fri 1:30-4:30pm
Serves points in Newton including Newton Centre and Newton Highlands on the Green D Line.

OWL—Onset Wareham Link   800/433-5995; 508/823-8828; www.gatra.org
Sponsored by GATRA, OWL runs 4 routes in and around Onset and Wareham from West Wareham to the Bourne Bridge. Service runs hourly Mon-Sat days. Fares are 75¢.

PAL—Plymouth Area Link   508/746-0378; www.gatra.org
Freedom and Liberty Links   :50 14 hourly loops; 12 Sat and Sun
Serves points in North Plymouth and Kingston including Plymouth and Kingston Commuter Rail stations (limited) and the Plymouth & Brockton Bus Terminal. Freedom runs counter-clockwise and Liberty runs clockwise.

Mayflower Link   :50 7 bi-hourly trips, 6 Sat and Sun
Runs along the Plymouth coast from the Plymouth & Brockton Bus Terminal to south of Manomet serving Plimoth Plantation, White Horse Beach, and other points.

	Trip Time	Rush	— Weekday Trips — Day	Night	Sat Trips	Sun Trips

Puritan Link :50 6 bi-hourly trips, 5 Sat and Sun

Runs from Kingston to West Plymouth. Stops include Kingston Commuter Rail station, Plymouth & Brockton Bus Terminal, and Plimoth Plantation.

Paul Revere Transportation Co. 617/889-5899

Pt Shirley—Orient Heights (T-bus 712)	:22	10/11	11	7	32	12

Pt Shirley (outbound only, see next listing for inbound) to Orient Heights (Blue Line) via Winthrop Beach and Winthrop Highlands. This route is subsidized by the MBTA.

Pt Shirley—Orient Heights (T-bus 713)	:23	10/11	11	7	30	12

Pt Shirley (inbound only, see above listing for outbound) to Orient Heights (Blue Line) via Winthrop Beach and Winthrop Ctr. This route is subsidized by the MBTA.

Peabody Transit 978/531-2254

Salem Depot—Peabody	:40	4/4	—	—	—	—

Salem Commuter Rail station to Peabody Sq, North Shore Mall, Centennial Industrial Park, and Northway Industrial Park (one trip).

Peter Pan and Greyhound 800/343-9999; www.peterpanbus.com
800/231-2222; www.greyhound.com

Most runs do not make all stops along a given route.

Boston—Albany, NY 4:00 8-10 trips each way daily

South Station to Albany via Newton, Framingham, Worcester, Springfield, Lee, Lenox, and Pittsfield.

Boston—NY, NY (express) 4:30 19 trips daily, 26 trips on Fri and Sun

South Station to Port Authority via Framingham and Newton.

Boston—NY, NY via Hartford, CT 5-7:00 11-15 trips each way daily

South Station to Port Authority via Worcester, Hartford, New Haven and other points in MA, CT, and NY.

Boston—NY, NY via Providence, RI 6-7:00 9 trips daily, extra on Fri and Sun

South Station to Port Authority via Worcester, Providence, Foxwoods Casino, New Haven, White Plains, and other points in MA, CT, and NY.

Boston—Amherst or Greenfield 3-4:00 8 trips daily, extra on weekends

South Station to UMass via Worcester, Palmer, Springfield, Northampton, Hampshire College and others. One daily trip serves Greenfield via Deerfield. Extra runs serve UMass, Hampshire College and other points on Friday afternoons and Sunday evenings during the school year.

Boston—Bradley Int'l Airport, CT 3:30 2 trips each way daily

South Station to Bradley via Newton, Worcester, Palmer, Springfield, Six Flags New England (seasonal), and Suffield, CT. One extra trip from Boston runs on Friday and Sunday.

Boston Area Colleges—NY, NY 4:50 2 trips Thur; 5 Fri; 1 Sat; 3 Sun

Seasonal service from Boston University and Northeastern to Hartford (one trip) or New York. Saturday trips are outbound; Sunday trips are inbound.

Boston—Foxwoods Casino, CT 2:15 1 trip each way daily

South Station to Foxwoods via Newton, Framingham, and Worcester.

Boston—Sturbridge 1:40 2 trips each way daily

South Station to Sturbridge Center and Old Sturbridge Village via Worcester.

	Trip	Weekday Trips			Sat	Sun
	Time	Rush	Day	Night	Trips	Trips

Boston—Worcester and Framingham 1:35   4/4   4   2   14   14
Copley Sq, Park Sq, State House, Post Office Sq, and South Station in Boston, express to Framingham then Worcester. Additional trips run express to Framingham and make local stops in Framingham.

Plymouth & Brockton Street Railway   508/746-0378; www.p-b.com
Bikes allowed for small extra charge when space available.

Boston—Hyannis or Provincetown 1:55   8/12   13   3   21   21
Logan Airport, Park Sq, and/or South Station to Hyannis via Rockland, Plymouth, Sagamore, and Barnstable. Six trips daily also serve Provincetown via Truro, Wellfleet, Eastham, Orleans, and Harwich.

Boston—Rockland and South Shore 1:20   11/13   10   2   —   —
Logan Airport, Park Sq, and/or South Station to Rockland. Seven of the trips continue from Rockland to Plymouth via Kingston, two continue to Duxbury via Marshfield, and one continues to Scituate via Hingham and Cohasset.

Marshfield—Braintree :30   2/2   —   —   —   —
Bus loops twice: Plymouth, Marshfield, Hanover, Braintree MBTA station, Marshfield, Braintree MBTA station, Rockland, Plymouth (pm trips are vice versa).

PVTA—Pioneer Valley TA   413/781-7882; www.pvta.com
PVTA serves 23 communities along the Connecticut River: Agawam, Amherst, Belchertown, Chicopee, Deerfield, East Longmeadow, Easthampton, Granby, Hadley, Hampden, Holyoke, Leverett, Longmeadow, Ludlow, Palmer, Pelham, Northampton, South Hadley, Springfield, Sunderland, Ware, West Springfield, Westfield, Wilbraham, and Williamsburg. Northern routes are mostly free and focus on the Amherst-Northampton area catering to the students of UMass at Amherst, Amherst College, Mt. Holyoke College, Smith College, and Hampshire College. Southern routes are 75¢ plus 25¢ per zone and are centered around the Greater Springfield area. Bike racks are available on many of the northern routes from April through November.

RIPTA—Rhode Island Public Transit Authority
401/781-9400; www.ripta.com
RIPTA operates all public transit in Rhode Island including many bus routes, seasonal ferry service to Newport, and two downtown Providence trolleys. Direct service is available from Providence to Newport, Pawtucket, East Providence, and Kingston (URI), in addition to the many routes within Providence and other towns. Altogether most towns and points of interest in the state are reached and many enjoy daily service. All RIPTA buses and trolleys plus Greyhound, GATRA, and some Bonanza routes stop at Kennedy Plaza which is 4 blocks south of the Amtrak and Commuter Rail station in downtown Providence. The main Bonanza terminal is located about two miles north of downtown, but they offer hourly shuttle service to Kennedy Plaza. RIPTA offers ferry service to Newport from the Point Street Dock just over a mile south of Kennedy Plaza (take RIPTA bus 1 or 3 or the Golden Trolley); see Boston Harbor Cruises below for ferry details. T.F. Green Airport is located several miles away in Warwick (take RIPTA bus 66).

SRTA—Southeastern RTA   508/997-6767; www.srtabus.com
SRTA runs buses primarily in Fall River and New Bedford with service to Acushnet, Dartmouth, Fairhaven, Freetown, Mattapoisett, Somerset, Swansea, and Westport. Most routes operate Mon-Fri 5am-6pm every 20-60 min and Sat from 7am-6pm every 40-60 min. Many routes also operate on Sunday, though Sunday service in New Bedford was discontinued in January 2003. SRTA bus terminals, also frequented by intercity buses, are located in downtown New Bedford and downtown Fall River. Fares are $1 per zone travelled. Of special note, bus 9 runs from New Bedford to Fall River hourly Mon-Fri 6am-7pm and weekends 8am-7pm via Dartmouth, UMass at Dartmouth, and Westport.

	Trip Time	— Weekday Trips —			Sat Trips	Sun Trips
		Rush	Day	Night		

Travel Pack
617/338-8222; www.travelpackusa.com

Boston—New York, NY 4:30 13 trips Mon-Fri, 14 on Sat and Sun

Harrison Ave & Beach St in Chinatown, Boston express to Forsyth St near Division St in New York, NY.

Trombly Commuter Lines
978/937-3626; www.tromblybuslines.com

Methuen—Boston :40 1/1 — — — —

Pelham St park-and-ride express to Haymarket (inbound only), Government Ctr, Park Street station (inbound only), Park Sq, Copley Sq (inbound only), and Essex & Tremont Sts in the Financial District.

Vermont Transit
800/642-3133, 800/451-3292; www.vermonttransit.com

In addition to the Boston routes below, Vermont Transit serves Springfield, MA; Hartford, CT; Albany and New York, NY; and others. Most towns in Vermont are served via transfers in Rutland and White River Junction.

Boston—Bangor or Bar Harbor, ME 6:00 7 trips daily

South Station to Bangor, ME via Newburyport, MA; Portsmouth, NH; and Portland, Brunswick, Lewiston, Augusta, and Waterville, ME. One trip continues to Bar Harbor via Ellsworth and three trips continue from Boston to New York, NY. Except for South Station, no stop is served by all trips.

Boston—White River Jct or Montréal 7:00 11 inbound, 12 outbound trips daily

Logan Airport and South Station to White River Jct, VT via Lowell, MA and Nashua, Manchester, Concord, New London, and Hanover, NH. Five trips continue to Montréal via Montpelier, Burlington, and St. Albans, VT. Other than South Station, no stop is served by all trips. One express trip leaves Boston at 9am and arrives in Montréal at 3:15pm. Two trips offer connecting service to Rutland, VT and two others connect to Newport, VT.

Boston—Rutland, VT 5:00 2 trips each way daily

South Station to Rutland, VT via [Lowell, MA; Nashua and Peterborough, NH] or [Newton, Fitchburg, Gardner, and Winchendon, MA; Fitzwilliam, NH]; Keene, NH; Brattleboro and Springfield, VT.

Waltham CitiBus
781/890-0093; www.128bc.com

Routes 11, 12, 14, 16, 17, 23 :20 hourly approx. 7am-8pm Mon-Fri*

This service is run by 128 Business Council TMA. Routes radiate from Waltham Center and serve Riverside on the Green D Line; Waltham, Brandeis/Roberts, and Waverley Commuter Rail stations; T-buses 70, 70A, 73, 500, 505, 553, 554, 556, and 558; Lexpress 2; Newton Nexus 1; and many points in Waltham. *Route 23 operates Saturday only, every 45 min from 8am-4:35pm. Other 128 Business Council shuttles operate from Alewife station (Red Line) and Newton Highlands station (Commuter Rail) to businesses along Rte 128. These primarily serve employees of the member institutions but are open to the public for a small fee.

WRTA—Worcester RTA
508/791-WRTA (9782); www.therta.com

WRTA operates buses primarily in Worcester with service to Auburn, Boylston, Brookfield, Clinton, East Brookfield, Holden, Leicester, Millbury, Oxford, Shrewsbury, Spencer, Webster, and West Boylston. Most buses operate Mon-Fri from 5am-10pm every 30-60 min and on Saturday from 6am-9pm every 60 min. Some routes also operate on Sun from 11am-6pm. All buses depart from Worcester City Hall which is 4 blocks north of the intercity bus terminal and about 1/3 mile west of Union Station where Amtrak and Commuter Rail trains stop. Several WRTA routes offer service to these points. Worcester Airport is several miles away and is served by bus 2. Fares are $1-1.75.

Yankee Bus Lines
617/268-8890

Acton and Concord—Boston :45 1/1 — — — —

Acton and Concord to Copley Sq in Boston plus inbound drop-off at South Station by request.

🚢 More Ferries

	Trip Time	Rush	Weekday Trips Day	Night	Sat Trips	Sun Trips

A.C. Cruise Line   617/261-6633; www.accruiseline.com

| Boston—Gloucester | 2:30 | — | — | — | 1 | 1 |

Note this service was discontinued in 2002, but the carrier is considering offering it again in 2003. Seasonal service from Wharf 8 near the Fleet Pavilion in South Boston to Town Wharf in Gloucester with a stop at Pickering Wharf in downtown Salem.

Airport Water Shuttle   617/951-0255; www.massport.com

Boston—Logan Airport   :07   every 20 min, weekends: 30 min

Year-round service from Rowes Wharf to Logan Airport via Fan Pier in South Boston. Airport shuttle bus #66 stops at the dock every 15 min. and serves all Logan terminals. Weekday service runs from 6am-8pm; weekend service from 10am-8pm. The adult one-way fare is $10.

Bay State Cruise Co.   617/748-1428; www.baystatecruisecompany.com

Boston—Provincetown   1:30   3 trips daily

Seasonal high-speed service from Commonwealth Pier in South Boston to downtown Provincetown. One more trip runs on Friday, Saturday, and Sunday in high summer on the slower boat which takes 3 hrs. A round-trip costs $60 on the high-speed boat and $29 on the slower boat. Bikes cost $5 on either.

Boston Harbor Cruises

617/227-4321; 877/SEE-WHALE; www.bostonharborcruises.com

In addition to the routes below Boston Harbor Cruises operates the MBTA's Inner Harbor Ferry and Commuter Boat service detailed in Chapter 11, "MBTA Ferries & Commuter Boats."

Boston—Boston Harbor Islands   :40   3-9 trips daily depending on season

Seasonal service from Long Wharf to George's Island. Free water taxis take you from there to other islands. One trip each day in high summer stops at Deer Island.

Hingham—Boston Harbor Islands   1:00   3 trips daily or weekends only

Seasonal service from Hewitt's Cove Commuter Boat Landing in Hingham to George's Island. Free water taxis take you from there to other islands. Boats run daily in high summer and on weekends only in late spring and early fall.

Boston—Provincetown   1:30   1-3 trips daily in season

Seasonal high-speed service from Long Wharf to Provincetown. Round trip fare is $49.

Providence, RI—Newport, RI   1:25   4-5 trips daily in season

Seasonal service from Point Street Dock in Providence to Perrotti Park in Newport. Point Street Dock is just over a mile south of Kennedy Plaza, RIPTA's main bus terminal. Take RIPTA bus 1 or 3 or the Golden Trolley. In Newport the ferry lands just down the street from RIPTA buses at Gateway Visitors Center. This service is subsidized by RIPTA.

Capt. John Boats   508/747-2400; 800/242-2469; www.captjohn.com

Plymouth—Provincetown   1:30   1 trip each way in season

Seasonal service from Town Wharf across from the Visitor Center in Plymouth to downtown Provincetown. Round trip fare is $28 and bikes are $3.

City Water Taxi   617/422-0392; www.citywatertaxi.com

Boston Harbor   On-demand service, call for pick-up

On-demand taxi serving Burroughs Wharf (North End), Charlestown Navy Yard Pier 4, Fan Pier, FleetBoston Pavilion, Logan Airport, Long Wharf, Lovejoy Wharf, Museum Wharf/Congress St, Sargents Wharf (North End), South Boston Pier 4, and World Trade Center. Service is seasonal but operates from early spring well into fall.

| Trip Time | ——— Weekday Trips ——— | | | Sat Trips | Sun Trips |
	Rush	Day	Night		

Cuttyhunk Boat Lines

508/992-1432; www.cuttyhunk.com

New Bedford—Cuttyhunk Island   1-2 trips daily, less off-season

Year-round service from Pier 3 in New Bedford to Cuttyhunk Island. Cuttyhunk is about two miles long by one mile wide with a good harbor and beautiful beaches. Only about a third of the island is settled with its 26 year-round residents.

Falmouth Ferry

508/548-9400; www.falmouthferry.com

Falmouth—Edgartown   :45   5-6 daily trips, less in off-season

Seasonal service from Falmouth Marine on Scranton Ave to Memorial Wharf in Edgartown. Spring/fall schedule offers 3 trips Friday, Saturday, and Sunday.

Freedom Cruise Line

508/432-8999; www.nantucketislandferry.com

Harwich Port—Nantucket   :90   1-3 trips daily depending on season

Seasonal service from Saquatucket Harbor in Harwich to Nantucket Island.

Hy-Line Cruises

508/778-2600; 800/492-8082; www.hy-linecruises.com

Hyannis—Oak Bluffs   1:35   1-4 trips daily depending on season

Seasonal service from Hy-Line Dock off Ocean Ave in Hyannis to Oak Bluffs on Martha's Vineyard.

Hyannis—Nantucket   1:50*   5-6 trips daily, more in season

Hy-Line Dock off Ocean Ave to Nantucket Island. A first class lounge is available on some trips. *The high-speed ferry ($60 round trip) makes the trip in one hour and operates year-round. The regular ferry ($30 round trip) is seasonal.

Nantucket—Oak Bluffs   2:15   3 trips daily in season

Seasonal inter-island service.

Island Queen

508/548-4800; www.islandqueen.com

Falmouth—Oak Bluffs   :30   2-9 trips depending on day, season

Seasonal service from Falmouth Harbor off Falmouth Heights Rd to Oak Bluffs.

Steamship Authority

508/477-8600; www.islandferry.com

Falmouth—Martha's Vineyard   :45   17-26 trips daily

Frequent year-round service from Woods Hole to either Oak Bluffs (summer only) or Vineyard Haven (year-round). All boats take passenger cars by reservation. Steamship Authority also offers seasonal weekend "Relax & Ride" service from MBTA's 128 Commuter Rail station which is a one-ticket bus ride to the dock plus ferry ride to the island.

Hyannis—Nantucket   2:15*   8-12 trips depending on day, season

Year-round service from Steamship Authority Pier at the end of Pleasant St in Hyannis to Nantucket. These ferries take cars by reservation. *Some trips are via the high-speed ferry which makes the journey in 55 minutes.

New Bedford—Vineyard Haven   1:30   2-4 trips depending on day, season

Seasonal service from New Bedford to Oak Bluffs. This Steamship Authority service does not take cars.

USING TRANSIT

DESTINATIONS

ROUTE DETAILS

INDEX

Chapter 13:
New England and Beyond

Cape Cod

Cape Cod is easily reached from Boston by bus, and in season by ferry, too. Plymouth & Brockton buses offer over 20 daily trips, all stopping at Sagamore, Barnstable, and Hyannis; six continue to Harwich, Orleans, Eastham, Wellfleet, and Truro en route to Provincetown. Bonanza runs 8-11 daily trips to Buzzard's Bay, Bourne, Otis Air Base, and Woods Hole (Falmouth).

A ferry ride to Provincetown takes just 90 minutes aboard a high-speed boat. Boston Harbor Cruises and Bay State Cruises both make the trip from Boston, and Capt. John Boats runs trips from Plymouth. Ferries to Martha's Vineyard and Nantucket are available from Woods Hole (Falmouth) and Hyannis on the Cape as well as from New Bedford. The Steamship Authority even offers "Relax & Ride," a one-ticket trip by bus then ferry from the Route 128 Commuter Rail station in Westwood to Martha's Vineyard.

Many people use a bicycle for local transportation due to the mild summer weather, mostly flat terrain, and many bicycle paths; and most local buses, operated by Cape Cod Regional Transit Authority (CCRTA), are equipped with bicycle racks. For visitor information contact the Cape Cod Chamber of Commerce at 888/33-CAPECOD, 508/862-0700, or www.capecodchamber.org. Ask for a copy of their annual publication, "Smart Guide: Car-Free Ways to and around Cape Cod, Martha's Vineyard, and Nantucket," or visit www.smartguide.org.

Western Massachusetts

Amtrak runs six trains daily from Springfield to New York, NY and Washington, DC, one of which originates in Boston. The Lakeshore Limited, running once daily from Boston to Chicago, stops in Springfield and Pittsfield, and the Vermonter, running once daily from Washington, DC to Montréal, Canada, stops in Springfield and Amherst (not Boston).

Peter Pan runs 8-10 buses daily from Boston to Albany, NY via Springfield, Lee, Lenox, and Pittsfield as well as a number of other routes that stop in Agawam (Six Flags, seasonal), Chicopee, Deerfield, Greenfield, Holyoke, Palmer, and/or South Hadley.

Regional Transit Authorities serve many of the towns in Western Massachusetts. The two biggest operate in the two main regions—Pioneer Valley Transit Authority (PVTA) and Berkshire Regional Transit Authority (BRTA). Greenfield-Montague Transit Authority (GMTA) and Franklin Regional Transit Authority (FRTA) offer more limited service. Of special note, FRTA has teamed up with Montachusett Regional Transit Authority (MART) in Central Massachusetts to provide "The Link" which meets Fitchburg

Commuter Rail trains seven times per day and serves Athol, Gardner, Greenfield, Orange, Phillipston, Templeton, and Winchendon.

For visitor information contact Greater Springfield Convention and Visitors Bureau at 800/723-1548, 413/787-1548, or www.valleyvisitor.com; or the Berkshires Visitors Bureau at 800/237-5747, 413/443-9186, or www.berkshires.org.

Connecticut

Amtrak runs 24 daily Northeast Corridor trains from Boston or Springfield to New York, NY and Washington, DC—18 take a coastal route, and six take an inland route. Coastal route trips begin in Boston and serve Providence, RI; Mystic, New London, Old Saybrook, New Haven, Bridgeport, and Stamford, CT; then continue to New York, NY and Washington, DC. Inland trips begin in Springfield, MA (except one which starts in Boston) and serve Windsor, Windsor Locks, Hartford, Berlin, Meriden, and Wallingford before joining with the coastal route from New Haven, CT to Washington, DC.

New Haven, Bridgeport, and Stamford are transfer points from Amtrak to Metro-North Commuter Railroad (800/638-7646; 212/532-4900; www.mta.nyc.ny.us/mta) which has a route along the shoreline plus inland routes to New Canaan, Danbury, and Waterbury. Shore Line East commuter trains (800/ALL-RIDE; 203/777-7433; www.shorelineeast.com) serve New London, Old Saybrook, Westbrook, Clinton, Madison, Guilford, Branford and New Haven. The Bridgeport and New London stations are adjacent to ferry docks offering service to Block Island and Long Island.

Peter Pan and Greyhound bus lines make 11-15 daily inland trips from Boston to New York City via Hartford, Farmington, New Britain, and Meriden; and nine daily coastal trips via Foxwoods and New London. As with Amtrak, both routes serve New Haven, Bridgeport, and Stamford. Bonanza runs four daily bus trips from Boston serving Hartford and other points in Connecticut via transfers in Providence, RI.

For information about local bus service within Connecticut, call CTTransit at 860/522-8101 or visit www.cttransit.com. For visitor information contact the Connecticut Office of Tourism at 860/270-8080 or visit www.ctbound.com.

Maine

Amtrak service aboard the Downeaster runs from Boston to Portland four times daily and stops in Wells, Saco-Biddeford, and Old Orchard Beach (seasonal). Concord Trailways has 12 daily bus trips to Portland, some of which continue to Bangor, plus two Maine Coastal Route trips. Vermont Transit makes seven daily trips to Augusta and Waterville, one of which continues to Bar Harbor. Stops served by these bus companies include Brunswick, Lewiston, Ellsworth, Camden/Rockport, Belfast, and other towns, plus the University of Maine at Orono and Bowdoin College during the school year.

Additionally, Mermaid Transit connects Boston's Logan Airport to Portland with limited service to some colleges.

For information about local transit within Maine, call the Department of Transportation at 207/624-3000 or visit www.state.me.us/mdot. For visitor information call the Maine Office of Travel & Tourism at 888/624-6345 or visit www.visitmaine.com.

New Hampshire

Concord Trailways runs 18 daily buses to Concord and/or Manchester along with more limited service to Berlin, Conway, Franconia, Gorham, Jackson, Laconia, Lincoln, Meredith, Pinkham Notch, Plymouth, and Tilton Junction. Vermont Transit runs 11 daily trips to Nashua, Manchester, Concord, and Hanover en route to Vermont and Montréal with an alternate route making stops at Keene, Peterborough, and Fitzwilliam. C & J Trailways runs to Durham via Portsmouth 18 times Mon.-Fri. and 16 times on weekends, and additional direct service to the University of New Hampshire in Durham when school is in session.

Less frequent than the above service, the Coach Company offers limited commuter service from Plaistow, and the Downeaster Amtrak train makes stops in Exeter, Durham (during school year), and Dover on its way to Portland, ME.

Concord Area Transit (603/225-0989), Manchester Transit Authority (603/623-8801; www.mtabus.org), and a few other RTAs offer local service within the state. For visitor information go to www.visitnh.gov or call 800/FUN-IN-NH (800/386-4664).

Rhode Island

Bonanza offers frequent bus service from Boston including 17 trips to Providence and T.F. Green Airport from South Station, 12 trips from Logan Airport, and seven trips to New York, NY via Providence. Bonanza also runs eight daily trips (six on weekends) to Newport via Portsmouth and Middletown.

The MBTA Commuter Rail Attleboro Line makes 11 trips to Providence Mon.-Fri. scheduled to favor Boston-bound commuters. Amtrak runs 18 trains and Greyhound runs 9 buses to New York, NY along a coastal route via Providence, and GATRA offers a bus route from Attleboro, MA to Providence.

All public transit within Rhode Island is operated by Rhode Island Public Transit Authority (RIPTA). The main terminal is Kennedy Plaza in downtown Providence where RIPTA, GATRA, Peter Pan, and some Bonanza buses stop. The train station is about 1/2 mile north of Kennedy Plaza, and Bonanza's main terminal is about two miles north. Some Bonanza routes stop at both terminals, but for those that do not, there is hourly shuttle service between them.

Call 800/556-2484 or go to www.visitrhodeisland.com for Rhode Island tourist information.

Vermont

Most intercity buses in Vermont are operated by Vermont Transit, a private company. They offer 12 daily trips from Boston to either White River Junction or Rutland, and virtually all points in the state can be reached via a connection at one of those hubs.

The Amtrak Vermonter train stops in the Western Massachusetts towns of Springfield and Amherst (it does not serve Boston) en route to Brattleboro, Bellows Falls, Windsor-Mt. Ascutney, White River Jct., Randolph, Montpelier-Barre, Waterbury-Stowe, Burlington-Essex Jct., and St. Albans in Vermont. Service then continues to Montréal via a Vermont Transit bus connection.

For visitor information call 800/VERMONT or see www.travel-vermont.com.

New York City

Many transit companies operate along the well-worn path from Boston to New York City. Amtrak offers 19 trips daily, many aboard the Acela Express which makes the trip in just 3 hours, 45 minutes. The Peter Pan and Greyhound schedule lists over 25 trips on weekdays and even more on weekends, and Coach New England and Bonanza each offer seven daily trips. Chinatown to Chinatown buses (Fung Wah Transport Vans and Travel Pack) offer express service for as little as $10 one-way (off-peak hours) or $20 round-trip. All bus service takes as little as 4 hours, 30 minutes running express and as much as 7 hours for longer routes with local stops.

For information on public transit in New York City contact the Metropolitan Transportation Authority (MTA) at 718/330-1234 or www.mta.nyc.ny.us. For visitor information contact the New York Convention and Visitors Bureau at 212/397-8222, 800/NYC-VISIT, or www.nycvisit.com.

Montréal, Canada

The best current transit option between Boston and Montréal is by bus. Vermont Transit has five daily trips, one of which runs express leaving Boston at 9am and arriving in Montréal by 3:15pm—a trip of only 6 hours, 15 minutes. Peter Pan teams up with other carriers to offer four outbound and two inbound trips daily, but with transfers and local stops these rides often take 10 hours or longer.

There is no easy rail connection between Boston and Montréal, but high-speed rail service is being considered (visit www.bostonmontrealhsr.org or email info@bostonmontrealhsr.org). In the meantime, the Vermonter Amtrak train, running through Springfield and Amherst, MA (but not Boston), reaches Montréal, but even that requires a bus connection in St. Albans, VT.

To learn about Montréal's excellent local transit system, call STM at 514/280-5100 or visit www.stm.info; for visitor information call 514/873-2015 or 877/BONJOUR (877/266-5687) or visit www.tourisme-montreal.org.

Chapter 14:
Regional Airports

Boston's Logan Airport is one of the nation's busiest airports, serving over 20 million passengers per year. The three other most widely-used airports within 60 miles of Boston are also listed below (note: commercial flights to Worcester Airport were discontinued in February 2003). All are listed with summaries of ground transportation options. Note that all fares given in this chapter are one-way unless marked "round-trip."

Logan International Airport

East Boston; 800/23-LOGAN; www.massport.com

Located less than a mile across the Inner Harbor from downtown, Logan is served by major national airlines, a variety of regional and commuter carriers, and a dozen international airlines. The airport's five terminals, A through E, are arranged counter-clockwise around a central parking garage (Terminal A is under construction). Call 800/23-LOGAN for up-to-the-minute information on an airline's terminal location or public transportation options.

The Massport shuttle buses listed below under "Rapid Transit" connect the terminals to the Airport subway station on the Blue Line. In addition, shuttle 11 circles around all terminals (7am-10pm), shuttle 77 links employee parking with all terminals (employees only, 24 hours), and shuttle 88 links all terminals with economy satellite parking (24 hours). While shuttle buses and the Water Shuttle Dock are wheelchair accessible, Airport subway station is not, so handicap connections to rapid transit must be made via Wood Island station, one stop north of Airport on the Blue Line. Accessible-van pickups and drop-offs at Wood Island can be scheduled 6am-11pm daily from any of the Visitor Information desks in the airport terminals, or by calling 617/561-1770.

Logan Airport – Rapid Transit

Airport station on the Blue Line is linked to all terminals by the following free Massport shuttle buses (every 8–12 minutes, 365 days per year, hours listed below). Allow an extra 20 minutes from Airport station for the shuttle trip.

- shuttle 22—Airport (Blue Line) and Terminals A and B (7am-10pm)
- shuttle 33—Airport (Blue Line) and Terminals C, D, and E (7am-10pm)
- shuttle 55—Airport (Blue Line) and all terminals (4am-7am, 10pm-1am)

Logan Airport – Buses and Limousines

MBTA buses 448, 449, and 459 stop at the upper level of Terminal C en route between downtown (South Station and Downtown Crossing) and several communities north of Boston (Revere, Saugus, Lynn, Swampscott, Marblehead, and Salem). Bus 171 runs early morning only from Dudley Station (Silver Line BRT) and Andrew (Red Line) to all terminals. See Chapter 10, "MBTA Buses" for more details about these routes.

Blue Line train arriving at Airport station. Shuttle buses serve all airport terminals. See text for the many transportation options to Logan airport.

ANDREW RUBEL

Additional ground transportation, described below, is available from most Boston hotels, South Station, many towns throughout Eastern Massachusetts, and nearly all neighboring states.

Massport-sponsored Logan Express buses
Four express bus routes run between suburban communities and Logan. All four operate every day and stop at signposted curbsides outside the baggage claim areas of each passenger terminal. Paid overnight parking is available at all Logan Express destinations (see below) and costs $7-8 with every seventh consecutive day free.

Braintree, Framingham, and Woburn buses cost $9 or $16 round-trip and the Peabody bus is $8 or $14 round-trip. All four offer discounts for seniors and children, and all run daily every 30-60 minutes from early in the morning until late at night. Call 800/23-LOGAN for more details.

- Braintree Logan Express—from Forbes Rd., opposite South Shore Plaza (see p. 91), off Rte. 37 near the junction of I-93 and Rte. 3
- Framingham Logan Express—from Shoppers World (see p. 90) between Rtes. 9 & 30, off Mass. Pike Exit 13
- Peabody Logan Express—from 164 Newbury St. (Rte. 1 South); if heading north, make U-turn at Exit 26, Lowell St.
- Woburn Logan Express—from Anderson Regional Transportation Center (on the MBTA Commuter Rail Lowell Line), I-93 Exit 37C

Private buses (see Chapter 12 for details)
- Bonanza Bus Lines—from Providence, RI via South Station
- C & J Trailways—from southern New Hampshire via South Station
- Concord Trailways—from northern Maine and northern New Hampshire via South Station

- Plymouth & Brockton—from Hyannis (17 departures daily, 3:15am-8:30pm) via Plymouth; six trips originate from Provincetown
- Vermont Transit—from Montréal, Québec via New Hampshire and Vermont

Scheduled shared vans

The following companies operate on regular schedules. Advance reservations for specific departures to Logan are recommended in order to guarantee a seat, but outbound trips from Logan do not require a reservation unless you're travelling with a group, have a large quantity of luggage, or require service to a private residence. All prices are one way unless noted.

- Back Bay Coach (888/222-5229 or 617/746-9909; www.backbay-coach.com)—serves every town inside of Rte. 128 ($9-50)
- Boston Beats Limo (617/267-5856; www.bostonbeatslimo.com)—serves any destination in New England with advance notice, but primarily Boston area hotels ($9 and up)
- City Transportation (617/561-9000)—serves towns within Rte. 128, but primarily Boston area hotels ($9 and up)
- Flight Line (800/245-2525; www.flightlineinc.com)—daily arrivals 9am-11pm every 30 minutes from Andover, Billerica, Bradford, Chelmsford, Dracut, Haverhill, Lawrence, Lowell, Methuen, North Andover, Tewksbury, Tyngsborough, and Westford ($29 and up). Also serves southern New Hampshire.
- Flight Line-Seacoast Service (888/942-5044; www.flightlineinc.com)—daily arrivals 9am-11pm every 60-90 minutes from Amesbury, Boxford, Danvers, Georgetown, Groveland, Hamilton, Ipswich, Lynnfield, Merrimac, Middleton, Newbury, Newburyport, North Reading, Reading, Rowley, Salisbury, Topsfield, and Wenham ($29 and up). Also serves southern Maine.
- JC Transportation (800/517-2281 or 781/598-3433; www.jctransportationinc.com)—daily arrivals 6:05am-9:05pm every 20 minutes from all Boston, Brookline, and Cambridge hotels ($9-12)
- Mermaid Transportation (800/696-2463 or 207/772-2509; www.gomermaid.com)—arrivals five times daily 8:30am-5pm from Portland, ME ($45), plus seasonal academic vacation service direct from Bates, Bowdoin, and Colby colleges ($45-50)
- Zebra Shuttle (800/242-0064 or 508/481-7300; www.zebrashuttle.com)—daily arrivals 5:30am-11:30pm every 45 minutes from hotels in Boxborough, Framingham, Marlborough, Milford, Southborough, and Westborough ($38)

On-demand door-to-door vans and limousines

- Knights Airport Limousine Service (800/822-5456; www.knightsairportlimo.com)—serves most of Eastern Massachusetts
- Worcester Airport Limousine (800/660-0992; www.wlimo.com)—serves most of Eastern and Central Massachusetts

• Zebra Shuttle (800/242-0064 or 508/481-7300; www.zebrashuttle.com)—
serves Berlin, Bolton, Boxborough, Boylston, Clinton, Grafton, Harvard,
Hopkinton, Hudson, Marlborough, Milford, Millbury, Northborough,
Shrewsbury, Southborough, Stow, Westborough, and West Boylston
($45)

Logan Airport – Taxis
Taxicabs between downtown and Logan are metered, but tolls are extra, and
passengers boarding at the airport must also pay a surcharge. Taxis are available at all terminals at all times.

Flat-rate fares are in effect to points beyond a 12-mile radius from downtown
Boston. You should confirm the fare in advance with the driver or the Logan
taxi dispatcher.

Logan Airport – Boats
Year-round, the **Airport Water Shuttle** ($10, $17 round-trip) links Logan
Airport with Rowes Wharf in downtown Boston (Mon.-Fri. 6am-8pm every
20 minutes; Sat-Sun 10am-8pm every 30 minutes). Free Massport shuttle bus
66 connects all terminals with the Water Shuttle Dock. There is no service
on New Year's Day, July 4, Thanksgiving, and Christmas. Bicycles are carried
at no extra charge. For more information call 617/951-0255.

Connections between the Logan Dock and a dozen points around the Inner
Harbor is provided daily 7am-7pm Apr. 1-Oct. 15 by the **City Water Taxi**
($10). Ask the Logan shuttle 66 driver to radio ahead for a pick-up, or call
the captain directly at 617/422-0392.

Direct daily ferry service to Logan from the South Shore is provided by the
MBTA Commuter Boat F2 and F2H (Boston-Quincy or -Hull); for details
see Chapter 11, "MBTA Ferries & Commuter Boats."

T. F. Green Airport
Warwick, RI; 401/737-8222; www.pvd-ri.com
Located south of Providence, RI, 60 miles from Boston, T.F. Green Airport
is the most popular alternative to Logan thanks to less congestion, extensive
regional ground transportation connections, and the influence of budget carrier Southwest Airlines. T.F. Green is served by all major domestic airlines
including Southwest, most regional commuter affiliates of the national carriers, and Air Ontario.

T. F. Green Airport – Rail
At press time a new Warwick station on the main Amtrak Boston-New York
rail line is under construction. When complete, service will be provided by
Commuter Rail (Attleboro Line) from Boston's South Station, with a connecting shuttle bus between the rail depot and all airport terminals.

T. F. Green Airport – Buses and Limousines
Bonanza Bus Lines offers direct service from South Station until 11pm daily ($31 round-trip; 90 minutes trip time). Other Eastern Massachusetts locales served include Bourne, Fall River, Falmouth, Foxboro, Hyannis, Logan Airport, New Bedford, Woods Hole and Worcester. Call 800/751-8800.

Knights Airport Limousine Service (800/822-5456; www.knightsairport limo.com) and Zebra Shuttle (800/242-0064 or 508/481-7300; www.zebra shuttle.com) offer door-to-door van service to various towns in Eastern Massachusetts by advanced reservation.

From Providence and other Rhode Island cities, bus service is provided by the Rhode Island Public Transit Authority (RIPTA); call 800/244-0444 or 401/781-9400 for information. Additional scheduled van service between the airport and downtown Providence hotels, campuses, train station, and convention center is provided by Aero-Airport Limousine Service (401/737-2868), a.k.a. the Providence Shuttle.

Manchester Airport
Manchester, NH; 603/624-6556; www.flymanchester.com
Located 60 miles northwest of Boston, off I-93 in southern New Hampshire. Currently served by most major domestic airlines, including Southwest Airlines; Air Canada, and a number of commuter affiliates of the major national carriers.

Manchester Airport – Buses and Limousines
Vermont Transit offers a handful of buses throughout the day. Trip time is 65-125 minutes depending on number of stops and the fare is $21.50 for the round-trip.

Zebra Shuttle (800/242-0064 or 508/481-7300; www.zebrashuttle.com) offers reserved, door-to-door van service to towns in Central and Eastern Massachusetts. Mermaid Transportation (888/MERMAID; www.gomermaid .com) offers five daily scheduled vans to the University of New Hampshire.

Hanscom Field
Bedford, MA; 781/869-8000
Located just west of I-95/Rte. 128 about 20 miles from downtown Boston, Hanscom is a former Air Force base that's now used primarily as the region's leading civil aviation facility for private corporate and personal aircraft. However, it also has a limited amount of scheduled passenger service via US Airways Express and Boston-Maine Airways.

Hanscom Field – Buses and Limousines
MBTA bus 76 runs hourly Mon.-Sat. from Alewife (Red Line); trip time is about 40 minutes and the fare is $1.25. Zebra Shuttle (800/242-0064 or 508/481-7300; www.zebrashuttle.com) offers reserved door-to-door vans from communities along Rte. 128.

Index

*Map page references in **bold**; ⓣ denotes rapid transit or Commuter Rail station.*　　**175**

Index

Ⓣ *denotes rapid transit or Commuter Rail station*

The Esplanade 26, **27.**
See also Charles
River Basin
Essex. *See* CATA
Essex Junction, VT
169
Everett 100
Exchange Conference
Center 81
Excursions 25–52.
See also specific
place name
Exeter, NH 168
EZ Ride 157

F
ⓣFairbanks St. 124
Fairhaven 100
ⓣFairmount 133
Fairmount Line 132.
See also Commut-
er Rail
Fall River 100
Falmouth 166. *See
also* CCRTA
Falmouth Ferry 165
Faneuil Hall **30–31,**
32, 33, 55, 69, 89
Fan Pier 152
fares. *See* specific
service or carrier
name
MBTA Fast Facts 2
Farmington, CT 167
Faulkner Hospital 85
ⓣFenway **34,** 125
Fenway/Kenmore
34–35, 100
Fenway Park **27.** *See
also* Red Sox
ⓣFenwood Rd. **34,**
126
Fernald Center 85
ferries, MBTA 9–10,
152
fares 10. *See
also* passes,
MBTA
special 13
hours of opera-
tion 10
to Logan Interna-
tional Airport 173
ferries, non-MBTA
18, 164–165. *See
also* specific carrier
name
ⓣFields Corner 120
Financial District
30–31, 32
Fisher College **27,** 73
ⓣFitchburg 133
Fitchburg 101
Fitchburg Line 131.
See also Commut-
er Rail
Fitzwilliam, NH 168
flag stop 16

FleetCenter **29,** 69
Fleet Boston Pavilion
69
Flight Line 172
Fogg Art Museum
40, 55
Foothills Theatre Com-
pany **52,** 66
Footlight Club 67
ⓣFordham Rd. 123
ⓣForest Hills 128, 133
Fore River Shipyard
152
ⓣForge Park/495 133
Forsyth School of Den-
tal Hygienists 73
Forsyth School of
Dentistry **34**
Fort Point Chan-
nel 101. *See
also* South Boston
Foxborough 101
Foxwoods Casino,
CT 167
ⓣFramingham 133
Framingham 101
Framingham/
Worcester Line
132. *See also* Com-
muter Rail
Framingham State
College 74
Franciscan Children's
Hospital 85
Franconia, NH 168
ⓣFranklin 133
Franklin 101
Franklin Line 132. *See
also* Commuter Rail
Franklin Park 36, 62.
See also Emerald
Necklace
Franklin Park Zoo
36, 55
Frederick Law Olmsted
National Historic
Site 55
Freedom Cruise Line
165
Freedom Trail 28, **29,
30–31,** 55
Freetown 101
French Library & Cul-
tural Center 88
Fresh Pond Mall 89
FRTA 157
Fuller Museum of
Art 55
Fung Wah Transport
Vans 157

G
Gardner 167. *See
also* GMTA; MART
Gardner Museum.
See Isabella
Stewart Gardner
Museum

GATRA **48,** 157
Georgetown 101
Gibbs School, Kather-
ine 74
Gibson House Mu-
seum **55**
Gillette Stadium.
See Patriots (NFL)
Glass Flowers 41
ⓣGloucester **44,** 133
Gloucester 44, 101
GMTA 157
Goethe-Institut 88
Gore Place 55
Gorham, NH 168
Government Build-
ings 81–83. *See
also* specific build-
ing name
ⓣGovernment Center
4, **30–31,** 122, 129
Government Center 32
ⓣGrafton 133
Grafton 101
Granary Burial Ground
30–31
Granby. *See* PVTA
Greater Attleboro-
Taunton Regional
Transit Authority.
See GATRA
Great Barrington.
See BRTA
Greenfield 166. *See
also* FRTA; GMTA;
MART
ⓣGreenwood 133
Green Line 3, 117,
118, 122–126. *See
also* rapid transit
B Line 123
C Line 124
D Line 125
special fares 5
E Line 126
special notes
about 4
ⓣGreen St. 128
ⓣGreycliff Rd. 123
Greyhound 17, **30–31,
48, 52,** 161
ⓣGriggs St., Long
Ave. 123
Groton. *See* LRTA
Groveland 101
Guilford, CT 167
Gulbankian Bus Lines
30–31, 158

H
Hadley. *See* PVTA
ⓣHalifax 133
Halifax 101
Hallmark Health Sys-
tem 85
Hamilton 101
ⓣHamilton/Wenham
133

Hampden. *See* PVTA
Hancock-Clarke
House. *See* Lex-
ington Historical
Society
Hancock Tower **27**
handicap accessibility.
See disabled per-
sons, services for
Hanover 102
Hanover, NH 168
Hanscom Field 174
ⓣHanson 133
Hanson 102
Harrison Gray Otis
House 55
Hartford, CT 167
ⓣHarvard **40,** 119
ⓣHarvard Ave. 123
Harvard Film Archive
40, 64
Harvard Museum of
Natural History **40,**
41, 56
Harvard Semitic Mu-
seum **40,** 56
Harvard Square **40,** 41
Harvard University **40,**
41, 74
Medical School **34**
Radcliffe **40**
Harwich 166.
See CCRTA
ⓣHastings 133
Hasty Pudding Theatre
40, 67
Hatch Memorial Shell
26, **27,** 69
ⓣHaverhill 133
Haverhill 102
Haverhill/Reading Line
131. *See also* Com-
muter Rail
ⓣHawes St. 124
ⓣHaymarket 4, **29,**
122, 127
ⓣHeath St. 126
Hebrew College 74
Hebrew Rehabilitation
Center 85
Hellenic College/Holy
Cross Greek
Orthodox School of
Theology 74
ⓣHerald St. 130
ⓣHersey 133
Higgins Armory Mu-
seum 56
ⓣHighland 133
Hingham 102
Hingham Shipyard
152
Hinsdale. *See* BRTA
Holbrook 102
ⓣHolbrook/Randolph
133
Holden. *See* WRTA
holiday service,

178

Ⓣ *denotes rapid transit or Commuter Rail station*

Index

Ⓣ *denotes rapid transit or Commuter Rail station*

Index

Ⓣ denotes rapid transit or Commuter Rail station; Map page references in **bold**.

Transit Telephone Numbers and Websites

MBTA (www.mbta.com)

Routes and Schedules **617-222-3200**
  Toll free 800-392-6100
  TDD/TTY..................................617-222-5246
  Police..617-222-1000
    Emergency.............................617-222-1212
  Main switchboard........................617-222-5000
  Hingham Ferry.............................781-749-8009
  Charlestown Ferry 617-227-4321
  Monthly, Weekly, and Visitor Passes
    Customer Service 877-939-0929
    Purchase by Mail 617-222-5218
    Purchase by Phone...................877-927-7277
    Senior Citizens and TAPs...........617-222-5976
    TDD/TTY.................................617-222-5854
  Semester Pass Program...........617-222-5218

Elevator updates 617-222-2828
  TDD/TTY..................................617-222-5854
Lift Bus requests 800-LIFT-BUS
  TDD/TTY..................................617-222-5854
The Ride program 617-222-5123
  TDD/TTY..................................617-222-5415
Lost and Found
  Rapid transit or bus 617-222-5000
  Commuter Rail, North Sta.........617-222-3600 ✔
  Commuter Rail, South Sta 617-345-7456
Customer Relations.....................617-222-5215
  Complaints/Commendations.....617-222-5216
  "Write to the Top" ....see p. 15
  Advisory Board 617-426-6054

More Local Transportation

Caravan for Commuters
  ....www.commute.com; 888-4-COMMUTE
Zipcar .... www.zipcar.com; 866-4-ZIPCAR

Massachusetts Bicycle Coalition
  ....www.massbike.org; 671-542-BIKE

Amtrak (www.amtrak.com)

Information and Reservations 800-USA-RAIL

Wheelchair accommodation......617-482-3660
  TDD/TTY..................................800-523-6590

Buses

A&A Metro ....www.aametro.com
  ....800-437-3844; 508-697-0017
American Eagle Motor Coach......508-993-5040
The B Line .. www.burlington.org; 781-270-1965
BAT 508-580-1170
Bedford Local Transit
  .... www.town.bedford.ma.us; 781-275-2255
Beverly Shoppers Shuttle.............978-232-9559
Bloom's Bus Lines
  .... www.bloombus.com; 508-822-1991
Bonanza Bus Lines
  ....www.bonanzabus.com; 401-751-8800
BRTA 413-499-2782; 800-292-BRTA
Brush Hill Tours 781 986 6100
C&J Trailways
  .... www.cjtrailways.com; 603-430-1100
CATA...........www.canntran.com; 978-283-7278
Cavalier Coach...........................617-330-1234
CCRTA
  .... www.capecodtransit.org; 508-775-8504
The Coach Company
  ....www.coachco.com; 800-874-3377
Coach New England
  ....www.coachne.com; 800-310-9900
Concord Free Bus 978-318-3035
Concord Trailways
  .... www.concordtrailways.com; 603-228-3300
Dartmouth Coach
  .... www.concordtrailways.com; 603-448-2800
Dedham Local Bus .... see JBL Bus Lines
EZ Ride.......... www.ezride.info; 617-8-EZ-INFO

FRTA....http://users.rcn.com/frta; 413-774-2262
Fung Wah Transport
  ....www.fungwahbus.com; 617-338-0007
GATRA (www.gatra.org)
  Attleboro...................................508-222-6106
  Taunton 508-823-8828
  TDD/TTY.................................508-824-7439
GMTA ...... www.gmta-transit.org; 413-773-9478
Greyhound
  .... www.greyhound.com; 800-231-2222
Gulbankian Bus Lines 508-460-0225
Interstate Coach.. 508-583-2225; 781-344-2231
JBL Bus Lines 781-843-4505
Lexpress....................................781-861-1210
LIFT 508-620-4823
Longwood Medical Area Shuttle
  .... www.masco.org; 617-632-2800
LRTA.. www.lrta.com; 978-452-6161 or 459-7101
MART......................www.montachusettrta.org
  ....800-922-5636; 978-345-7711
Mass Bay Limousine
  ..www.massbaylimousine.com; 781-895-1100
Mission Hill Link.........................617-566-5509
MVRTA.........www.mvrta.org; 978-469-MVRTA
Natick Neighborhood Bus
  ....508-647-6446 (7-11am)
Newton Nexus............................617-796-1288
NRTA 508-228-7025
OWL .... see GATRA
PAL .... see GATRA
Paul Revere Transportation 617-889-5899

Peabody Transit............................978-531-2254
Peter Pan
.... www.peterpanbus.com; 800-343-9999
Plymouth & Brockton Street Railway
.... www.p-b.com; 508-746-0378
PVTA...................www.pvta.com; 413-781-7882
RIPTA..................www.ripta.com; 401-781-9400
SRTA..............www.srtabus.com; 508-997-6767
Travel Pack
.... www.travelpackusa.com; 617-338-8222

Trombly Commuter Lines
...... www.tromblybuslines.com; 978-937-3626
Vermont Transit........... www.vermonttransit.com
.... 800-642-3133, 800-451-3292
VTA .... www.vineyardtransit.com; 508-627-9663
Waltham CitiBus
......................www.128bc.com; 781-890-0093
WRTA.............. www.therta.com; 508-791-WRTA
Yankee Bus Lines.........................617-268-8890

Ferries

A.C. Cruise Line
.... www.accruiseline.com; 617-261-6633
Airport Water Shuttle
.... www.massport.com; 617-951-0255
Bay State Cruise Co. 617-748-1428
.... www.baystatecruisecompany.com
Boston Harbor Cruises
......................www.bostonharborcruises.com
.... 877-SEE-WHALE; 617-227-4321
Capt. John Boats .... www.captjohn.com
.... 508-747-2400; 800-242-2469
City Water Taxi
.... www.citywatertaxi.com; 617-422-0392

Cuttyhunk Boat Lines
.... www.cuttyhunk.com; 508-992-1432
Falmouth Ferry
.... www.falmouthferry.com; 508-548-9400
Freedom Cruise Line....................508-432-8999
.... www.nantucketislandferry.com
Hy-Line Cruises.......... www.hy-linecruises.com;
.... 508-778-2600; 800-492-8082
Island Queen
.... www.islandqueen.com; 508-548-4800
Steamship Authority
.... www.islandferry.com; 508-477-8600

Airports

Logan Airport (www.massport.com)
Main Line................................. 800-23-LOGAN
Handicap Van service................617-561-1769
TDD/TTY......................................800-262-3335

Logan continued:
Airport Water Shuttle.................617-951-0255
More Logan transportation .... see Chapter 14
Other airports .... see Chapter 14

Out-of-State Local Transit

Concord Area Transit (NH)...........603-225-0989
CTTransit (CT)
.... www.cttransit.com; 860-522-8101
Maine Department of Transportation
.... www.state.me.us/mdot; 207-624-3000
Manchester Transit Authority (NH)
.... www.mtabus.org; 603-623-8801

Metro-North Commuter Railroad (NY, CT)
....................................www.mta.nyc.ny.us/mta
.... 800-638-7646; 212-532-4900
Metropolitan Transportation Authority (NY)
..................www.mta.nyc.ny.us; 718-330-1234
Shoreline East (CT) ......www.shorelineeast.com
.... 800-ALL-RIDE; 203-777-7433
STM (Montréal)..... www.stm.info; 514-280-5100